# THE SPIRAL PATH

David Fernbach

# THE SPIRAL PATH

**a gay contribution
to human survival**

Alyson
Publications
Boston

GAY
MEN'S
PRESS
LONDON

First published in Great Britain 1981 by Gay Men's Press,
27 Priory Avenue, London N8 7RN; and in North America by
Alyson Publications, PO Box 2783, Boston, Mass. 02208 USA.

ISBN (UK) 0 907040 07 1
    (US) 0 932870 12 0

Photoset by Alyson Publications, Boston


BRITISH LIBRARY/LIBRARY OF CONGRESS CIP DATA

Fernbach, David
  The spiral path.
  1. Communism
  I. Title
335.43    HX36    80-42322

# Contents

# Preface

> The epoch of world communism will be
> reached when all humanity voluntarily and
> consciously changes itself and the world.
>
> MAO ZEDONG[1]

In his poem, 'Praise of Communism,' Bertold Brecht wrote:
'It is the simple thing/So hard to achieve'.[2] Simple, because
anyone can understand the idea of reorganizing society so
that it genuinely does meet our individual and collective
needs; but hard, because we have the weight of millenia of
hierarchy and conflict to overcome.

In the West today, communism, and even the far less ambitious term of socialism, has long been a dirty word. Not
surprisingly, given the terrible connotations it has been burdened with by the abysmal failure of the Soviet experiment.
Yet there is no better word for this goal of a unified humanity consciously determining its social institutions and its
direction of development. Communism was the label adopted by Marx and Mao, by William Morris and Edward Carpenter, by Rosa Luxemburg and Alexandra Kollontai, and I
believe the communist ideal is powerful enough to shake off
the associations of Stalin and Brezhnev and reassert its
original utopian dimension.

The dialectical tradition, from Hegel through to Mao, has
always used the metaphor of the spiral to describe the evolution of matter, life and consciousness. In this great movement there are no straight lines, but a process of twists and
turns that often looks as if it has doubled back and is facing
the opposite way. This is certainly true of the communist

movement itself, which has had so many failures as well as successes, but is now poised, especially in our particular part of the world, to go forward on a new and higher basis.

Just like any other human enterprise, there is no guarantee of success for communism. If our species fails to make this new evolutionary leap, it will undoubtedly be made on other planets — it undoubtedly has already been made. Yet humanity stands today at a crucial point of decision. For if we do not manage to navigate this next twist in the spiral, the alternative can only be self-destruction, i.e. a downward spiral of decline.

This critical decision will depend most of all on what happens in the industrialized countries, as it is we, with our hydrogen bombs and ecocidal processes of 'production', who threaten to destroy intelligent life on the planet. Yet despite a steadily increasing awareness of the problem, we are still far indeed from pulling ourselves over the hump, and the official Marxist representatives of the communist ideal seem unable to generate anything like the enthusiasm that is needed.

As I see it, there is a key strand in the spiral that is still missing. In the last decade the feminist and gay liberation movements have developed, out of our practical activity, a radical critique of the present social order that is quite distinct from the traditional Marxist critique, yet ultimately capable of fusing together with this in a new and more powerful synthesis. The present book is written as a contribution towards this goal.

At the turn of the 1960s, when I was in my mid teens, I was already committed to communism. I was active in the Campaign for Nuclear Disarmament, joined the Young Communist League for a time, while my rather theoretical turn of mind led to a deep and lasting interest in Marxism. I spent much of the 1960s at university (London School of Economics), but was very involved in the campaign against the American war on Vietnam, and through this, in the 'revolutionary' student movement at the end of the decade. In 1968 I rushed over to Paris to take part in the May events, and for the next couple of years my main concern was to try and build up a similar movement in Britain.

By this time the themes of feminism, ecology and the counterculture were beginning to question far more of the conventional wisdom of the Left than the student movement had ever done. In September 1970 I met up with gay liberation, and the heady years of GLF were a period of great new discoveries for all involved, about the world and also about ourselves.[3]

If I came into GLF as a communist, the gay movement led me to expand my vision of a liberated society by a whole new dimension, adding the abolition of gender to the abolition of class as a communist goal. The writings of the American feminists helped a lot towards this, in particular Shulamith Firestone, whom we studied in the group that drafted the London GLF *Manifesto* of 1971. Yet although it was not hard to make certain connections between the systems of class and gender, these fell far short of a really coherent theory. The traditional Marxists had a ready answer, that the gender contradiction was simply a function of class, to which a certain tendency in the women's movement retorted that class was rather a function of biological sex. Those of us unable to accept either of these simplistic reductions found ourselves on increasingly shaky ground in between.

When the first great wave of gay liberation spent itself, and the movement split up under the weight of its own contradictions, the *Gay Marxist* magazine of 1973-74 provided a focus in which the very diverse group of gay radicals, finding ourselves suddenly isolated from a mass base, debated what to do next. But by 1974 the fragmentation of GLF had extended to the fragmentation even of the Gay Marxists, and the small group whose views I shared found ourselves out on a limb, virtually outside of the gay movement as now defined.

As a communist, I had naturally taken a great interest, both before and during the GLF time, in the Cultural Revolution in China (1966-76). It so happened that the decline of the radical gay movement in Britain coincided with a new upsurge of feminism in China, in which the Chinese Communist Party vigorously encouraged women to struggle against male domination.[4] A considerable number of feminists in Britain and other Western countries began to pay close attention to what was going on in China, and, given the intimate connection that we saw between women's and gay oppression, our own small group followed suit. We had some interesting discussions with women cadres at the Chinese embassy, and prepared material which they asked for on the gay movement, while some of us visited China ourselves to study conditions there at first hand and to raise the question of homosexuality. But though many Chinese feminists could appreciate lesbianism, as a support for women's struggle against male oppression, male homosexuality was still seen solely as a form of decadence, and we were unable to make any contact with gay men in China.

In this respect, my connection with China proved a failure, but I don't in any way regard it as a wasted effort. For throughout the mid 1970s I was able to acquaint myself very intimately with the political ideas of Mao Zedong, which had not only brought China out of an abyss of misery and dependence, but led in the 1960s to an unprecedented challenge to the hierarchical division of labour that is always the nitty-gritty of the class division — even under the 'dictatorship of the proletariat'. I came to see the world far more from the standpoint of the great underprivileged majority of the South of the planet. I came to see the Soviet Union as a vicious system of class oppression and imperialism. I came to see in a new and more ominous light the rivalry between the two superpowers, with the United States on the wane after its defeat in Indochina, and the more 'up to date' imperialism of the Soviet Union aggressively aspiring to world hegemony. And through a better understanding of the arduous dynamics of people's revolution, I came to a clear realization that the class struggle in our part of the world had taken a different course, and that the rhetoric of 'seizing power' indulged by the British Trotskyist and Communist parties completely failed to engage with the real needs and possibilities of the situation today.

One particular respect in which the ideas of the Chinese Communists have shocked Western opinion is their contention that a new world war is highly likely. After the Soviet invasion of Czechoslovakia in 1968, the Chinese increasingly came to expect attack from their north, rather than from across the Pacific, and like so many other visitors to China,

I was quite stunned in 1976 to see the scale and sophistication of their provision of deep shelters in every urban area, designed against atomic, biological and chemical weapons. Yet the Chinese determination to survive even nuclear attack has been slandered as 'warmongering' — particularly of course by the Soviet imperialists.

I came to see the pro-Soviet bias of the British Left as at best a relic of past illusions, at worst due to the belief that trade-union bureaucrats and party secretaries would make a more efficient ruling class than the one we have now: particularly, of course, if elections could be managed as well as they are in Eastern Europe, and opponents denied any legal protection or access to the nationalized mass media. At the same time, though, there is a very genuine tradition on the Left of anti-militarism and pacifism, and the attempt to keep our country from embroilment in the struggle of the superpowers had inspired the Campaign for Nuclear Disarmament which was my own first political experience. Contrasted with China, and even with Sweden or Switzerland nearer home, the British military system was evidently very far from meeting the real defence needs of our people, and I became involved for a while with a study group which produced a few pamphlets under the name of Democratic Defence. Its key principles were: European defence cooperation instead of reliance on the United States; conventional defence instead of deterrence by nuclear weapons; the regular army to be democratized, and backed by a militia system open to both sexes; and the full provision of shelters.

One important thing, however, I had lost through no longer being actively engaged in the gay movement, and this was the lesson of relating my political ideas to personal experience, seeking in my own oppression a basis of solidarity with others in the struggle for communism. The question of violence particularly required this connection. We are surrounded from our earliest years by the culture of masculine violence and the glorification of war. My own adolescent response to the demand that I train as a soldier was a simple rationalization: I didn't believe in it. Only through GLF, a decade later, did I come to understand my deep-seated antipathy to violence as basically good, and an integral part of my personality as a gay man. In the period between, however, a contradiction between my repugnance for violence and my commitment to revolution cropped up time and again. In the late 1960s, for example, it gave me an ambiguous attitude towards the militant demonstrations against US imperialism I helped to organize. In GLF, I was at least able to begin to tackle this question in some kind of objective way. Yet I was still far from able to resolve it. Carried along by the GLF tide, I shared in the radical critique of violent masculinity that our movement developed. But as the movement ebbed, I retreated to the safer ground of orthodoxy, and could once again endorse the need to smash the state apparatus even in the democratic capitalist countries.[5]

There is certainly no easy answer to the problem of how to effectively defeat oppression without resort to the oppressor's own means. It has long been a problem in the communist movement, even if women and gay men are today seeking to tackle it at a new and deeper level. But we are still far too cowed by the dogmatized Marxism of the masculine Left, and it is an uphill struggle to try and rethink the communist perspective from an anti-gender standpoint.[6]

By the late 1970s, I was at last beginning to see my own way through this knotty problem, one necessary precondition being a renewed personal commitment to the gay movement. I argue in this book that the crisis which makes possible and necessary the advance to a communist society is a global contradiction between scientific technology and the system of social relations based on violence, its present form being the twin threats of nuclear war and ecological catastrophe. In our part of the world, marked by a far-reaching integration of the working class into capitalist society, there is little prospect for the traditional Marxist strategy of violent revolution. Today it is the whole society that is threatened with destruction, so the communist movement must take a form that can mobilize all classes. Particular responsibility, as always, falls to those fortunate enough to have become aware of the awesome choices we face. But in this new situation, the feminist and gay liberation movements also have a special contribution to make, by working to erode the masculine specialization in violence that underpins class society, the state and the endemic warfare between states.

Like everyone who will read this book, I've read quite a lot on sexual politics, and on politics and history in general. Yet I have not attempted to establish my argument by appeal to authorities. This method is scarcely better than any other, as there are enough conflicting authorities around to prove anything. It appeals rather to the common ground that can be established, I believe, between people who share an ultimate common goal, on the basis of shared elements of individual and collective experience. In this perspective, what I have tried to produce is a hypothesis made of bits and pieces from different sources, which will convince, if at all, by showing how apparently disparate elements of the human kaleidoscope can be seen as part of an overall pattern.

Just as important as anything written, moreover, is the constant process of informal discussion. Many people have made an essential contribution to my development in this way: other gay men, women, and even the occasional heterosexual man, particularly of course those I have lived and worked with over the years. I would also like to remember here Mike Silverstein of Berkeley, California, one of the pioneers of gay liberation, in the full sense of the term, but who was far worse affected than I was by the collapse of GLF, and finally took his own life in 1977, unable to wait for the new wave of gay radicalism that he himself predicted. It is almost impossible, in our movement, to separate emotional support from political support, and those who have sustained me through the troubled times we live in are in a certain sense co-authors of this book, though happily free from responsibility for what I write.

Rather than dedicating this book to a friend, which strikes me as somewhat quaint in this day and age, I'd like to invoke the Buddhist saint Kuan Yin, who, 'in the very process of attaining Buddhahood. . . "hearing the cries of the world", turns back and vows to renounce her own divinity until, with her aid, all the suffering of the world is extinguished, and all beings have attained the same highest level of spiritual existence'.[7] Let those of us with the time and energy to debate revolutionary ideas, so privileged as we are by that fact alone, take this as an example to follow.

*London, January 1981*

# Chapter One:
## The Gender System

### 1. *Sex and Gender*

The division between female and male that our species shares with the animal world in general, and our mammalian cousins in particular, is a fundamental fact which every human society has had to take into account in building its particular pattern. The social relevance of the sexual division is always visible, yet it is only recently that we have learned to make a distinction between sex and gender. In so far as this is one instance of a wider distinction between nature and culture, between the human raw material and what human society constructs, it signals an increased awareness of the relative character of our institutions, and hence of the possibilities of change. The opposing of gender to sex is very definitely something progressive.

Between sex and gender, moreover, it is possible to mark the nature-culture boundary in a sharper fashion than in certain other fields. The division of sex is a genetic one, clearly inscribed in our chromosomes. In all but an insignificant fraction of individuals, this genetic difference is translated into a visible anatomical difference at birth, from which it is safe to predict that the infant will develop into one particular kind of adult or the other. Everything that is not attributable to the workings of our genes is a difference not of sex, but of gender.

Far more important to human society than any other aspect of the sexual division is the difference of function in procreation (menstruation, intercourse, conception, gestation, childbirth and lactation). Some other differences, however, are also significant, in particular the greater average size of the male, the difference between female and male orgasm, and the fact that heterosexual intercourse is not necessarily dependent on female consent (the possibility of rape). These four aspects of the sexual division are beyond dispute, even if their bearing on social organization is quite complex. There is however still a grey area, the question of how strongly human females and males are differentially predisposed to certain forms of temperament and behaviour by hormonal (i.e. genetic) influences, in the way that other animals very definitely are.

Fortunately we have got beyond the stage at which those committed to change felt they had to deny the very possibility of such influence a priori. Today it is perfectly legitimate for feminists to investigate the possible effects of different female and male hormonal levels on aggressiveness, for example, or the effects of the menstrual cycle.[1] What is quite clear, however, both from cross-cultural comparison and from the study of deviant individuals within our own society, is that any differences between the sexes at this level are in no way adequate to explain the different functions ascribed to women and men by human society. In this respect, at least, culture has already triumphed over nature. A girl can readily learn to be a warrior, and a boy to tend for infants, if placed in the right milieu. The ascription of childcare to women and warfare to men, which is so widespread in human society, is simply a more viable adaptation given that one sex bear children and the other do not, and it could have scarcely been different even if the human female were slightly more predisposed to aggression by nature than the male.

What is peculiar about the division of gender is that it is a cultural division, but along the line of sexual demarcation already given by biology. In this area, more than in any other where a distinction between nature and culture is made, it is impossible to see the sphere of culture as already free from the constraints of its natural boundaries. In the most extreme case, the degree of freedom is virtually zero, and the distinction between sex and gender simply disappears, as in the example of procreation itself. For no matter that human beings have to learn any form of sexual intercourse (as indeed do other primates), as well as learning how to handle childbirth and lactation, no human society could have survived for more than a few years if its culture had not included penis-vagina intercourse, as well as inculcating a positive attitude towards child-bearing in its female members. Even today, while any individual woman can reject pregnancy, this is not yet possible for women as a whole, except at the price of an end to our society altogether.

If the sphere of culture is statically counterposed to that of nature, it becomes impossible to comprehend the multifarious ways in which our biological endowment impinges on our social constructions, making some choices more workable than others, and even making some absolutely necessary, as in the above example. In everything to do with relations between women and men, i.e. between female and male human beings in their roles ascribed by human society, this impingement of biology is particularly significant. Rather than already complete in itself, the cultural aspect of human society must be seen as a sphere of becoming, which expands by a steady rolling back of the natural boundaries as our ability to manipulate the material world increases. Since we are not creatures of pure spirit, but material beings ourselves, this process can never reach a point at which the biological base disappears or becomes unimportant for the way that we organize human society. The distinction between sex and gender is made in the interest of eroding the confinement and oppression of the present cultural pattern, and it rightly points out that there can be a radical rapprochement between women and men. But this is a struggle to roll back the natural boundary, and it is not surprising that it leads to putting in question the biological distinction of sex that underlies the very phenomenon of gender.

The gay movement, like the movement of women, is a challenge to the existing configuration of gender. The gender system stipulates that, if you are female, you must be a certain kind of person, in behaviour and temperament, and if you are male, you must be a certain other kind of person. In the form that we know it today, the gender system places women in a subordinate position vis-à-vis men. Because this is not just the result of men's arbitrary action, but a structural element in the overall pattern of social organization, it is by no means always possible for women to wage a struggle for liberation, or even to conceive of a change in their situation. If such a struggle does develop, it generally indicates that the existing social pattern is in crisis, and the time is ripe for its replacement. But because women are indeed oppressed by men in the gender system, a liberation struggle invariably does develop once the conditions are ripe. What this struggle demands, as a minimum, is a significant redefinition of the gender division, allowing women to develop in ways that were previously proscribed.

Gay men start out from a very different relationship to the gender system than do women, and the same applies to lesbians in so far as they struggle on the specific basis of their gayness. While women are oppressed by being what the gender system requires them to be, offering them a certain reward of legitimacy for being a 'proper' woman and accepting oppression, gay people are oppressed by our inability — or refusal — to be 'proper' women or men. For our homosexuality, unlike the prevalent forms of homosexuality met with in other societies, or even some marginal forms found in our own, is incompatible with the gender definitions of femininity and masculinity. The minimum starting-point of the gay struggle, accordingly, is the demand for our right to exist, for a basic social tolerance.

These two very different starting-points explain how it is that the women's and gay movements have by no means immediately recognized each other as allies. Heterosexual feminists have been able to see themselves as essentially 'proper' women, who simply wanted access to particular privileges that men had withheld from them: the right to vote, access to professions and property, economic support for child-rearing, etc. While gay men have conversely accepted that we were indeed 'improper', a deviant minority, and sought an end to legal and social persecution without calling into question the norms of gender that define what is 'proper' masculinity.

This absence of mutual recognition has been more pronounced on the feminist side. For the women's movement is a more massive force in society than the gay men's movement, and in a more central position. Feminists speak not only as representatives of a biological sex, but also as representatives of the economic category in which the great majority of women in our society are placed by virtue of their dependence on men. This can lead, and still sometimes leads today, to even the more radical tendencies in the women's movement viewing the gay men's struggle as having no bearing on their cause. This is the case on the one hand with those feminists who see their oppression in terms of orthodox Marxism, and seek liberation on the basis of a socialist revolution. And it is also the case with those very different feminists who see the root of their oppression as lying in male biology, and seek liberation through the ultimate elimination of the male sex as such. I do not believe that either of these routes can bring a solution to women's oppression: the first is inadequate, while the second is impossible, in as much as a biological fix of this kind could only work out as the common action of women and men, once the gender contradiction was already resolved. But this is for women themselves to determine.

What is relevant to us as gay men, however, and a very hopeful sign, is that besides these two forms of reductionism, the economic and the biological, a third tendency in the women's movement developed at the turn of the 1970s, with a perspective that was far more compatible with the requirements of gay liberation. This was the tendency that located the roots of women's oppression not simply in economic dependence, nor in a biological difference that structured human society without any cultural mediation, but precisely in the *gender system*, i.e. the way that the biological distinction between female and male was taken as the basis for a pattern of social organization. Given that child-bearing, as opposed to child-rearing, now took up such a small portion of women's time and energy, there was no reason why women should not do everything that men do, and vice versa, apart from the strictly procreative function. Instead of two radically different types of human being, feminine women and masculine men, with this distinction involving a very definite relationship of oppression into the bargain, all human beings could combine the positive aspects attributed at present to one sex or the other alone, and jettison the negative aspects. Both women and men could be sensitive and caring, and both could be emotionally independent and technically competent. Love would become a relationship between equals, rather than between dominant and subordinate.

The gay movement, for its part, has always been more aware of the relevance of feminism to its own cause, even if this was simply from the attempt to hitch its chariot to a brighter star. From the gay point of view, even the women's movement of the late 19th and early 20th century, with its far more limited goals, challenged the extreme polarization of feminine and masculine roles and thus made the gay minority seem a little bit less freakish. It was against this background that Edward Carpenter, our great foreparent, developed his characteristic ideas, so far ahead of their time. And if even he was still not completely free, at the turn of the century, from ideas of a 'third sex', the dominant tendency in his writing was to see the liberation of the gay minority in terms of the liberation of homosexuality in general and a convergence between women and men.[2]

When the second wave of the women's movement broke with such explosive force in the late 1960s, the new gay movement was able not just to follow in its footsteps, a couple of years later, but also to make its connection with feminism in a far more explicit and theorized way than ever before. When we heard the gender system come under attack, this immediately struck a resonant chord. For we had ourselves been put down all our lives for being inadequately masculine, less than 'proper' men, long before we gave outward evidence of this in homosexual behaviour. And if the gender division could really be broken down, as many women were suggesting, then the present categories of homosexuality and heterosexuality would cease to have any meaning.

This connection was by no means universally recognized in the gay movement, any more than it was on the feminist side. The majority even of those men involved in the Gay Liberation Front, and its radical counterparts in other countries, were concerned less with theory and the broader perspectives of social evolution, than with the very pressing struggle against the immediate symptoms of our oppression, with the attempt to create a wider social space and an alternative to the traditional institutions of the gay ghetto. Yet just as in the women's movement, and indeed in all movements of social liberation, the minority of theorists had a certain recognition, and their influence percolated through, however unevenly, to the movement as a whole.

In Britain, the key document of this stage was the London GLF *Manifesto* of 1971, which is still reprinted today, if with certain significant bowdlerizations.[3] Yet although this shows the influence of Shulamith Firestone, the first feminist to champion extra-uterine gestation, it still describes the present system underlying gay and women's oppression as the 'gender-role system', rather than simply the 'gender system'. And in this little word lies a whole world of confusion.

There is no doubt whatsoever that the socially defined patterns of femininity and masculinity confront the individual as a role to which she or he is expected to conform, both in outward behavior and in inward temperament and desire. For gay people, indeed, the term 'role' has a peculiar piquancy, in that we precisely fail to fit at all properly into our ascribed category of feminine woman or masculine man, and are forced so much of our lives to act a part which we do not feel is really ourselves. Yet as a theoretical concept, in the sense of the 'gender-role system', this 'role' belongs to idealist sociology, with its claim that norms and values, i.e. ideas, are the ultimate social reality, the sphere of culture standing aloof from and uncontaminated by the crude material world in which human beings produce their subsistence and procreate their next generation, in circumstances that allow them only a limited area of choice. As an individual, the human being is amazingly plastic, and can adapt to a great variety of roles. But the pattern of social organization is not plastic in the same way. It changes gradually over time, but not in any arbitrary direction. And only in the evolutionary timescale does it show the same adaptability as the individual.

Ideas do indeed have a real force, but the material constraints on human society to date have been heavy ones. Our biological nature requires us to obtain food, to maintain our body temperature, etc. by a regular metabolism with our material environment, and it is not so very long since we found, with agriculture, a way of conducting this that was radically different from any other animal. The material force of violence, too, has played a steady part in human development, sometimes more so than others, and is still very much with us today. And the gender division is precisely a way of coping with the biological differences of sex, so that the abolition of gender is quite unlike, say, the replacement of a monarchy by a republic, or private by collective ownership of the means of production. Rather than just a reshuffling of cultural elements, the abolition of gender must be seen in the broader perspective of human evolution, in which culture gradually supplants nature. Either it is possible, and necessary, as an integral and central aspect of this process, or it is not possible at all.

The problems that the gay movement had to confront in the 1970s were many, and it is not just the fault of inadequate theoretical understanding that the promise of its radical early years has so far been disappointed. The stagnation we are caught in today has its parallel in the women's movement, and in the communist movement as a whole. The period between about 1966 and 1972 saw the birth of so many new hopes for the future, which we are still painfully struggling to fit together, in a practical way, for the purpose of building a better society. But the struggle for correct ideas has an essential part to play in resolving the present stagnation, and an accurate perspective of where we are coming from and where we are trying to go is today more essential than ever, if change is to succeed.

I am firmly convinced that the *abolition of gender*, a goal put forward by both a section of the women's movement and a section of the gay movement at the turn of the 1970s, is absolutely crucial. It is the perspective that alone can unite all those directly oppressed by the gender system: women, gay men, and increasing numbers of 'men against sexism' too, while the anti-gender movement has a vital part to play in the struggle for human survival and evolution, which it is the aim of this book to show. But by defining the problem as essentially a system of 'roles', far too little attention was paid to the material conditions underlying the present crisis, and to the evolutionary dynamic that is inherent in these conditions. Much of the support that the anti-gender interpretation of women's and gay liberation gathered was accordingly lost to those who had something more concrete to say about the material conditions, even if what they had to say was wrong.

Both biological and economic reductionism are still very influential in the women's movement today, and from this base they exert a certain force of attraction on the gay men's movement as well, despite having nothing at all to offer us.[4] A new school of biological reductionism, in which Mary Daly is particularly influential, metaphysically opposes a timeless female 'being', founded in the chromosomes, to the timeless oppression of the male, even if this trenchancy has led to certain important new insights into the phenomenology of women's oppression.[5] The socialist feminists, on the other hand, genuinely do try to integrate a certain feminist consciousness into historical materialism, yet they are held back by their unwillingness to challenge the dogmas of orthodox Marxism, which cannot accommodate too radical a feminist perspective. Socialist feminism does not define all men as the enemy, gay men included, on the simple basis of our biology; but it has certainly not succeeded in offering a basis for a common struggle against the gender system.

The precondition for this struggle, I believe, is a better understanding of the 'dialectic of gender', how the gender system arose in the course of human evolution, and how it is now due for abolition. The reflections that follow are very incomplete, and are bound to be flawed in all kinds of ways. But I hope they will at least serve as one base among others on which the gay men's movement can regain its radical dimension, link up with the women's movement and the movement of men against sexism in a convergent struggle against the gender system, and in this way make what I believe is an essential contribution to human evolution.

## 2. *The Dialectic of Gender*

Our closest primate relatives of today, as we presume our common ancestors as well, are already to a limited extent social animals, deriving certain important advantages from living in bands of a certain size. The more meticulous studies of primate behaviour conducted over the last couple of decades have shown what a large part learning plays for the chimpanzee or the gorilla, and how false it is to attempt to understand their behaviour in terms of mere instinct or imprinting. Yet what decisively marks out the social life of chimpanzees (with whom we share 99 per cent of our genes) as still an animal one, rather than even proto-human, is that the behaviours that are learned are themselves quite rigidly circumscribed by the ecological niche of the species and its corresponding patterns of social organization. You can bring up a baby chimpanzee in a human household, and it will learn the rudiments of human language if this is expressed in signs it can imitate. But this surprising adaptability of the chimpanzee as individual is not matched by any such adaptability on the part of chimpanzee society, which has continued essentially unchanged for ten million years, and can only either continue the same in the future, if we let it, or die out, if we destroy its habitat.

It is impossible for anyone sensitive to the gender system as we know it today to observe the behaviour of chimpanzees without being struck by certain similarities — features which are in fact common also to many other social animals. There is a dominance hierarchy which ranks adult males by their success in competing for scarce resources. Even the most junior adult male is dominant over all females, with the one exception of his own mother. The care of infants is the exclusive province of females. When the band needs defence against predators, this is the special task of the males. Male sexuality is linked with aggression, sex being a behaviour in which a male mounts a subordinate individual who may be female or another male; conversely, presentation for mounting signals acceptance of subordination.

These similarities with a very widespread form of human social organization go together with major distinctions. For example, no enduring pair-bonds are formed between female and male chimpanzees, and each individual, once weaned, must basically forage for itself. But the similarities themselves can only be understood if set in the very different overall system of human society. What makes our society characteristically human, as opposed to any animal society, is that the capacity for learning, and for manipulation of the environment, is so greatly extended that a genuine sphere of culture comes into being. Human society learns collectively, not just individually. It evolves ever new patterns of social organization, ever new ways of providing for its subsistence, as well as systems of religion, art, etc. that answer the peculiar needs of the expanded cerebral cortex, and not just the needs of material metabolism. As one major aspect of this rise of culture, the biological differences between the sexes cease to determine an inevitable division of functions, apart from those immediately involved in the process of procreation. Beyond this, there is nothing a man can do that a woman cannot do also, and vice versa. Our biological evolution points us in this direction not just by our big brain, but also by a reduction in the sexual dimorphism of size and strength, and a relative convergence between female and male sexuality. The decline of the oestrus cycle and the development of the characteristic female (clitoral) orgasm gives heterosexuality a more egalitarian form, at least capable of being an equally pleasurable activity for both parties, and not just a seasonal one.

Yet while the biological division of sex narrowed, a new and specifically human division of gender came into being. For all the diversity shown by human societies, there are certain basic common features of gender differentiation that have proved very long-lived indeed. Although not rigidly determined by our biology, and in this sense a cultural construction, the phenomenon of gender has had this relative constancy to it as a function of the very limited control human beings had over their material environment. Only today is it at all feasible to arrange things differently.

The starting-point for explaining the gender division is the very protracted period of infantile dependence. Our characteristic adaptation of the big brain, with its greatly increased capacity for learning, means that it takes much longer for the human infant to reach maturity, while it is also expelled from the womb at a relatively early stage of maturation. A baby chimpanzee can hang onto its mother as soon as it is born; it is weaned by the age of twelve months, and can soon gather its own food. A human baby cannot stand on its feet for one year; and even if suckling continues till the age of three or four, it still has a long way to go before its contribution to the procuring of food matches its consumption.

A whole distinctive pattern of human existence grew up around this protracted dependence. 1) The greater burden of childcare makes it highly desirable that males should contribute to the subsistence of children and those caring for them. 2) Hunting animals, a high-protein food source that was indispensable to our early development, however barbaric it seems today, developed as a masculine specialization, while women still concentrated on gathering activities around the domestic base. 3) The sharing between the sexes of their respective produce was promoted by a pair-bond reinforced both by a more constant and convergent sexuality, and by the strong emotional memories of the mother-child relationship. These three elements together made up the matrix of the family, which is still to be found, in one form or another, in all human societies to date, even if it does not always stand out in full relief as the 'nuclear' unit.

The example of the family, and the basic gender differentiation it enshrines, shows the constraint that biology continues to exert on the sphere of culture. The human family is clearly not inscribed in our biology in the way that the pair-bonding of certain other mammals definitely is. Yet in the gathering/hunting stage that was the only human way of life over an evolutionary timescale, from the period of homo erectus, three million years back, until just a few thousand years ago, no human society managed to organize things differently, and the advantages of the family enabled it to persist even when our species gained a new degree of freedom with agriculture and the beginnings of industry. The gender phenomenon, as already argued, must be seen as a transition between nature and culture. It is still a division along the line of biological sex, which remains a tremendously powerful constraint in structuring social relations. Once human society gains a greater degree of freedom, and can roll back its natural boundaries a bit more, it will no longer need to organize its relations in this way. In the gender division, human culture still mimics, as it were, the animal world around it, as yet unable to leave its inherited organizing principles behind and strike out on its own.

A further element that fits together with the family matrix as a characteristic feature of human social organization
in the gathering/hunting stage is the system of kinship. The
nuclear family form as we know it today is in fact also characteristic of the earliest known forms of human society,
while the development of kinship systems is especially associated with the later stages of the gathering/hunting
adaptation. But the formation of the heterosexual pair-bond
is never left simply to the individuals involved. The sexual
division of labour requires marriage to be institutionalized
under the control of the environing society. Marriage does
not have to be permanent, 'till death do us part', nor need it
rule out a certain space for extra-marital sexuality (itself
within regularized limits), but marriage is an essential cement for the sexual division of labour, and given that this is
the institutionalizing of heterosexuality, it also serves to
hold in check potentially destructive rivalries for a sexual
partner.

In the earliest gathering/hunting societies, bands are generally limited to a very few families, having only occasional
contact with others who share their language. Exogamous
marriage, however, is a means by which alliances can be
formed between families and bands, leading in due course to
a kinship system, a larger and more structured society capable of handling its environment more successfully. Kinship
was for a long while the only principle that could weld
human beings together into larger groups, and in many
societies it has been carried to amazing lengths — the
extreme case being the indigenous peoples of Australia. In a
developed system of kinship, the individual family appears
submerged. The husband may have no particular economic
obligation to his wife and children, as opposed to the wider
social unit, and in a matrilineal system his paternal role
may be displaced in favour of his wife's brother. But the
family matrix is still very much present at the heart of the
kinship system, with marriage both regularizing the heterosexual pair-bond, and tying men to women in the sexual
division of labour.

In the gathering/hunting stage of human society, therefore, which ceased to be the way of life of the majority of

human beings only 2,000 years ago, we can already see certain basic elements of what we criticize today as the gender system. The primary division of labour, between childcare + gathering and hunting, forms female and male individuals into two significantly different types of person, with differing mentalities and subcultures. Heterosexuality is institutionalized, and this means a relationship not simply between persons of different biological sex, but between persons of different gender. Heterosexuality means the woman's attraction to a hunter, and the man's attraction to a 'homemaker'. It means something very different, in other words, for the woman and for the man. Yet even so, the more primitive gathering/hunting societies, of which some examples such as the !Kung bushpeople have survived into our own day, display less of a polarization in terms of the differential feminine and masculine personalities than do any of our modern complex societies. And in many of them women enjoy so much more favourable a position that some observers have even been led to describe them — however misguidedly — as matriarchal. Male domination, therefore, is not coterminous with the gathering/hunting form of society, but only becomes universal with the transition from the gathering/hunting way of life to the settled existence based on agriculture.

The key argument against the existence of a primitive matriarchy is that there are simply no examples of this to be found, even though the primitive societies that have survived into modern times number many hundred, and present a comprehensive spectrum from the earliest forms of gathering and hunting, little changed since the emergence of modern homo sapiens 40,000 years ago, through to those peoples already in the process of developing a complex and stratified society. The New World, in particular, offers a virtually complete range of examples, which were able to develop or not to develop, as the case may be, in relative isolation from one another.[6] The question of 'who rules?' in the early gathering/hunting societies, men or women, is impossible to abstract from a context in which the respective spheres of female and male existence are particularly distinct. But at one extreme, there are many societies where male domination over women can be very definitely recognized, while the other extreme is not one of female domination, but at best of a relative equality between women and men in their separate respective spheres of competence.[7]

Two factors can give the illusion that women rule over men. The first is quite simply the contrast with our own society. The same thing led certain observers of Soviet Russia in the 1920s to speak of a 'new matriarchy',[8] which seems quite ridiculous to us today, despite the undoubted advances Russian women made at this time. The second is the existence of matrilineal kinship systems and matrilocal residence. This is undoubtedly associated with a relatively favourable position for women. In gathering/hunting societies, it is almost always women who make the greater contribution to food supply, even if the men's more erratic contributions from hunting are a valuable source of protein. Contrary to what orthodox Marxism might assume, there is no case where women manage to translate this into a dominant position in society. But where women's share in food provision is especially great, supplying more than the two-thirds of calorie intake that is a rough average for these societies, then descent tends to be through the female line, though there is no indication whatsoever that this was a universal primordial form. It would seem, therefore, as if men's biological endowment of a larger average musculature, plus the specialization in aggressive activity that is less the result of this than of their freedom from suckling infants, gives a bias towards male domination even at the gathering/hunting stage, unless this is countered by women's preeminent role in the economy, which can then bring about a relative balance.

This balance, however, is only possible because one crucial human institution was not developed until the gathering/hunting adaptation was already in crisis and on the decline — warfare. The earliest gathering/hunting societies were quite innocent of warfare, and there were many isolated peoples who were spared this invention until the advent of European colonization. The use of stone tools and fire had given humankind, even before we had fully evolved our modern biological form, an unprecedented freedom from predators and command over our environment. Almost the whole of Earth's land surface was open to human habitation, while population expanded only slowly. (The late weaning practised by gathering/hunting societies in the absence of animal milk and cereal leads to a spacing of several years between pregnancies, and on top of this infanticide is common, to restrict the band to the size that the area within its reach can support.) Until a relatively late point in their development, accordingly, most gathering/hunting societies have no occasion for conflict with their neighbours, and many are scarcely aware of the existence of other human populations than their own. If a conflict over resources does arise, it is far easier for the weaker side to move elsewhere than to defend 'its' territory, and this is indeed what happens.[9]

The rise of warfare dates from the time when available land was taken up, and became scarce in relation to the very considerable requirements of the gathering/hunting adaptation. There was no question as to who would specialize in this new task. As with hunting, only men were free for activities that took them away from the domestic base for protracted periods, and from a technical point of view, the skills of warfare and hunting were not unrelated. To many societies, moreover, peoples who did not speak their language seemed like a different species. But the social effects of warfare are very different from those of hunting. The hunter has the ability to kill another human being, and this may have been a factor in the bias towards male domination that seems to characterize even gathering/hunting society. But he is still restrained by the strong taboo against murder, which makes the killing of another person in these societies extremely rare. The avoidance of potentially murderous conflict between hunters, in fact, is always institutionalized in various ways.[10]

The warrior, however, is the man who does kill other humans, and even if these are only the members of another society, they are still potential friends, lovers, marriage partners and in-laws. A society needing to engage in warfare — which, even if intially defensive, soon reaches a point where defence and offence are inextricably linked — must produce large numbers of violent men, and this has three major effects on the social pattern. Firstly, it strengthens the tendency to male domination, while depriving women of any means to resist this. They are now dependent on men in a completely new way, for protection against the enemy; and warfare also leads to the capture of prisoners, including women taken as booty for their sexual services, thus degrading the position of women in general. The second effect of warfare is as a new way of uniting societies into larger groups, particularly as the same pressure on resources that leads to the spread of warfare also leads to a more sedentary way of life based on a broader spectrum of food sources, as the first step towards agriculture. Thirdly, the cultivation of masculine violence, and its rewards in the form of domination over other peoples and over women, is the necessary foundation for the development of hierarchical organization, initially with the separation of a warrior elite at the top, and captured slaves at the bottom.

As far as the gender system is concerned, it is the masculine development of warfare that gives this its developed form, which we are still burdened with today. The sexual division of labour is not only expanded with the addition of warfare onto hunting as a masculine specialization. It is now the unambiguous foundation for a relationship of domination and subordination. And this also means that the rivalry inherent in heterosexuality, which the institution of marriage serves to control, becomes more particularly a rivalry between (violent) men for women, with women now deprived of any independent subject role in the sexual relationship, and relegated to the position of sexual object.

I mentioned above how the contrast between the position of women today and that in the early gathering/hunting societies could create the illusion of a primitive matriarchy. In a somewhat similar way, another illusion current in certain sections of the women's movement arises from comparing the role of aggression in human society with that among primates. In this perspective, males are the 'violent sex', and male domination is directly anchored in our biology, without any cultural mediation.[11] The existence of many gathering/hunting societies where aggression is carefully restrained, and women enjoy a position of relative equality, shows the falsity of this theory. Yet just as the illusion of matriarchy arises from exaggerating certain very real differences, so there are also certain real similarities on which the illusion of the 'violent sex' is based. Among primates, the biological dimorphism gives rise both to a dominance hierarchy among the males themselves, and to the subordination of females. In those human societies where violence is cultivated as a masculine specialization for the purpose of warfare, it has a similar effect, both in degrading women to a subordinate position, and in fostering the development of hierarchy among men themselves. Of course, just as masculine violence is the product of culture, and not of mere biology, so its effects on social organization are also culturally mediated. Warfare itself develops in a particular economic context, the competition between separate societies for resources that have become scarce. And the particular forms taken by male hierarchy and female subordination are similarly the product of economic factors as well. Yet while it is not human males who are the 'violent sex', but at most a certain form of masculinity that makes men the 'violent gender', the emphasis on the role of violence, and a violence of which men are the agents, is a very real element of truth.[12]

## 3. *Gender and Class*

In the previous section, I showed how the differentiation of gender differed from the characteristic sexual differentiation of primate society, yet had certain common features that persisted through an evolutionary timescale. The matrix of relations embodied in the family comprises, firstly, a primary division of labour between women and men, in which women specialize in childcare and a gathering activity in the vicinity of the domestic base, while men specialize in hunting, which takes them further afield. Secondly, it involves a sharing of their respective produce. And thirdly, it comprises a heterosexual pair-bond, which is asymmetrical for the woman and the man in that each of them is respectively either 'feminine' or 'masculine', and their partner the opposite category.

In its original form, the family matrix gives a system of gender relations that is characteristic of the gathering/hunting adaptation. In this first basic stage of human society, for all the great innovations that already mark our advance over the animal world — language, systematic preparation of tools, art and religion, etc. — we were still tied to a quasi-natural existence in the crucial respect that we simply appropriated our food where we found it, whether vegetable or animal, and thus had not yet genuinely embarked on the great trajectory of production that has led, through agriculture and industry, to the scientific technology of today, with at each stage a specific pattern of social organization to match.

The decisive subordination of women, together with the beginnings of social hierarchy, has its immediate cause in the expansion of the masculine sphere in the division of labour from hunting to warfare, and the systematic rearing of large numbers of violent men. Yet the rise of warfare corresponds to a particular stage in the evolution of human society as a whole, i.e. the expansion of the human population to the point where the original gathering/hunting adaptation comes up against its limits, and has to give way to something else. This 'something else', at the basic level of how human society supplies itself with the material necessities of life, is the settled existence of agriculture; even if this was not reached at one stroke, but developed via a transition phase of 'broad spectrum' adaptation, such as was typified by the Natufian culture of the Near East, some 12,500 to 10,000 years ago, and survived through to modern times with the Northwest Coast Indians of the American Pacific.[13]

If the gathering/hunting peoples, until the final phase of their existence, could avoid violent conflict by running away, agriculture ties a society down to the land, and makes escape of this kind impossible. It soon leads to a tremendous expansion of population, as ten and later a hundred families can live where one lived before, also ruling out any return to the earlier way of life by the extermination of wild animals and plants, redefined as pests and weeds. It also establishes a permanent competition between different societies for the scarce resource of fertile land. In agricultural society, accordingly, warfare becomes endemic; there is a great reward to be gained from capturing the land of others, and a permanent need to defend one's own land against such attack.

The acquisition of fertile land by conquest, as the Israelites captured Canaan, is inscribed in the legends of all agricultural peoples. So, too, is the arduous character of agriculture as opposed to the earlier stage: the expulsion from the garden of Eden, with God forcing Adam to 'gain your bread by the sweat of your brow' (*Genesis 3*, 19).

It is the settled existence, too, that lays the basis for the rise of an exploiting class. It would be quite wrong to imagine that agriculture had this effect through the production of an unprecedented surplus on which the first class of mental workers could live. The gathering/hunting peoples, in this respect, had a far higher productivity per unit of labour, and have even been called the first affluent society, needing to work no more than a few hours a day to provide for their basic needs. Yet as long as land is abundant in relation to the demand on it, there is no way that a would-be privileged class can force the majority to produce a surplus for their consumption. Even a warrior elite cannot stop their people running away, so long as there is somewhere for them to go.[14]

With the development of agriculture, however, there is no longer anywhere to run to. Even if agricultural peoples must work much harder simply to meet their own subsistence needs, they can now be enslaved by a political power that forces them to work still more hours of the day to produce a surplus for a privileged class. It is true that the settlement of especially fertile land, such as river valleys, or the lake-shores of the Valle de Mexico, greatly increases the possible surplus and is generally associated with the first rise of 'civilization', but this is still based on a labour productivity that is low compared with the early gathering/hunting societies. The decisive factor is that the direct producers now have no way of resisting exploitation, and also there are far more of them to exploit.[15]

It is the development of agriculture, as seen by Marxism, that signals a decisive break with a merely natural existence. 'Men can be distinguished from animals by consciousness, by religion or anything else you like. They themselves begin to distinguish themselves from animals as soon as they begin to *produce* their means of subsistence.'[16] It is certainly beyond question that agriculture marks an entirely new stage in the human relationship with our natural environment, deliberately modifying this in an unprecedented fashion, and thus enabling a vast increase in population and the rise of complex and stratified societies. The agricultural adaptation, as already stated, also fits together with a built-in competition between societies for fertile land, and an endemic state of war that simmers just beneath the surface even in times of so-called peace.

For this reason, it is legitimate to associate with agriculture, too, the development of the family matrix into the systematic subordination of women to men; for even if warfare predated the discovery of agriculture, it was a symptom of the crisis of the gathering/hunting adaptation that led to agriculture as a solution, arising out of the same scarcity of land that agriculture was to make permanent. The family, in other words, is the level of the gender system that corresponds to the original gathering/hunting stage of human evolution, while male domination, both within the family and in society at large, corresponds to the stage of agriculture.

In the course of the last century, the study of primitive societies has taught us a painful but necessary lesson in modesty. Though there is a very real sense in which these societies are indeed primitive, i.e. in terms of their level of technology, and their consequent low degree of freedom from the constraints of their natural environment, yet in many of the higher things of life, from interpersonal relations through to their art and oral literature, they prove in no way inferior to ourselves — however different the forms they have developed in their particular circumstances. We have slowly had to abandon the comfortable illusion that the indigenous peoples of Africa, Australia, the Americas, etc. lead a merely animal existence, and to recognize that some of them at least are more civilized that we are — in particular, in the greater harmony of their social relations, free from the structured patterns of domination and exploitation that are an integral characteristic of our own complex societies.

Even though the Marxist theory of historical materialism recognized the development of technology as the guiding thread of human evolution, thus in one sense reinforcing a Eurocentric perspective, their commitment to communism also enabled Marx and Engels to appreciate earlier than most social theorists the relatively harmonious way of life displayed by the primitive peoples. So much so, in fact, that by 1884 Engels could take over, in *The Origin of the Family*, the verdict of the American anthropologist Lewis Henry Morgan, on whose work his own book was largely based, that 'the next higher plane of society to which experience, intelligence and knowledge are steadily tending' would be 'a revival, in higher form, of the liberty, equality and fraternity of the ancient *gentes* [= clan system]'.[17]

In this light, the violent social antagonisms of the class system, which the *Communist Manifesto* of 1848 had seen as marking 'all hitherto existing society',[18] came to appear as a distortion of human social organization from an originally harmonious pattern, which was necessary in order to develop material technology and give humankind greater command over our environment, but has now served its purpose and become redundant. And though it would be quite wrong to idealize gathering/hunting society, where people may not face the terrors of class oppression, but do face all too often the terrors of their own imagination, the expansion of ethnographic knowledge in the last hundred years has certainly confirmed the basic shape of this dialectical process. If anything, the distortion of class society appears even more as a temporary kink, now that the history and prehistory of our species is known to be far longer than Engels suspected.

Yet there are many aspects of the traditional Marxist view of the main lines of human development that must be reformulated, if they are to remain contemporary with the progress of scientific discovery, and not ossify into useless and harmful dogma. And one of these, which particularly concerns us here, bears on the relationship between gender and class. It is indisputable today that a certain bias towards male domination already exists in gathering/hunting societies, that actual male domination can be demonstrated in those many gathering/hunting societies where this is not counterbalanced by a decisive economic preeminence on the part of women, and that with the rise of warfare, women are decisively relegated to the subordinate position in society they have occupied ever since. Gender oppression, in other words, predated class oppression, even if the two things ultimately form part of the same development, i.e. the reorganization of human society around the principle of violence, associated with the transition from gathering/hunting to agriculture.

The orthodox Marxist conception, however, as classically expressed by Engels, wrongly posits a universal stage of matrilineal descent or 'mother right' (though Engels was correct in associating matriliny with a more equal relationship between women and men), and wrongly depicts this as overthrown in favour of patriliny and male domination only with the development of individual private property (in the form of herds of domesticated animals). Since this happened to arise in the masculine sphere of the division of labour, it made women economically dependent on men. It is sad to see these arguments, now almost a century out of date, being repeated today in the name of an orthodoxy that has degenerated into dogma. A detailed debate with 19th century conceptions seems pointless, so I shall simply put forward what I believe, on the available evidence, should be the general position of historical materialism today.

This reformulation of the relationship between gender and class, however, also requires the introduction of what is quite rightly the third term in Engels' argument: the origin of the family, private property, and the *state*. Here I shall take up the detailed analysis of the relationship between private property and the state developed by the East German exile Rudolf Bahro in his book *The Alternative*, perhaps the most important work in the historical materialist tradition to have been written for many years.[19]

The orthodox Marxist thesis holds that systematic economic inequality first arose in the form of individual private property, originally herds of animals. This subsequently developed into commodity production, which also gave an impetus to the exploitation of slave labour. To protect this exploitation, the privileged class eventually established the state, with its monopoly of armed force to enforce class rule. Engels took the rise of the Athenian state as a model, yet this was more than 2,000 years after the empires of the

Near East, which had so great an effect on Greek development, were already well established.

Bahro builds on advances already made within the Marxist tradition, which are grouped under the concept of the 'Asiatic mode of production', to conclude that a system of economic exploitation first came into being in the form of the state itself. The origins of the state, however, lie much further back in time, when private property, even in animal herds, was still relatively undeveloped. The specialization by the first mental workers (priests) in determining the calendar, in particular the rise and fall of rivers that was so important in the rich alluvial plains where this development took place, enabled them to set themselves up, necessarily in some kind of combination with a warrior elite, as a privileged corporation, entitled not only to direct society's labours in the interest of more effective production (irrigation works, etc.), but also to channel surplus labour into their own luxury consumption. We can still see the monuments of this today, in the great stone structures that almost all these early states forced their workers to build. But these first gigantic results of the extraction of surplus labour, whether in Egypt, Mesopotamia, China, Central America or Peru, are all the work of ruling classes whose 'property' existed only as the collective property of the state they directed, never as the private property of individuals. Private ownership of productive slaves, of land, or the purchase of wage-labour, came only at a much later date, becoming a characteristic system of production only in the Graeco-Roman world.

Bahro accordingly sees the mental-manual division of labour enshrined in the state as a 'geological stratum' that underlies the rise of individual private property, and can thus easily survive its demise, as is most clearly seen in the case of Soviet society. Private property is only one particular form of the class system, its most general form being the separation of a class of mental workers and the existence of a state that they direct.

This advance on orthodox Marxism has several implications of tremendous importance to understanding the relationship between the systems of gender and class. The existence of the state, as was already recognized by Marx and

Engels, involves a special public force to enforce the system of exploitation.[20] For Engels, in developing this concept, the sexual division of labour was taken as simply natural, yet from today's perspective, the fact that this is precisely a special force of armed *men* gives call for reflection. From what I have argued above, it is a precondition if the state is to develop that this 'special force' is available, i.e. that men already do specialize in violence against other human beings, a violence that insidiously spreads from its original direction, purely outward against other societies, into a violence against members of their own, as the boundaries between different societies are broken down by the capture of slaves, and eventually by conquest. And if the state is the primordial form of the class system, then this arises much more directly from the division of gender than in the orthodox Marxist presentation.

Far more is involved here than simply a case of 'which came first?', class oppression or the oppression of women. It is not just that the orthodox Marxist conception places class oppression, women's oppression and the state in a wrong order; the error bears on the specific forms that these three systems take, and on the consequent causal relationships between them. The orthodox conception sees the class system only in terms of individual private property, whereas the first form of class privilege was the corporate form in which the mental workers separated themselves off from manual work. It sees the state, accordingly, as always external to the class system, supporting this from without, whereas it was precisely in the state itself that the privilege of the mental workers was first embodied, this original form of the state always combining a priestly and a military elite. And it sees the oppression of women only in those respects that can be attributed to economic dependence, remaining blind to the deeper level at which this is already a function of the masculine specialization in violence. Thus although orthodox Marxism is correct in seeing women's oppression, class oppression and the state as bound up together in a single pattern, characteristic of a certain stage in the development of human society, it is incorrect in its definition of what precisely each of these elements involves, and this has an important bearing on the relationship between the three elements still today, when the overall system is in crisis, and we are searching our way forward to a new social harmony.

In seeking to explain women's oppression as an effect of private property, the classical Marxists were attempting, quite understandably, to link the movement of women with the movement of the working class, in a common struggle against private capital. Yet as Bahro so cogently argues, the orthodox explanation of class oppression in terms of private property has itself proved defective. Under the Soviet system, the basic social hierarchy remains very similar to that in the West; private property in the means of production has been as good as completely done away with, yet the whole society is organized on the basis of a division of labour running from the unskilled farm labourer up to the managing directors of state corporations (not to mention the completely parasitic 'politbureaucracy').

It was understandable that Marx should have concentrated, in his analysis of working-class oppression, on private capital, as in the heyday of laissez-faire manual work was very largely coterminous with wage-labour, and wage-labour with manual work. Yet even in mid 19th century Britain, class privilege could not simply be equated with capital ownership, and as capitalism has developed into its monopoly and state monopoly phases, the gap between the two things has steadily widened. In the dogmatic insistence that the oppression of the working class is reducible to private capital, Marxism has been distorted from a weapon of liberation into a justification for the new ruling class of the Soviet system and their would-be counterparts in the West.

What is wrong with the Marxist theory of women's oppression, therefore, is also wrong with the Marxist theory of class oppression. In both cases, to put the theory right it is necessary to start not from private property, but from the oppressive division of labour that underlies both private property and the gender system. This was indeed the original perspective of Marx himself, as expressed for example in the *Economic and Philosophical Manuscripts* and *The German Ideology*. But as Marx came to focus his analysis more and more on the specificities of the capitalist mode of production, leaving his general theory of history very much un-developed, this perspective was overshadowed. In *Capital*, the division of labour is introduced only as a division among equals, i.e. the division between commodity producers, or between workers within the factory. The *unequal* division of labour, which Marx took as his starting-point in *The German Ideology*,[21] has all but disappeared.

Faced with the negative example of the 'socialist' countries, it is clear enough today that any communist critique of the present society, East or West, must take up the original Marxist perspective. And when this is done, we find not only that the division between mental and manual labour, between those who give orders and those who take orders, runs through every form of class society from the early empires to capitalism and beyond, but also that the sexual division of labour existed before the class division, and formed its precondition in so far as the class division requires a state which institutionalizes masculine violence.

The gross inadequacy of the orthodox Marxist theory of women's oppression, lacking as it does any concept of gender, cannot be attributed simply to the theoretical failures of Marx and Engels, still less to their personal male chauvinism. If they were unable to see women's specialization in childcare and men's specialization in violence as a product of history, let alone to see heterosexuality as anything but natural, these things were not challenged either by the feminist movement of their time. When Engels wrote that, in communist society, women will never have 'to give themselves to a man from any other considerations than real love', or 'to refuse to give themselves to their love for fear of economic consequences',[22] this undoubtedly read very differently to European feminists of the 1880s and 1890s than it does to their descendants today.

The women's movement of the late 19th century, which Engels certainly had in mind when he wrote *The Origin of the Family*, was above all a movement of middle-class women (I use the term without any pejorative connotation whatsoever), for whom economic dependence on their husbands was the most immediate form of subjugation. It was not as if they absolutely couldn't earn their own living; after all millions of women did, as millhands, domestic servants, etc., but it was taken for granted by all concerned that this sacrifice of class privilege, in the conditions of Victorian capitalism, was an impossible one to make. In *The Origin of the Family*, Engels is quite correct to contrast this abject dependence with the far more equal position that women enjoyed, for example, among the Iroquois studied by Morgan, where the economy was communal. He could also explain why among the proletariat, for all the brutality of family relations, women generally had a greater degree of independence than among the bourgeoisie. Yet by accepting the sexual division of labour as quasi-natural, Engels could proceed, quite falsely, to attribute all forms of women's oppression simply to private property. In class society, with its individual family unit, housework had become a private service, making women economically dependent on men; under communism, 'private housekeeping is transformed into a social industry',[23] and women's problems are thereby solved. The whole dimension that the present-day women's movement describes as 'patriarchy' (particularly those socialist feminists who see patriarchy as existing alongside capitalism) is simply whisked away.

I have argued above that the structure underlying women's oppression is the sexual division of labour. This not only ascribes childcare and housekeeping to women (an activity Engels naturalistically depicts as women's 'family duties');[24] it also ascribes warfare, and violent activity in general, to men. The Marxist theory explains why houseworkers are economically dependent; it does not explain why houseworkers are women. And the incessant round of bullying and battering, demands for ego-placation and sexual services that men presently inflict on women goes far beyond anything that can feasibly be attributed to economic dependence; the capitalist does not behave like this to his employee.

The comparison that Engels does not make, but should have done, is between the position of women in capitalist society and that in peasant societies, which is how most people have lived since what he describes as the 'world-historical defeat of the female sex'. Here, there is no economic dependence of women on male incomes in the way characteristic of exploiting classes in general, and partially among the proletariat in capitalist society, yet the symptoms of male domination are still very much present. In many peasant societies, indeed, they take a far more vicious form than anywhere else, with such phenomena as foot-binding (China), the marriage of young girls to middle-aged men (India), suttee (also India), the tortures of clitoridectomy and infibulation (Africa and elsewhere) being an everyday fact of life.

Even the most strongly feminist of orthodox Marxists, Alexandra Kollontai, failed to challenge the primary sexual division of labour, or the theoretical explanation of women's oppression in terms of private property. Though she was in many ways far ahead of her time (certainly in Bolshevik Russia), and her writings are of interest to the women's movement even today, Kollontai still saw women in socialist society as having primary responsibility for child-rearing, which implicitly meant leaving the defence of the revolution primarily to men. In her *Revolution in Life and Morals*, for example, written in 1923, Kollontai wrote:

> After breast-feeding, the remaining cares for the growing generation can be passed onto the collective. Naturally the maternal instinct is strong and we should not let it die out. But why not let this instinct, so precious for working humanity, branch out and rise to its highest level — that of caring for other children?

And discussing the problem of abandoned children, Kollontai actually warned: 'The women of the Workers' Republic have not yet fully realized that motherhood is not a private matter but a social obligation.'[25] Kollontai herself, of course, was sufficiently in a privileged position, both before and after the revolution, that she never had to do any form of housework, and could have her own children looked after by others.

If the socialist feminists of today, well aware of the impossibility of reducing male domination to economics, have introduced a principle of 'patriarchy' as something that exists alongside the capitalist system, this itself shows how they still pay too great allegiance to Marxist orthodoxy. They have criticized the sexual division of labour, and seek the abolition of both class and gender, yet despite this advance, they are not ready to challenge traditional Marxism on its own ground. But it is an untenable half-way house to grasp the gender system as a system of social relations, yet to leave the Marxist concept of the social formation otherwise unaffected. The whole structure of society must appear different, once the gender system is understood. Rather than being afraid to examine it afresh, we should be glad of the opportunity to advance the materialist conception of history in this way; it is certainly in need of modernization, being in so many ways ossified in the 19th century and an inadequate instrument for understanding — and transforming — the present. I am well aware how inadequate is the synthesis I am trying to present here, particularly how it fails to cope with the full complexity of the historical process. But I am convinced that we must struggle forward to a unified conception of gender and class, that the concerns of women's and gay liberation should not be hived off from the social totality under the rubric of 'patriarchy.'[26]

A major reference-point for discussion of the Marxist theory of women's liberation is of course the historical experience of the Marxist-led revolutions. In all these cases, women undoubtedly took great strides forward. Yet this advance was always most evident in the more backward countries, where even the democratic transformation of social relations (i.e. essentially along modern Western lines) already meant the abolition of the most extreme forms of female servitude (e.g. foot-binding in China, the legal subordination of women to their fathers and husbands in Russia). In terms of the specifically socialist programme, a certain progress was undoubtedly made, particularly in providing economic support for mothers and collective childcare facilities. Also, helped by a high demand for labour and the shortage of men after major wars, women encroached on many fields of work that had previously been a male preserve. In these respects, at least, the position of women in the 'socialist' countries still remains in advance of that in the West today, though Western women seem belatedly to be catching up. On the other hand, however, these countries have defined motherhood as a social obligation (Kollontai), and erected strict barriers to any form of life outside the 'socialist family', in a way that seems very backward from the contemporary Western standpoint.

In China, the greatest of all Marxist-led revolutions, both what women put into the revolutionary movement and what they got out of it was more substantial than anywhere else. It is no coincidence that Mao Zedong's first published writings were on the topic of women's oppression, i.e. his articles of 1919 on 'Miss Chao's Suicide'.[27] And more than fifty years later, in the campaign to criticize Lin Biao and Confucius, the Chinese Communist Party could still encourage women to struggle against male domination in a way that would be quite impossible in any other 'socialist' country. Yet despite the inroads that Chinese women have made into productive activities traditionally monopolized by men, at no time, even during the heady days of the Cultural Revolution, has any group of Chinese feminists yet criticized the basic sexual division of labour itself. Women may 'hold up half the sky', yet it is still they who specialize in childcare, even when this is socialized. And although many women receive basic weapons training in the militia, the People's Liberation Army remains an all-male institution, aside from certain auxiliary roles (medical, etc.)

It would be impossible to discuss this question fully without placing it in the context of the problem of the 'socialist' countries in general. In the Soviet bloc in particular, it is clear that the planned economy is not geared to the overall needs of society; indeed, there are very few democratic channels through which social needs can be expressed. It is the rulers of the state who define economic and social goals, and the needs of women suffer accordingly, as do those of working people in general. Now that the women's liberation movement of the last ten years, not to mention the gay movement, has begun to criticize the gender system as such, our sights are set at a level that the Soviet countries cannot even accept as within the realm of legitimate debate. In July 1980, the writers of the first feminist *samizdat* in the Soviet Union were expelled to the West,[28] while the official press simultaneously excoriated the film-maker Sergei Paradzhanov who, having been convicted for homosexuality, had not only got sent to a labour camp, but, according to

*Pravda*, 'placed himself outside society and consequently outside art'.[29] 'Society', as defined by the Soviet state, cannot tolerate any challenge to the gender system, even the most involuntary.

From the limited progress that women did make in the Marxist-led revolutions, it is possible to argue that a socialist transformation in a Western country today, if it built on existing democratic traditions and did not abolish these, would at least help to undermine the gender system. The contribution of Marxists to discussion of the gender contradiction in recent years has been precisely to point out the important part played in the position of women in our present society by their economic dependence on men. They have thus kept attention focussed on the situation of the majority of women in our society, who are still tightly enmeshed in the family in a way that the vanguard of women's liberationists, almost by definition, are not. Undoubtedly, the struggle for economic independence, which means in particular that the costs of child-rearing should be borne by society as a whole, is a crucial one. Yet some progress in this direction has already been made with the welfare state, and as women become ever less ready to bear children under the present economic conditions, this makes a strong pressure for further advance. Would it occur automatically after a proletarian revolution? As I shall argue in Chapter Four, such a revolution is not on the agenda in Britain, and the orthodox Marxist position also ignores the very real possibilities that women have today, as opposed to any time in the past, for a radical struggle against the sexual division of labour as such. For these reasons, the appeal of Marxism to the women's movement in the West today is strictly limited, and will remain so until it can speak to them in a way that genuinely does tie in with the real problems and opportunities of the present situation. The same applies still more strongly to the relationship between Marxism and the gay movement, as discussed in Chapter Two.

## 4. *The Abolition of Gender*

I argued in the previous sections that the gender system is not just historically prior to the system of class, but actually forms its necessary precondition, through the extension of the sexual division of labour into the male specialization in warfare. This does not in itself mean that it is impossible to do away with class without simultaneously tackling gender; that question I shall come on to discuss in the final chapter of this book. What should be noted here, however, is that the socialist movement, and orthodox Marxism in particular, has invariably proceeded to struggle against the class system without taking the gender system into account, as it has had no understanding of this. And so, if today the abolition of gender has been placed on the historical agenda (no pun intended!), it has been introduced not from the socialist side, but rather from the side of feminism — i.e. from women and gay men who are immediately oppressed by the gender system, subsequently joined by a section of 'men against sexism'.

What, though, are the objective conditions that lie behind the feminist and gay liberation movements, enabling us to struggle for a change in rigid definitions of gender 'role', and ultimately to set our sights on the abolition of the gender system altogether? For if the movement against the gender system is indeed 'history conscious of itself', then it must be possible to demonstrate the objective forces at work in society that are pressing in this direction, of which the conscious formulation of the anti-gender goal is in the last instance simply the subjective expression. These forces are indeed to be found.

Taking the history of the women's movement from the late 18th century onwards, its developing demands can be seen first of all as part of the struggle of the oppressed masses for democracy and socialism. In the first phase of this struggle, the demands of the working class were particularly directed to winning full rights of citizenship, above all the suffrage. This was also the specific demand of the women's movement, from the first petitions for female suffrage in the French revolution through to the militant campaigns in America, Britain and Europe of the late 19th and early 20th centuries. Once the working class had gained a foothold in the body politic, it used its strength above all to win a certain economic security against the hazards of the capitalist labour market. And together with the struggle for unemployment insurance, sickness benefit and old-age pensions, women struggled to gain family allowances and maternity benefits. At the present time, when the working class is focussing on winning new rights in the workplace, there has also been a women's struggle on this front, for equal pay and access to skilled jobs.

The feminist and working-class struggles have never been waged in mutual isolation. Their origins were separate, yet they have time and again at least partially coalesced. Middle-class feminists, in solidarity with the majority of their sex, have consistently got involved with working-class women and their double oppression, in the way that led Sylvia Pankhurst, and many like her, from feminism on to communism. While the working-class movement, which in its earliest forms did not even support female suffrage (the Chartists in England, the disciples of Proudhon in France), soon recognized that the class struggle would be greatly strengthened by embracing the particular needs of working-class women.

Other economic factors have given a more specific stimulus to the women's movement. The development of industrial capitalism made millions of women into wage-earners, giving them an income independent of their husbands, which had a very definite effect in extending their horizons. In parallel with this, the capitalist market extended to supply to women, in return for their wage, goods that had previously been more arduously produced in the home. The household economy contracted in favour of the factory economy, in a development running from processed foods through to vacuum cleaners and washing machines.

All this had a certain undermining effect on the gender division, yet a still stronger effect resulted from the reduction in family size that the middle classes pioneered in the 1870s and 1880s, and which spread to the broad mass of the working class within a generation or two. The greatest factor that has enabled women to raise their sights, recognize their present position as bad and struggle for change, is that instead of having eight, twelve or even more pregnancies (if they survived to menopause), seeing most of their children die and being worn out from the physical and mental burden, women in the advanced countries today have an average of just over two pregnancies, in a lifespan that has lengthened to approach eighty years. The cycle of pregnancy, childbirth and lactation now takes only a minor part of women's time and energy, instead of completely dominating this as it had done in the past, especially since the beginnings of agriculture.[30]

The preconditions for this reduction in fertility, of course, have been the great advances in nutrition, hygiene and medicine that have marked the last century or so. These are certainly the product of the capitalist epoch (in the sense in which the struggle of the working class to better its conditions is ultimately an integral part of this). Yet they have a dynamic that is relatively independent of both the course of the class struggle and the specifically economic 'laws of motion' of capitalist production, and an effect that amounts to a world-historical transformation in the relationship between the sexes; at first only as a potential, but sooner or later requiring a change in all aspects of relations between women and men as a result.

The women's movement has long been aware of the liberating potential of birth control, and it is an important strand in the feminist struggle still today to improve the quality and availability of birth-control techniques. The effect of this transformation on gender relations, however, is in no way dependent only on the campaigns of the women's movement as an organized force. Far more than is the case with class relations, gender relations can change in a relatively molecular way, with each new generation of women facing a different objective situation and making individual choices that in the long run add up to a profound cultural change. One aspect of this, in recent years, has been the changing relationship of women to their own sexuality.

In the not so distant past, women learned to regard (hetero)sex as a dangerous activity, threatening to produce unwanted children. It was always men who made sexual de-

mands on them, and they who had to restrain these demands, and thus their own sexuality into the bargain. This
tendency was actually reinforced in the early period of family planning, when even within marriage women sought to
avoid further pregnancy, at a time when contraceptive appli-
ances were still rudimentary and hard to come by. In the last
twenty years, however, the great improvement (though no
one could say 'perfection') of birth-control technology, and
its near-universal availability, have finally enabled women
to release these restraints on their own sexuality, to undo a
repression they had to impose for the sake of maintaining
themselves above primary poverty. Besides the value of
being able to enjoy sex for its own sake, this has undoubtedly led women to pose new demands to their male partners
for sexual satisfaction, and by beginning to overcome their
relegation to mere objects of sexuality and reassert themselves as equal subjects, their self-confidence and strength
in struggling to improve their condition is undoubtedly enhanced in other fields of life as well. If the first effect of the
pill in the 1960s was to give men a new excuse for demanding sexual services (particularly pre- and extra-marital), this
was soon overshadowed by a stronger tendency promoting
women's independence.

The traditional feminist movements, very understandably, focussed their demands on access to spheres that had
previously been a male monopoly: the vote, education,
skilled jobs, ownership of property, political office, participation in artistic and cultural life. This struggle was constantly fuelled, from one generation to the next, by the increasing time and energy that was not taken up with pregnancy, childcare, and the mundane activities of housework.
Yet as I pointed out with the example of Alexandra
Kollontai, it was a long time before it even occurred to feminists, in anything but a marginal way, that there was something wrong with the basic sexual division of labour itself.
Finally, however, this realization burst through with the
new wave of feminist consciousness that broke in the late
1960s. At last, women were no longer content to be child-
carers who *also* worked in industry or services, voted, wrote
books or flew airplanes. They demanded that the basic task

ascribed to women in the sexual division of labour should itself be the equal responsibility of men.

This cast a radically new light on a tendency that had
hitherto been subordinate in the women's movement,
though never quite unvoiced. Feminists had very often had
the feeling that, just as there was something wrong with the
present society's definition of femininity, so there was conversely something wrong with masculinity too. It was never
possible to demand that women should change, in their
activities and in their minds, without demanding at least a
certain complementary change from men as well. This feeling had often been articulated in terms of opposition to masculine violence, and militarism in particular. Yet until the
gender division as such was radically challenged, it was
never possible to demand that men should stop being violent altogether, i.e. that girls and boys should be brought up
in a non-gendered way, and that the mentality underpinning
war and the state should not be produced. The new feminism of the late 1960s very accurately defined itself as 'radical', by contrast to the 'liberal' and 'socialist' feminism of
the past. It represented a qualitative leap forward, with altogether new and major implications for society as a whole.

The struggle of gay men, if inevitably on a more modest
scale than that of women, has similarly experienced different stages of development. And in our case, the immediate
determinants of a new push forward have generally depended on the rhythms of the feminist movement. Every up-
swing of the women's movement has found itself faced with
the reactionary ideology that the existing gender definitions
were natural, and has had to oppose this with the correct
idea that they were a cultural product — or should at least
become so. The rise of feminism has thus always provided a
certain shelter for the gay minority to demand our right to
exist, and the ups and downs of the women's movement in
the past have always had their reflection in the gay men's
movement.

In the new movement of women's liberation, however,
the convergence with the gay movement was altogether
more pronounced than ever before. The radical critique of

the gender system made by feminist writers now directly
enabled the gay movement, for the first time, to adopt the
scientifically justified position that homosexuality was acquired rather than innate, as it could at last see this acquisition as something altogether good, i.e. a relative erosion of
the norms of gender, which the eventual triumph of feminism would abolish altogether, making homosexuality as
universal a human relationship as heterosexuality.

In the last analysis, the same precondition underlies the
feminist and gay struggle for the abolition of gender, as the
socialist struggle for the abolition of class. In each case, the
advance of the productive forces characteristic of the capitalist epoch has made what was previously a necessary social pattern, if society was to develop, into something redundant. It is the scientific technology that has come into its
own with capitalism, as its lasting legacy to the human
race, that enables the majority of the population, i.e. the
working class, and that other majority, women and gay
men, to seek the radical overthrow of the systems by which
we are oppressed, and to point out that these systems actually *have* to be overthrown in the interest of human progress
as a whole. In this process, capitalism has acted not just as a
contingent mode of production, but as a world-historical
turning-point in the development of our species. Human
control over our environment has reached a level that places
on the agenda a fundamental readjustment of certain basic
conditions of human existence: the class system, which has
been with us for several thousand years; male domination,
which has been with us even longer; and the sexual division
of labour with its institutionalized heterosexuality, which
has been with us since the very dawn of our species.

I have sought to show in this chapter how male domination and the class system are intimately related, in a common matrix with the state and the endemic warfare between
competing societies. All these are different strands in the
kink of human evolution, the disruption of an earlier
more harmonious pattern of social relations and the reorganization of human existence on the principle of violence.
Today, this disruption is no longer required; from being a
help to human development, it has turned into a hindrance.
It is both possible and necessary to overcome it, and to re-

establish a new social harmony on the surer basis provided by our increased knowledge of the world and ourselves.

As far as the gender system in particular is concerned, the present crisis bears differentially on the feminine and masculine spheres of the division of labour. The two-pregnancy revolution certainly makes it possible for women to reject their confinement to a childcaring role, and demand that men should take equal responsibility for this so that women can share equally in other social tasks. Yet women endured far greater oppression in the past than they do in the West today, and still endure in many other parts of the world. However necessary a radical change seems to the minority of conscious feminists, the gender system could survive more or less indefinitely, out of inertia and the force of habit, if this were the only problem it presented.

What has been far less emphasized in the anti-gender movement, but if anything is even more vital, is the bearing that the crisis has on the masculine sphere in the division of labour, i.e. the specialization in violence. Given the unprecedented amplification of violent action by scientific technology, this becomes ever more destructive. We have already seen two world wars in this century, with more than sixty million people atrociously killed, not to mention the echoes of these in several dozen minor wars following similar logic on a smaller scale. Just as it was the increasing and inescapable proximity of one society to another that originally brought warfare into being, so today it is a still greater degree of inescapable proximity on our planet that makes warfare intolerable. The potential effects of a new world war would embroil us all to the extent of precipitating a downward spiral from which our species might well not recover; war must be made impossible, and very soon, if the human race is to survive and take its next step forward.

This means a unified global society on our planet — for there is no way we can put an end to war unless the underprivileged of the South receive their (over)due share of the planet's resources, and unless the competing systems of East and West can inaugurate a process of learning from each other's good points and abandoning their respective bad ones. But at a different level, though an equally necessary aspect of the process, it means abolishing the masculine specialization in violence. This is not merely possible, on the basis that scientific technology has provided. It is absolutely essential, in the interest of survival itself.

The abolition of the gender system has been alternatively conceived in terms of women becoming like men, men becoming like women, or both meeting somewhere in between. It is now possible to define more precisely where the convergence will take place. The gender system arose, like the class system, as a division of labour, in this case between women's specialization in childcare and men's specialization in hunting, subsequently extended to warfare and violence in general. As with the later division between mental and manual work, this sexual division of labour immediately brought with it a dimension of oppression. The warrior came to face the childcarer as dominant to subordinate, just as the mental worker later faced the manual worker. But this relationship of oppression can only be understood as a result of the functional relationship that underlies it. The oppression of women by men, in other words, like the oppression of manual by mental workers, is part of a social system, not just the voluntaristic act of the oppressors.

There is of course much more to the sexual division of labour, in contemporary Western society, than the primary division between childcare and warfare which I have focussed on in this chapter. And while the enforced specialization of women in childcare has rightly been a particular theme of the women's liberation movement, this has more usually been discussed in relation to those spheres of masculine activity from which, unlike warfare, women experience their exclusion as an oppression: the whole range of skilled jobs that are largely a masculine monopoly. I believe it is essential in understanding the gender system to keep in mind the distinction between the primary sexual division of labour, and the other, secondary aspects of this division. Not only are the feminine specialization in childcare and the masculine specialization in warfare universal features of human society at a certain evolutionary stage; this primary division is the foundation of women's oppression, and these two things in turn structure the psychological dimension of gender.

The secondary aspects of the sexual division of labour, on the other hand, are merely a by-product. They are in part a direct function of the primary division, i.e. women in the caring professions; in part a function of women's oppression, i.e. women in subordinate positions to men. (A job like that of secretary embodies both these things.) In some respects, moreover, the secondary division of labour can be quite flexible. During the world wars, women were temporarily drafted into skilled engineering jobs on a mass scale, and in some contemporary class societies, particularly in the Soviet countries, this is not nearly such a masculine monopoly as it is in the West. Yet no real conflict arises between a woman working in a job like engineering, and her psychological femininity that is a function of the primary division of labour, directly as mother and indirectly as subordinate to men. While every encroachment that women make into fields of social life that were formerly a masculine monopoly is a step in the right direction, the breakdown of the gender system requires a struggle against the primary sexual division of labour, and cannot be achieved by anything short of this.

As the gender system is eroded, those differences between women and men that are due to the relationship of oppression will simply disappear, i.e. everything that is a product of male domination and female subservience. In this respect women and men will meet in the middle. The same will apply to the secondary sexual division of labour. But the situation is quite different as far as the underlying primary division of labour goes. Here, the tasks ascribed to women and men were formerly all socially necessary. What has happened today, however, is that the male specialization in warfare and violence has become redundant, while the feminine specialization in childcare can accordingly be shared equally between the two sexes. In this respect, therefore, women and men will not meet in the middle, but at a point that is more on the traditional feminine side. *Not* the weak femininity that expresses women's subservience to men, but the strong femininity of the maternal role, which must indeed, as Alexandra Kollontai put it, 'branch out and rise to its highest level,'[31] this time, however, as a caring by both women and men alike, not just for our children, but for the planet as a whole.

There is no guarantee that our species will succeed in bringing a communist society into being on Earth, though the greatest single driving force towards this today is the fate that awaits us if we do not overcome the present contradictions. And just as the transition from the relatively harmonious stage of the early gathering/hunting adaptation to the stage of agriculture and violence was a complex one, its different elements emerging at different points in time and only later fitting together into a new pattern, so the different elements of a communist society, for example the resolution of national, class and gender divisions, and the development of an ecologically stable system of production, cannot arise simultaneously. As far as human intention is concerned, we must naturally concentrate on resolving those contradictions that immediately jeopardize our survival, and leave the less urgent ones until later.

But if we do manage the advance to communism, how will this form of society appear when considered as an entire new pattern, a new adaptation in the sense that gathering/hunting and agriculture are each a basic stage in human development, ultimately defined in terms of the way that human society obtains its means of subsistence, or conducts its material metabolism with its environment? Gathering/hunting, as already noted, is the stage at which production, in the full sense of the term, is not yet even commenced. Human beings certainly manipulate the material world around them in ways that are qualitatively in advance of anything of which the apes are capable, yet food and fibre, the most basic of all use-values, are still directly appropriated where they are naturally found. Agriculture, by contrast, replaces mere appropriation by a deliberate production, giving human development a decisive new impetus. A progressive improvement in technology, despite occasional setbacks due to social disorganization, leads in a continual line to the industrial revolution and the establishment of technology on a scientific basis, still in the context of a society organized by class and gender, the state and warfare.

The original Marxist argument holds that scientific technology makes it possible to overcome the class division in that the demands of the superstructure, which led in the past to the majority having to toil to support a privileged few priests, philosophers, artists, scientists, etc., can today be met by a sharing of mental and manual work, with the latter (in fact, menial tasks in general) reduced to a minimum, leaving enough time and energy for all to take part in super-structural activity of one kind or another. As we have seen, this argument can be simply extended to apply to the other major divisions that set one group against another. Yet if scientific technology is the characteristic adaptation that makes it possible to straighten out the kink in human development and establish a new social harmony, this demands a redefinition of the concept of production as important as that involved in the transition from the mere appropriation of gathering/hunting to what Marxism sees as production proper.[32]

It already begins to seem strange, to those of us whose particular oppression lies in the gender system, that while the production of material use-values left the original phase of quasi-natural appropriation behind some several millenia ago, and has had such an exciting development since then, the way that we procreate ourselves as human beings still remains essentially at this spontaneous, 'paleolithic' level. To obtain a new human being, we still depend on the random exchange of genetic material, between individuals who select themselves not on the basis of genetic suitability but for quite different reasons, and as effected by penis-vagina intercourse. If conception takes place, then gestation is generally allowed to proceed in a quite spontaneous fashion, with no conscious control, and it is hoped that the end-product is a viable human infant.

This is at least how the majority of us still happen. But even now, there are a growing number of technological interventions made in the process. Birth-control techniques of various kinds make it possible for the penis-vagina intercourse that is still generally de rigeur in the heterosexual milieu to be practised without leading to pregnancy. Artificial insemination, on the other hand, makes it possible for a woman to conceive quite independent of sexual intercourse of any kind (even if, in the present social system, this technique is applied far more to shore up the family than to transform it). An increasing number of tests can be performed to check on the normalcy of foetal development, and if significant deformity is indicated, it is a simple operation to abort. As soon as a critical position is adopted towards the gender system, it seems only sensible that the intervention of scientific technology in this field, which is as yet at its very beginnings, should be extended so that women are freed from internal gestation, genetic recombination is effected in a way designed to improve our biological material, and the division between female and male individuals is ultimately phased out altogether. When this happens, then the transition from a quasi-natural process to a deliberate process of production, which already took place several thousand years ago in the field of material use-values, will also have been extended to the production of human beings ourselves. Humankind will then truly *make itself*, in the full sense of the term. How could anyone who looks forward to communism wish it otherwise?

A quotation from Engels that is often bandied around is taken from his Preface to *The Origin of the Family*:

> According to the materialist conception, the determining factor in history is, in the final instance, the production and reproduction of immediate life. This, again, is of a twofold character: on the one side, the production of the means of existence, of food, clothing and shelter and the tools necessary for that production; on the other side, the production of human beings themselves, the propagation of the species.[33]

This has frequently led to confusion among those who seek to reconcile an anti-gender perspective with orthodox Marxism. It seems to offer a place in the Marxist sun for those whose concern is with 'reproduction' in the sense of procreation/propagation. Yet it is clearly impossible to put procreation as we know it today, let alone as Engels knew it a century ago, on a par with the production of material use-values. The latter has millenia of historical development behind it, and a vast infrastructure of means of production in the present. The former still remains, even today, a quasi-natural activity, no matter how much it takes place within a complex system of social relations, as indeed it always has done. Yet Engels does seem to show at least an anticipatory glimmer that human procreation should be viewed, 'in the final instance', as 'the production of human beings', i.e. as a conscious practice, however far ahead of his time was the realization of this potentiality. Might his views on this subject have possibly been influenced by his own early practice of birth control, from the mid 19th century on?[34]

From this point of view, the Marxist dialectic of forces and relations of production, at least in the form put forward by Marx and maintained by his orthodox followers, applies only to one of the major adaptations that mark the evolution of our species, namely that centred on agriculture, in which the procuring of material use-values has left its quasi-natural phase of appropriation behind, and become a genuine production, and yet the procreation of new human beings is still stuck in its own quasi-natural phase. It is not hard to see why there is this great discrepancy in time between the two take-off points. For the first forms in which material use-values were produced, whether biological (domesticated plants and animals) or mineral (pottery, metallurgy, etc.), depended only on a very simple technology. In the 'production of human beings', moreover, it is impossible to pursue a eugenic policy, such as was practised with the earliest domestication of animals, as long as conception depends on penis-vagina intercourse, and gestation is intra-uterine. Only the most viciously repressive of regimes, such as the Nazis, have even attempted this. It is only in a society where people can be sure such a policy is not applied in any sectional interest, but in the interest of society as a whole (and certainly not a society 'represented' by the state), that human procreation can undergo its own 'neolithic revolution'.

The biological reductionism that sees feminine and masculine psychology as a matter of genes, leads naturally on to seeing the solution to women's oppression in the elimination of the male sex. Conversely, feminists of this tendency often perceive a more or less deliberate plot by men to perpetuate their position by an artificial parthenogenesis of their own. Male-to-'female' transsexuals, those unfortunate victims of the gender system, are indicated as the spearhead of a 'gynocide' of this kind. If the gender system is rooted not in biology, however, but in the sexual division of labour, then both problem and solution appear very differently. The dominating masculine personality, and its counterpart in the submissiveness of 'normal' femininity, are the effect of the social structure, not its cause. For all the oppression that women still suffer from men, not to mention the oppression that we gay men suffer from all upholders of the gender system, whether male or female (Anita Bryant and Mary Whitehouse), there is ultimately the basis for a common cause. The gender system is part of a social pattern that today endangers human survival, and the great majority of people, including heterosexual men, can and must be won to the struggle against it. A biological fix, such as reducing the number of male babies, [35] cannot possibly provide a sufficient solution. At worst, it might even antagonize men and make a common struggle against gender more difficult. But if humanity does succeed in overcoming the gender division and the other divisions linked with this, then the way will be open for us to adopt a eugenic policy that is genuinely in the interest of all. The biological convergence of the sexes will thus follow as a consequence of the breakdown of gender. And at this point, human procreation will finally link together with the production of material use-values as two halves of a common (and communist) harnessing of scientific technology: the production and reproduction of the human world.

# Chapter Two:
## Homosexuality and Gayness

### 1. Marxism and the Gay Movement

Orthodox Marxism has always recognized women as an oppressed group in class society, and championed their 'emancipation'. The problem is simply that the Marxist understanding of women's oppression has been very limited. Marxism has grasped the relationship of economic dependence that is typical of relations between the sexes among classes of privileged private proprietors, and to a lesser extent also among the working class of capitalist society, but it has had no concept of the gender system that underlies this.

For this reason, the relationship of Marxism to the gay movement has been altogether different from that to the women's movement. Even the 'bourgeois feminist' wing of the women's movement could be seen by Marxists as a potential ally in the right circumstances, but never has orthodox Marxism risen above regarding the gay minority as mere 'victims of capitalism', deserving more humane treatment, perhaps, but in no way having anything positive to contribute to the new society.

At times, indeed, the Marxist movement has viewed gay people in a far worse light, and from a superficial reading of Engels, it might even seem as if the founders of Marxism built an unjustified hostility to homosexuality into their doctrine right from the start. The reality, however, is somewhat more complex. It is true that Engels' *Origin of the Family*, the only text of classical Marxism where homosexuality is specifically discussed, refers to the 'distasteful practice of boy-love' among the ancient Greeks, and to the 'gross, unnatural vices' acquired by the early Germanic tribes.[1] Yet this was written in 1884, and only a few years later the early Marxists showed themselves to be in the vanguard of progressive opinion as far as the rights of the gay minority were concerned. Eduard Bernstein, Engels' literary executor, who had lived in England during the 1880s and returned to Germany to become a leader of the Social-Democratic Party (later famous as the founder of 'revisionism'), wrote a particularly vigorous defence of Oscar Wilde in the party's theoretical journal *Neue Zeit*.[2] And in 1898, when Magnus Hirschfeld and his Scientific Humanitarian Committee began the campaign for law reform, their first petition was introduced to the Reichstag by August Bebel, the Social-Democratic parliamentary leader.[3]

This liberal tolerance for the gay minority was based on seeing gays as a 'biological anomaly'. Yet when some form of homosexuality is practised by an entire male population, this explanation evidently breaks down, and sociological categories must be applied. Engels' moralistic labels of 'distasteful' and 'unnatural' clearly reflect only his own subjective distaste. Yet in his reference to Greek homosexuality, at least, there is something more involved, i.e. a genuine social criticism, which cannot simply be reduced to homophobia.

This reference appears in connection with Engels' discussion of male domination in Greek antiquity, where he goes on to add that 'this degradation of the women was avenged on the men and degraded them also till they fell into the distasteful practice of boy-love and degraded alike their gods and themselves with the myth of Ganymede'.[4] Male homosexuality as a general social practice, in other words, or institutionalized homosexuality as I shall refer to this form, was associated, not altogether wrongly, with male domination. Indeed, male homosexuality was glorified in ancient Greece (and elsewhere) as the highest form of love precisely because it did not involve those 'inferior' beings, women. In this perspective, Engels' critique of this institutionalized homosexuality can even be seen as progressive, whereas the defence of 'Greek love' that played so great a part in the apologetics of the early gay movement was ultimately reactionary. It only added grist to the Marxist mill that the Greek institutionalization of homosexuality was confined purely to the slaveowning class, while being to all intents proscribed for the working masses. Homosexuality was thus a practice typical of leisured men who oppressed women and lived off the backs of the producers.

If Engels and the classical Marxists had known more about primitive societies, they would have had to abandon this characterization as grossly simplistic. Yet without any comprehension of the gender system, it was quite impossible for Marxism to understand homosexuality in general, or gayness in particular. There was simply no way it could advance beyond a liberal tolerance in relating to the movement of gay people that began to get under way at the turn of the century.

This situation was certainly not helped by the fact that the early homosexual rights movement, concentrated in Germany under the leadership of Magnus Hirschfeld, obstinately adhered to the false theory that homosexuality was innate. This undoubtedly made it easier to gain support for the abolition of anti-homosexual legislation. And if gay people still regarded themselves as 'born that way', then who were the Marxists to contradict them?

Freud, however, did indeed contradict Hirschfeld and his disciples on this point, despite being a vigorous champion of their campaign. And when the gay movement entered a new and more international phase after the First World War, with the World League for Sexual Reform,[5] Freudian ideas were very definitely on the ascendant, becoming among other things the framework in which the question of homosexuality was viewed in the new world of Soviet Russia.

It was hardly surprising that Marxists, stressing in their own field the ascendance of culture over nature, should be attracted to the Freudian explanation of how psychological characteristics, too, were acquired rather than innate. Yet this brought them into an ambiguous relationship with the gay movement of the time. While stressing that there was nothing anti-social about homosexuality, in modern terminology that it was a 'victim-less crime', spokespeople for the gay cause were still unable to argue that gay was positively good, and this explains the attractions of the theory that a homosexual disposition was simply innate.[6] The social policy of the Bolsheviks, however, prefiguring a pattern that would be adopted throughout the modern world a generation or so later, actually saw tolerance for the homosexual individual as the best way to combat the 'sickness' and promote a healthy heterosexuality.

This was the explicit purpose of the Bolshevik legislation, as explained in 1922 by Dr. Grigorii Batkis, in a pamphlet often quoted by Marxists today to demonstrate the 'pro-gay' position of the Russian revolutionaries:

> While understanding the wrongness of the development of homosexuality, society does not place and cannot place blame for it on those who exhibit it. This breaks down to a significant degree the wall which actually exists between the homosexual and society and forces the former to delve deeply into himself.

Even John Lauritsen and David Thorstad, who seek to present the traditional Marxist organizations as the natural 'protectors' of gay people, have to admit that 'there is no indication that the Soviets reached a point of attempting to positively integrate homosexual behaviour into society'.[7] On the contrary! They precisely sought a more subtle way of dis-integrating it — even if from the gay standpoint liberal counter-measures are infinitely preferable to fascist (or Stalinist) ones.

This ambiguous relationship between the gay movement and Marxism took a decisive turn for the worse with the events of the inter-War years. Given the association that Marxism had already established between male homosexuality (at least in its institutionalized form), male supremacy and parasitism, it was in no way surprising that the exposure of homosexuality in the fascist organizations, especially the Nazi SA, was taken up by the Left as an added stick with which to beat the enemy. This was after all a descendant of the homosexual traditions of Prussian militarism, and cousin to its counterpart in the British public schools and elite universities.[8] The result, however, was that while in 1929 the Socialist and Communist parties had voted solidly in the German Reichstag for the abolition of the anti-homosexual law, by the time of the Röhm purge in 1934 homosexuality had got firmly tarred with the fascist brush. This was the background against which homosexuality was once again made a criminal offence in the Soviet Union, as part of a general tightening up of social discipline to meet the threat of invasion.[9] Withdrawal of Left support spelled the end of the early homosexual rights movement, which was always far more fragile than the gay movement of today, and it took a long time indeed for us to shake off the vicious charge that there was something 'fascist' about homosexuality. Even in the early 1970s, the left-wing Greek students opposing the fascist junta could still taunt the police with the dreaded accusation '*pustis*' (someone who gets fucked in the arse).

In no way can this slanderous attack be simply attributed to 'Stalinism', as it is by John Lauritsen and David Thorstad. What their pamphlet omits to say, though David Thorstad has since acknowledged it,[10] is that his own organization, the American Trotskyist party (known as the Socialist Workers Party, but apparently unconnected to its homonym in Britain), also refused until the 1970s to accept openly gay people as members, and even after this became impossible to maintain, with the rise of the new gay movement, he found himself compelled to leave the party because of its inability to take gay liberation seriously.

This should show how impossible it is to graft a new attitude towards homosexuality onto orthodox Marxism as a mere accessory, and how empty are resolutions passed by party congresses (or congresses of would-be parties) in support of gay rights, if these are not backed up by a genuine grasp of what gayness is all about. But a theoretical understanding of the gender system would require a fundamental reworking of Marxist doctrine, and there are precious few organizations of the Left, in any country, that do not prefer to cling to established dogma. Short of coming to grips with the gender system, attempts at a 'Marxist theory of gay oppression/liberation' are absolutely pathetic. It has sometimes been argued, for example, that we are oppressed because we reject the economic dependence of women upon men that is 'necessary to capitalism'.[11] But this cannot even explain certain aspects of state policy. What about those non-homosexual women and men who live an honourable existence as 'spinsters' or 'bachelors'? Nor can it begin to explain the deep-rooted emotional hostility towards gayness on the part of the mass of ordinary people. Recourse must therefore be made to a crude conspiracy theory, and gay oppression becomes 'an oppression started by the ruling class and purveyed through every form of media at their disposal — schools, press, tv and radio...'[12]

Wishing to avoid such an absurd conclusion, the alternative choice of some Marxists today is to justify gay liberation in terms of the 'right to one's own body'.[13] Yet this is to completely abandon socialism for libertarianism. It is evidently modelled on the feminist demand for the right to contraception and abortion. But just as, in the last analysis, any human society must regulate its fertility collectively (even if only women take part in this regulation), and not just as the sum total of individual decision, so too there must always be some social organization of sexuality. Even consensual acts that cause no harm to anyone individually may come into conflict with social needs if practised on a mass scale. Gay liberation demands that homosexuality be accepted because society will thereby be improved, i.e. by the abolition of gender. To justify our movement in the name of 'do your own thing' only plays into the hands of those reactionaries such as Anita Bryant or Mary Whitehouse who do have a concept of social needs — the needs of the status quo. That allegedly Marxist organizations have recourse to libertarianism of this kind is a very clear sign of their own weakness, i.e. the inability of their ossified theory to come to terms with the question of gender, as indeed with many other things in the world today.

As I shall go on to show later in this chapter, the roots of our oppression lie in the challenge we present to the gender system, not being 'proper' women or men in the terms that our society ascribes, and that normal girls and boys have had to internalize so rigidly, often involving a high degree of repression. A theory of gay oppression and liberation, in other words, requires that the primary sexual division of labour is put in question, and this means a complete restructuring of historical materialist theory, leaving orthodox Marxism behind as superseded, however much it is on the Marxist tradition that we can usefully build.[14]

The failure of Marxism to integrate the ideas of gay liberation is thus in no way accidental; paradoxically, it derives from the very strength of orthodox Marxism, its achievement of a relatively coherent theory of human society as the premise for a 'scientific' practice of revolution and liberation. Like any body of theory, there were many questions it could not solve, but it flourished so long as its visibly demonstrated strengths outweighed its weaknesses. The problem now is not to demolish its achievements, but rather to raise them to a higher level, in the way that any major scientific innovation builds on the work of its forerunners.

Outside the Marxist fortress, however, there were other more flexible schools of thought, which did not have to worry so much about whether new ideas would conflict with their revolutionary paradigm. The key historical figure here is Edward Carpenter, unique in his time, in England and in the world, for his integration of gay liberation, feminism and socialism. After decades of neglect, Carpenter's achievement is now beginning again to find due appreciation, being seen by the new gay movement as a vital part of our heritage. Carpenter's ideas have been discussed more fully by others,[15] and at least some of his writing is now being reprinted, both in English and in translations. Carpenter was not particularly concerned with Marxism, which, at the time he developed his characteristic ideas, in the 1880s and 1890s, had not yet hegemonized socialist thought in Britain. Yet the insights he was the first to formulate were so far ahead of their time that a century later they still indicate the basic directions in which the synthesis between class and gender politics has to be sought. To quote just a couple of passages:

> The Uranian [= homosexual] temperament in Man closely resembles the normal temperament of Woman in this respect, that in both Love — in some form or other — is the main object of life. In the normal Man, ambition, moneymaking, business, adventure, etc. play their part — Love is as a rule a secondary matter. The majority of men (for whom the physical side of sex, if needed, is easily accessible) do not for a moment realize the griefs endured by thousands of girls and

women — in the drying up of a wellspring of affection as well as in the crucifixion of their physical needs. But as these sufferings of women, of one kind or another, have been the great inspiring cause and impetus of the Women's Movement — a movement which is already having a great influence in the reorganization of society; so I do not practically doubt that the similar sufferings of the Uranian class of men are destined in their turn to lead to another wide-reaching social organization and forward movement in the direction of Art and Human Compassion.[16]

It is possible that the Uranian spirit may lead to something like a general enthusiasm of Humanity, and that the Uranian people may be destined to form the advance guard of that great movement which will one day transform the common life by substituting the bond of personal affection and compassion for the monetary, legal and other external ties which now control and confine society. Such a part of course we cannot expect the Uranians to play unless the capacity for their kind of attachment also exists — though in a germinal and undeveloped state — in the breast of mankind at large. And modern thought and investigation are clearly tending that way — to confirm that it does so exist.[17]

For Edward Carpenter, then, the gay struggle was far more than simply a question of civil rights, or tolerance by the heterosexual society. Gay men had a particular role to play, alongside women, in the struggle for the new social order. Absolutely crucial for Carpenter and this trend in radical thought, which found very limited expression in the intervening decades, and only fully surfaced once again with the anti-gender movement of the early 1970s, is the conception of a radical dissolution of the feminine/masculine dichotomy, as expressed in his poem 'These Populations':

> . . . a thousand women swift-footed and free —
> owners of themselves, forgetful of themselves, in all
> their actions — full of joy and laughter and action;
> Garbed not so differently from the men, joining with

them in their games and sports, sharing also their
labours;
    Free to hold their own, to grant or withhold their
love, the same as the men;
    Strong, well-equipped in muscle and skill, clear of
finesse and affectation —
    (The men, too, clear of much brutality and conceit) —
    Comrades together, equal in intelligence and
adventure,
    Trusting without concealment, loving without
shame but with discrimination and continence
towards a perfect passion.[18]

The gay movement of the early 20th century, however,
proved quite unable to rise to the heights proposed by Edward Carpenter, and form the advance guard of humanity.
Even though the movement led by Magnus Hirschfeld
always existed in association with the socialist movement,
and partly under its patronage, this stage of the gay struggle
was confined to a campaign for civil rights, and for tolerance
of homosexuality as a harmless sexual 'anomaly'. Only in
the 1970s, almost a century later, did we finally find a way
to integrate the tremendous vision of this great pioneer into
the mainstream of socialist thought, and in due course this
will inevitably undermine the ossified dogmas of Marxist
orthodoxy and enable the communist movement to rebuild
itself on a new and superior footing.


## 2. Sexuality and the Gender System

Homosexuality, like heterosexuality, can take a whole
range of possible forms. It can be separated from the emo-
tion of love, or it can combine with this in the way that
forms the specifically human pair-bond — whether temporary or permanent, exclusive or non-exclusive. It can display
the various 'perversions' in which a particular partial drive,
such as fixation to a certain fetish, comes to dominate sexual release. And as with heterosexuality, too, its object need
by no means be simply the same sex in general, but can be
restricted to a particular type of individual. Given the plas-

ticity and adaptability of human sexuality, it would be completely within the spectrum of possibility, therefore, that
the great majority of children should grow up to be preferentially homosexual, rather than preferentially heterosexual.
If there is so far no single human society that has not allotted heterosexuality pride of place, this is certainly not a
function of the biological need to procreate. For only a very
small amount of heterosexual activity is required, relative
to the general human need for sexual satisfaction, to bring
about an average of one pregnancy per adult woman every
few years. The real reason is the sexual division of labour
which is common in some form or another to all human
societies to date, and requires the heterosexual pair-bond as
its cement. This in no way rules out homosexuality, but it
ascribes it always a secondary role — even when exalted as
the 'highest form of love', as for example by the slaveowners
of ancient Greece. The position that homosexuality assumes in a society is circumscribed, in the first place, by the
parameters of institutionalized heterosexuality.

For the present purpose I am not concerned with those
human societies in which male domination is as yet virtually
undeveloped, but rather with the forms that homosexuality
takes in the context of the fully developed gender system.
If the sexual division of labour imposes a first set of
parameters on homosexuality, then male domination very
definitely imposes a further set. This is the situation in
which we find ourselves today, the combination in the
gender system of the sexual division of labour and male
domination. And it is not hard to see what this means for
the expression of male homosexuality.

In the gender system, male dominance over women is expressed in the sexual sphere by a relative suppression of
female sexuality. The man alone is brought up to be an
active subject; the woman is relegated to a passive object,
whose primary task in sex is to meet the needs of the man.
Within this context, the space left for female sexual satisfaction can vary. In certain societies, Japan for example, clitoral sexuality is recognized, and the successful satisfaction
of female desire is incumbent on the man, if he is to be
deemed a good lover. But so long as women are subservient
to men politically and economically, this is simply a bonus.

A more typical case is that of our own Western society, where female sexuality has been reduced to a 'vaginal' pleasure at best, if not annulled altogether. And there are many societies, especially in Africa, that practise the cruellest and most extreme forms of clitoridectomy and infibulation.

The normal man, then, is the man who fucks, the man for whom pleasing his partner is at best secondary, at worst simply unnecessary, even incomprehensible. It is no coincidence that the word for the 'male role' in sex, heterosex in particular, has come to be associated with violence and oppression.

If heterosexuality has always been institutionalized in the family, homosexuality has no such universal necessity. It is perfectly possible to do without it, i.e. to bring up children so that in the normal case they are exclusively heterosexual, and to use the system of social control to clamp down on any obstinate minority who persist in a homosexual preference. This is the pattern that our own society has favoured for thousands of years. As part of the campaign by the gay movement to gain social acceptance, it was understandable that we should turn to other societies where homosexuality is allowed a legitimate existence, and present these as a counter-example. But if the forms this takes are examined, they invariably turn out to be quite other than gay. For where homosexuality is permitted, and even institutionalized, this is always in forms that are consonant with the gender system, whereas our gayness is irredeemably contrary to the gender system and comes into being in objective opposition to it.

The Ford and Beach survey of homosexuality, in their book *Patterns of Sexual Behaviour*,[19] is still the most comprehensive of its kind. They found some form of homosexuality to be socially acceptable in 47 of the 76 societies in their sample. This study, which followed hard on the heels of the first Kinsey reports, and was directly inspired by Kinsey's own work, is often cited as evidence that homosexuality is quite normal to human society, and that our Western society is untypical in repressing it. Careful study of the Ford and Beach findings, however, gives little encouragement to gay liberationists. Right for a start, the 29 societies where homosexuality is 'not to be found', and even sometimes fiercely repressed, include many that are still firmly in the gathering/hunting stage, such as the Sanpoil Indians and the Trukese of Oceania, so that it is quite impossible to look back, as John Lauritsen for example does in his *Religious Roots of the Taboo on Homosexuality*,[20] to some assumed 'golden age' before the development of monotheism.

Among the 47 societies where some form of homosexuality is acceptable, the most common form, according to Ford and Beach, is that of the berdache. Though most commonly associated with the indigenous peoples of North America, this phenomenon is to be found in every continent. A certain proportion of young men here either decide, or it is decided for them, to reject the masculine role and live instead as 'women'. The extent to which they are subsequently differentiated from biological women may vary. In some societies a berdache can be married to a man in a very similar way as a regular woman; in others the berdache plays a religious role outside the family system, or may serve as a (very respected) prostitute.

It might seem strange that gay men should look back to the berdache as an ancestor, since his role is far more akin to the contemporary male-to-'female' transsexual, who refuses to define himself as gay, and clings to the quite false belief that he is really a woman. If we are justified in so doing, it is only to the extent that the berdache, like gay men today, is characterized by an effeminacy that brings him into conflict with the masculine role. Yet in societies where the berdache appears there is no real space for an intermediate category between 'proper' men and 'proper' women. If you can't be a 'proper' man, then you must at least try to be a 'proper' woman, in as much as this is at all possible for a biological male.

Far less common than the berdache, but still found in 13 of the 76 societies in this survey, is a form of homosexuality in which adult men have sexual relations with young boys, as yet uninitiated into manhood. Here the homosexual relationship may often be harnessed to an educational role, but this is not necessarily so. In the Egyptian desert, for example, 'prominent Siwans lend their sons to each other, and they talk about their masculine love affairs as openly as they discuss their love of women'.[21] In this form, male homosex-

uality is evidently constructed quite differently to the berdache. If the berdache phenomenon involves a small minority of males who are pressed back into normalcy through
transfer to the feminine role, man-boy relations of this kind
are completely normal for both parties involved, as part and
parcel of standard masculine behaviour. Yet there is still a
basic affinity between these two forms. In both, normal
adult men relate to their partners, whether berdache or boy,
in a way modelled on penis-vagina intercourse. Anal intercourse, with the adult man in the 'active' role, is the universal form. What pleasure the 'passive' partner receives is at
best secondary, just as it is for women in a male-dominant
society. For the berdache, this fact needs no justification,
since the berdache is defined as a woman. For boys who are
to grow up into normal men, however, the situation is more
complicated. Their need to be fucked may be justified in the
name of education, as in ancient Greece. Among the Kiwai
of New Guinea, 'sodomy is practised in connection with
initiation to make young men strong'[22], and similar myths
are retailed by the neighbouring Keraki. Ultimately, young
boys are smaller and weaker than their elders and betters,
and have to do what they are told. They can always console
themselves by knowing that the time will come when they
in turn will assume the adult role. But it is even less possible here than in the case of the berdache to see anything
corresponding to our contemporary conception of gayness.

Far more rare than anal intercourse, according to Ford and
Beach, is mutual masturbation between males, with only
three societies out of the 76 where this was practised among
adults. Here again, this is a standard part of adult male behaviour. But for men already used to coitus with women this
can only be a secondary outlet, possibly associated with the
long periods in which women are considered unclean, following childbirth or menstruation. And finally, 'oral-genital
contact', found only in one case, the native American Crow,
turns out to involve a kind of berdache, known as the *bate*.
Any sexual relationship between adult men on an equal
basis is thus virtually non-existent.[23]

Given not only the institutionalization of heterosexuality, but in most cases male domination into the bargain,
these data are in no way surprising. The gender system

offers men sexual satisfaction based on an unequal ascription to them of the role of active subject. Sex is thus their own pleasure above all, a mutual pleasure only secondarily at best. And the general form in which this unequal relationship is practised is that of the active man fucking his partner-object, whether this is a woman, a young boy, a berdache or even an animal. The masculine sexuality constructed in this way is certainly one-sided, but this does not mean that other components are repressed (for example homosexuality, in those societies where this is not to be found). There may well be a balanced 'sex economy' in the Reichian concept, which might actually have something to be said for it once it is freed from the false assumption that female sexuality is vaginal, and follows the same rhythms as male. Men do not necessarily have anything to gain, in this situation, from exploring forms of sexuality that are socially defined as deviant. And even in a situation of generalized sexual repression, such as our own society is just emerging out of, this repression, as far as most men are concerned, means the suppression of their heterosexual outlets, i.e. of the sexuality that society has brought them up to develop, but then not allowed them sufficiently to practise.[24]

The gender system is a system of domination of women by men, generally associated with a hierarchical order among men themselves. Both male and female sexuality, in this context, cannot but assume forms that the system impresses on them. As far as male homosexuality goes, there are only a very few possibilities. The berdache phenomenon and sexual relations between men and boys are two of these, each very different in content, but each equally consonant with the norms of the gender system. Within this system, there is very little room indeed for sexual relations between males on an equal basis.

Even in Western society, forms of homosexuality that are consonant with the gender system are not entirely absent. One of these is that characteristic of institutions such as prisons, where both male and female homosexuality have always carried on a furtive existence. Among men, here, the general rule is for the older or stronger to fuck the younger or weaker, reducing him not just in status, but in a very material sense, to the subordinate position of a woman.

(Which is not to say that the dominant male does not generally offer certain titbits, in the form of protection or even presents, in return for sexual services.) This is a form of homosexuality among normal men. As an emergency outlet when women are unavailable, it is largely free of the taboo and stigma that would otherwise attach to male homosexuality. Yet in the absence of the kind of institutionalization found in certain other societies, it is inherently unstable. It is maintained in the prison situation only by brute force.

A second quasi-acceptable form of male homosexuality is the mutual masturbation of adolescent boys, which again is considered perfectly normal. But this is similarly unstable. It breaks down precisely because the peculiar conditions of the prison situation do not obtain; the older boys generally do not have any means of forcing the younger boys to accept being fucked, and are free to seek a 'cavity' elsewhere, as Freud so inimitably puts it.[25] Homosexuality between normal men, in our society, exists only in these unstable interstices where heterosexuality is uncharacteristically excluded. But just as with the forms of berdache and man-boy sexual relations in certain other societies, our own forms of normal homosexuality also have nothing gay about them. However much it might provide material for gay fantasies, normal homosexuality is the diametrical opposite of gayness. Homosexuality between normal men is structured by the gender system, and can take a stable form only as a relationship between dominant and subordinate modelled on that between man and woman. Gayness, on the other hand, comes into being in objective opposition to the gender system, as a deviant form, and the more it escapes the vicious influences of the gendered society around it, the more it takes a form that is inherently egalitarian.

## 3. *The Reproduction of Gender*

I showed in the previous section how homosexuality, and male homosexuality in particular, need by no means assume the gay form characteristic of our own society, a form which is deviant in terms of the gender system and its ascriptions of masculinity. It can also assume forms that are consonant with the gender system, being in this sense an extension of the institutionalized heterosexuality that is indispensable to the sexual division of labour.

Heterosexuality is a part of the gender system, not the whole of it. What a society marked by the gender system is concerned to reproduce in the next generation, accordingly, is not just heterosexuality, but the wider norms of gender of which heterosexuality is part — even if it leaves room, unlike our own, for a form of homosexuality that is gender-consonant. And those of us who find ourselves marked out as deviant on account of our gayness, i.e. our obstinate preference for a same-sex partner depite the taboos against this, are the result of a failure of the gender system to reproduce itself in a perfect fashion. Not everyone who has failed to properly internalize the norms of gender gives such a visible sign of this as we do with our homosexuality. And there *may* even be a few homosexual men who, despite so serious a deviance from proper manly behaviour in this one respect, are masculine enough in others. Yet the explanation of our deviance as gay men must be set in the wider context of the reproduction of the gender system, from which we irredeemably deviate, no matter how hard we might try and pretend otherwise.

From the gay point of view, it is quite obvious that the process of growing up into a normal woman or man is by no means automatic, no matter how normal the parental models. Because our parents are, in most cases, passably feminine and masculine respectively, and thus among other things heterosexual, it is easy to retreat into the illusion that our deviance is innate (also a good excuse for the parents, letting them off the hook of 'where did we go wrong?'). The way forward to self-discovery, however, is through paying attention to the little subtleties of childhood experience, both within and outside of the family, that lead us to reject, in one way or other, the roles assigned to us, and to seek satisfaction elsewhere. These experiences are deviant in relation to a certain pattern of normality, the basic features of which are as follows.

Both female and male infants are born into a feminine world, i.e. the maternal culture that is ascribed to women by the sexual division of labour. The initial stage of human-

ization is conducted far more by the mother than by the
father, and in so far as the father does involve himself in
this, it is not in his specifically masculine capacity, but
precisely in an exceptional feminine role. (A sign that the
traditionally rigid barriers of gender are at least beginning to
soften.) The pink or blue blanket indicates the crucial importance of gender ascription from the very moment of birth —
to everyone but the baby itself! Yet although parents behave
differently to girl and boy babies right from the start, the
first couple of years is necessarily governed by the baby's
complete dependence and need for unqualified care and protection. The adult world is represented by the figure of the
mother, and in this sense the path trodden by all infants is
initially a feminine one.

Both girls and boys suffer the pain of being squeezed into
their alloted gender role, but this pain is very different on
either side. The little girl can continue undisturbed to gradually internalize and identify with her mother. The maternal
role is indeed spontaneously attractive to girls and boys
alike, as shown by the eagerness to play with dolls.
What is problematic for the little girl is not growing up to be
a mother herself, but rather growing into the other aspect of
the feminine role, i.e. accepting the domination of men.
The women's movement has catalogued in full and grue-
some detail the myriad little ways in which the spontaneous
inquisitiveness and independence of girls is suppressed, the
hundred and one labels by which girls who persist in wanting to be integral human beings are put down as 'tomboys',
'bluestockings', etc. — all variants on 'unfeminine' and
'mannish'. But the process only succeeds, at least in its own
terms, because acceptance of an oppressed femininity brings
with it certain compensations. The little girl is allowed the
privilege of beautification, and soon learns — from daddy —
how her desirability as a sex-object can be turned to advantage. In the normal case, this compensation disguises the
real situation of oppression, and is chosen without undue
force having to be used.

Growing up into a 'proper' man involves a quite different
combination of pain and reward. At an early stage of childhood, the little boy has to learn that his mother is not, after
all, the person with whom he must identify, but rather his

father — now appearing not as a second mother, but in his specifically masculine role. This is a painful transition, involving a break in the original tender relationship with the mother, and it only succeeds because the reward is far greater than anything the girl will receive. If he will learn to be a man like daddy, then the little boy has access to the independent adult status that is a masculine preserve, to manipulation of the material world, and the prospect of power over other human beings. (Every adult man has at least power over 'his' wife and children.) Even the original tenderness of the mother can be regained, via this circuitous route, when the little boy grows up and conquers a new woman to service his needs for sex and affection.

Yet however ego-syntonic the process of masculinization may appear, its characteristic reward has a sting in the tail. The masculine specialization in violence, in seeking satisfaction through the domination of others, rules out that tenderness which every human being has originally known, and for which no other reward can compensate. Even the tenderness of conjugal love is vitiated if based on domination. In this sense, masculinity involves a specific self-oppression, for all the superior status it gives, the modalities of which the movement of men against sexism has begun to investigate.[26] And this is why heterosexual men, too, have something specific to gain from a struggle against the gender system.

The primary locus for the reproduction of gender is the family. Yet in a complex society, where a million separate nuclear units independently bring up their young, it would be impossible for the gender system to reproduce itself in any viable way if the family were not supported by a system of education common to society as a whole. Without this, the polarization that the gender system maintains would erode in a few generations. But while each nuclear family necessarily deviates to a certain extent from the ideal norm, and many quite seriously so, there is also this standardizing influence to keep little girls and boys on their predestined rails. For boys, education in masculinity is particularly provided today by television (thanks to which the art of murder, as a masculine speciality, can easily be learned by the age of three), by school, by sport, by boys' organizations, by comics, etc., and the situation is very similar also for girls. All these forces, moreover, do not just operate on each individual separately, but also on the peer group as a whole, which thus exerts a further standardizing influence.

The reproduction of heterosexuality takes place essentially as a by-product of the reproduction of gender. Heterosexuality cannot be seen, any more than any other form of sexuality, as simply a behaviour imitated from others. Whatever imitation takes place evidently attaches itself to powerful desires that are already potentially directed to a heterosexual choice. And these desires are a function of the internalization of femininity and masculinity. As long as the little girl grows up into a 'proper' woman, and the little boy into a 'proper' man, then as a general rule they will fit together into a heterosexual pair-bond, even if their parents and educators, as was common until recently, have refrained from giving them any more specific instruction in matters of sex.

Heterosexuality, however, is very different from the feminine and masculine sides. It is quite significant that Freud, concerned in the first instance with male sexuality, referred to the chosen sexual partner as an 'object'. For in the field of sexuality, as elsewhere, it is the man who is posited by the gender system as subject, encouraged to define his needs and manipulate the material and social world so as to obtain satisfaction. At the level of the lowest common denominator, what he looks for in terms of sex is something to fuck, and the gender system makes women available for this, while making other men, in general, unavailable, and — what is more — competitors in the same market. A normal woman, moreover, is available not just to service men's immediate physiological needs, but also their emotional ones, as an extension of the maternal function. Even though the sensual and affectionate currents do not always run smoothly together, the man can at least hope in the heterosexual relationship to get two things for the price of one.

Heterosexuality is constructed quite differently in the woman. For the same reasons that make homosexuality less satisfactory for the normal (masculine) man would seem to make lesbianism more satisfactory for even the normal (feminine) woman. While the boy's original relationship with his mother was at least in one sense heterosexual, the same relationship, for the girl, was homosexual. And unlike the little boy, she was not forced to break this relationship for the sake of her adult identification, but could continue gradually to internalize and 'become' her mother. As an adult, she might expect to relate to another woman on a basis of equality, as subject to subject, rather than be relegated to an object of male heterosexuality. All this does indeed explain the rather greater facility with which women in the feminist movement can develop a lesbian orientation, even if they have been completely unaware of this possibility before, whereas even the tentative exploration of homosexuality in the movement of men against sexism is invariably altogether more fraught. In the normal case, however, heterosexuality is developed in the little girl as part of her compensation for accepting oppression: she can at least become the object of desire. To the extent that she learns to manipulate her environment, within certain limited parameters, from the feminine position — to twist men round her little finger — her heterosexuality is reinforced.

This, then, is the mechanism through which little girls and boys are brought up to be inwardly like their parents: a mechanism that is located partly within the family itself, and partly in the sphere of education (in the broad sense as above) that serves as a kind of adjunct to the family in the complex societies of today. But not even all heterosexuals completely meet the norms of the gender system. And for this reason a second and quite different mechanism is required, a system of control that enforces correct *behaviour*, even when this is not the spontaneous, ego-syntonic choice of the individuals involved.

Given that the ultimate rationale of the gender system is an economic one, the sexual division of labour, it is not surprising to find that it is backed up, even in a complex society, by economic forces. In simpler societies, there is a more direct functional need of a woman for a husband and a man for a wife, ultimately going back to the reciprocal provision of the proceeds of hunting and gathering respectively. Even in peasant societies, a separate household must generally be set up around a heterosexual unit. In our own society, where the exchange of services is mediated by money as the universal equivalent, the situation is more subtle. It is possible for a man, earning a man's wage, to purchase on the open market at least certain of the services that a wife might provide. But what he gets for his money in this respect is very much less than the investment in a wife — particularly if he has to start paying for sexual services. On the other hand, women's wages are still so much lower than men's that an independent life for a woman is generally a hard one, sinking into absolute poverty if she has dependent children.[27]

Yet the force of a deviant desire is sufficiently great that stronger forces than economic ones are required to maintain the gender pattern. The apparatus of ideological repression is also deployed on a massive scale, with the brute force of the state also standing ready in the wings. It cannot enforce a heterosexual orientation in men whom the gender system has failed to endow with this, any more than it can make men of a pacifist disposition into gung-ho warriors. But just as the less warlike men can be exhorted by priests and propagandists, and in the last instance forcibly conscripted, so those men inclined to a homosexual choice of partner can be told they are wicked and sick, and if this fails, they can be locked up in prison or worse. What the repressive apparatus directs its attack against is homosexual *behaviour*, yet the relative lenience shown towards the emergency homosexuality of normal men immediately signals that the real object of the exercise is to shore up the gender system by repressing the gay minority. It is we who rightly tremble in fear when we hear denunciations of homosexual 'vice', while the very agents of repression themselves, policemen and the like, are quite happy to beat us one day, and expect us to suck their cocks the next.[28]

Because the state has a monopoly of armed force, the worst that can befall the gay minority is that the state decides on an anti-gay pogrom, for reasons that may be complex and varied. We had this with the burning of faggots in the middle ages, and we have had it in living memory under the Nazis. Minor pogroms, decreed by local police chiefs or instigated by agencies to protect morality, are a regular occurrence. Yet we should not delude ourselves that this is more than the tip of the iceberg of gay oppression.[29] In so far as they are what they claim to be, in fact, and gay people are not simply cast into a scapegoat role, these sporadic police actions are very clumsy instruments. The main work of keeping the deviants in line is performed, day in day out, by the more routine operation of ideological repression, nowadays emanating not only from the church, but also from psychiatry, the mass media, and all the other agencies for managing public opinion. All these pump out the anti-gay message, as part of a general reinforcement of 'proper' masculinity and femininity. They may be directed, unlike the system of education, at adults whose emotional disposition is relatively unsusceptible to a major change. But they can make sure that deviant behaviour is very much less that deviant desire, forcing the very large numbers of people who feel uncomfortable in their ascribed roles to conceal their inner feelings and act in relation to one another in the ways laid down — making us all, in fact, a police force against one another.

## 4. *The Routes to Gayness*

As the data supplied by Ford and Beach so strikingly show, it is in no way possible to equate our own homosexuality, that of the gay minority, with homosexuality in general. Indeed, in the great majority of human societies where it appears, homosexuality assumes forms that are consonant with the gender system, and it is only relatively recently that the space has emerged for a gay way of life.

Gayness is a particular form of homosexuality, a homosexuality that is deviant from the gender system. What all gay men have in common, to be sure, is our preferential choice of another man as sexual partner. Yet even in our own society there is a certain amount of homosexuality, a considerable amount according to Kinsey, that goes on between straight men, who are 'properly' masculine and practise heterosexuality as part of their masculine role. And there are conversely many gay men who are not exclusively homosexual. To define yourself as gay, however, even in the minimal sense of accepting the judgement of the environing society that there is something different about you, is to recognize that your homosexuality has something about it that is radically incompatible with the prevalent normality — that you are 'bent', 'queer', i.e. in no way a 'proper' man. And given that the normal masculinity reproduced by the gender system leads automatically to a preferentially heterosexual choice of partner, a preferentially homosexual choice is quite rightly interpreted as the sign of a certain lack of masculinity.

Gay men, in other words, really are effeminate. Pejorative and inadequate as this word evidently is, it has a solid core of truth in implying that we have failed to complete the course of masculinization, having dropped out a significant way before the end of the process, and thus retain at least part of that femininity which masculinization is designed, among other things, to repress.

I argued in the previous section that the reproduction of gender takes place primarily in the family, but also with the indispensable support of the education apparatus which helps standardize the inevitable discrepancies between individual families and the social norm. Even though the little boy is never simply a passive recipient of indoctrination, but develops right from the start as a distinct agent in a system of interaction with his environment, his experience of the family and the education apparatus leads him to internalize a certain relationship to the gender system, ranging from complete consonance to the most extreme form of deviance (i.e. identification with the opposite gender), at a time when he has not yet reached the age of reason. However comprehensible the child's choices are in terms of the situation in which he finds himself, these are not choices made in an awareness of their wider social implications.

Our characteristic deviance from the norms of gender is therefore something that we 'couldn't help'; it is formed in early years, and can even give the illusion that we were 'born that way'. In as much as this gender deviance leads us to find ourselves attracted to a member of the same sex, this too is something involuntary. But it would be quite wrong to reduce our gayness to something simply thrust upon us from outside. As we grow up, we have still to make a choice whether to 'live according to our nature', or to make the effort to force ourselves into the behaviour prescribed for us, as the social control apparatus demands that we should. The greater the degree of our deviance, the more difficult this choice may be. Yet even many transsexuals, for example, who in later life prove to have so well-developed a feminine gender identity that they are prepared to try and live as a woman, have spent half a lifetime functioning outwardly in society as an apparently normal man. (Jan Morris is one of the better known examples.) In earlier forms of society, there is simply no space for a category of gay men, let alone lesbians. The steadily increasing size of the gay minority today is an indication that this social space is now greater than ever before. But even so, there are precious few of us who have not at least considered, at some point along the way, the possibility of bowing to the demands of the straight world around us and living as a 'proper' heterosexual man. It is simply that the choice of a gay way of life is that much easier now, and the choice of self-repression that much less inevitable.

Our gayness, then, is a function of two things: a deviance from the gender system that is anchored in our personalities in the course of childhood experience, and the choice to build our lives around the homosexual preference that this induces. In the next section, I shall go on to show how gay relationships have certain inherent characteristics that lead us an important step further away from the norms of gender. For the moment, however, I want to deal with the question of how our deviant experience of the family and education is translated into a homosexual preference.

Since the influence of education is precisely a standardizing one, designed to make up for the deficiencies of the individual family, it is particularly in our families that we should look for the roots of our deviance. It is our families that have not successfully induced us to complete the process of masculinization, and it is to our families, too, that we owe the fact that our exposure to the education system has been inadequate to bridge this gap.

The model of masculinization I put forward in the previous section was one in which this requires the repression of the original maternal culture of tenderness (a necessity if the little boy is to learn the masculine culture of violence, to 'harden his heart'), but this brings the reward of an adult independence and competence that are a masculine prerogative, as well as the specific rewards that the practice of violence might bring (in particular domination over women). In terms of this model, the effeminacy of gay men involves above all our refusal to repress the maternal culture and to cultivate masculine violence. This is not to say that all heterosexuality necessarily involves such a repression, simply that gay men can clearly see ourselves as differentiated from the masculine norm in this way.

If this is something we have in common with women, however, there is also something we have in common with other men. As males, we were offered not just the dubious privilege of cultivating violence, but also the quite unambiguous privilege of developing into independent and competent adults, in contrast to the restriction of ambition that is so integral to women's oppression. We have thus become as skilled in various forms of manipulation of the material and social environment as our heterosexual brothers. In this respect, the most effeminate gay man is quite distinct from the normal woman. So many gay men succeed in the various fields of 'design' — fashion, interior decorating, stage sets, etc. precisely because they are well placed to combine a certain feminine sensitivity with a whole bunch of practical skills to which being men gives readier access.

There is however also a certain differentiation among gay men ourselves. This is by no means rigid and watertight, and as I shall argue in the next section, the traditional ghetto categories of 'butch' and 'femme' are simply an attempt to squeeze our gayness into a pattern imposed by the heterosexual world around us. Yet the homosexual preference that leads us to choose a gay way of life is differentiated by the gender system, as a function of the particular family experience. Rather than 'butch' and 'femme', this gives rise to a whole range of possibilities, and the instances that follow should be seen as simply representing two opposing ends of this spectrum.

The route that leads to a greater degree of effeminacy is typically characterized by a conflict between the parents over the destiny of their child (or, if the father is absent from the family, a conflict between the mother and the forces of education). The mother resists the pressures that demand a break in the tender relationship with her son, whether this resistance derives from a bad personal relationship with her husband, her loneliness as an oppressed woman isolated within the family, or a conscious antipathy to masculinity. If the father is present in the family, then his inability to induce his son onto the path of masculinity will lead in time to his rejection of the boy on account of his effeminacy. At all events, the boy will be left free to continue his identification with his mother, and to do those girls' activities which he enjoys, even though, unlike a normal girl, he is not forced to abandon other activities simply because they are earmarked for boys. In particular, he can follow the example of his mother and other women (e.g. sisters) in beautifying himself as a desirable sex-object, while quite free from the oppressed position for which this is compensation.

At the other end of the spectrum, the route to gayness is characterized not by a conflict between the parents, but rather by father and mother jointly conspiring to shield their son from the extreme (normal) version of masculinity. In this case, the father is himself somewhat effeminate, a 'soft heterosexual', with his own maternal side relatively unrepressed. With the mother's agreement, the boy is indeed set on the specifically masculine path, but in a way that makes far less sharp demands and stops well short of a fully developed masculinity. The boy may be prevented from imitating his mother as desirable sex-object, but he is not forced to repress the maternal culture in himself and to cultivate violence.

How then are these two forms of deviance from the masculine gender role translated into a choice of sexual partner? In the first case, that of the more effeminate gay man, the beautification that he learns from his mother and other women is precisely designed to attract a masculine sexual partner, i.e. a 'man', and the little boy generally learns this long before puberty. Since his father can in no way respond to his son's effeminacy in the same way as he would to similar behaviour from a little girl, it is typical for the boy to look outside the family at an early age for a man to seduce. Yet this effeminate sexuality can by no means be simply equated with the normal sexuality of a heterosexual woman. Unlike the more extreme deviance of the transsexual, no gay man ever believes he is really a woman; he clearly recognizes any fantasies of womanhood as just fantasies. He seeks a specifically male sexual satisfaction, and he seeks this with a member of his own sex. It is notorious, in fact, that the partner's possession of the penis (in the direct physical sense, not just the 'symbolic phallus') is a more essential attribute for gay men, the most and the least effeminate alike, than it is for normally heterosexual women. Gay sexuality, in other words, always has an irreducibly inter-male dimension to it. It is never simply the attraction of feminine to masculine, and it is far less encumbered by the search for a father-figure as provider and protector than is normal female heterosexuality, in which the desire to be appreciated as an object of beauty is inextricably linked with the dependent position of women, dominated both by men's economic power and by their violence.

In this relationship to both masculinity and femininity, the gay man whom reactionary psychologists label 'masculine' is certainly a degree less deviant from the gender norm. Whereas the more effeminate gay man can be recognized as such even in early childhood, in this case it is only in the course of adolescence that there is a decisive parting from heterosexual development. The boy has failed to internalize the masculine culture of violence and to repress the original maternal culture, but he has not made a homosexual choice on the basis of a narcissistic femininity; he is not looking for a 'man'. Yet he is equally removed from developing into a 'proper' man himself, being unprepared for the inter-male struggle for dominance and unable to view women like his mother as objects to fuck. The solution is generally found in the context of the adolescent homosexual stage. As I explained above, this is inherently unstable as a form of relationship between normal adolescents. It is typically mutual masturbation oriented by a common fantasy of prospective penetration; and any emotional charge threatens a resurgence of that effeminacy which the adolescent is still striving to repress. But for the boy who is not striving for manhood this way, there is no such barrier to a form of sexuality that involves him in a 'feminine' role, or to falling in love with one of his peers, whether a normal boy or someone more likely to reciprocate.

A successful relationship of this kind evidently reinforces a gay orientation, whereas the homosexual play of normal adolescents is soon grown out of, as they separate to seek a 'cavity' in the sex ascribed to that purpose. But the education apparatus, speaking traditionally the language of religion, and more recently that of psychiatry, is aware of this danger to the gender system and intervenes against it as far as possible. The 'masculine' homosexual, at least, *should* be able to make a heterosexual adjustment, and all the stops are pulled out in the attempt to get him to do so. In the rhetoric of the 'psychonazis', as they are known to the gay movements of the Latin countries, the undertones of religion, defining us as wicked and calling on us to seek salvation, are still to be heard quite clearly beneath the official vocabulary of sickness.[30]

In this case, therefore, the question of which road to choose is posed particularly sharply. It is relatively easier for this gay man to convince himself that he is — or should try to be — a 'proper' man after all. If he does opt for normality, then the kind of man he becomes can again vary as a function of his social milieu. In a middle-class situation, for example, where the demands of masculine violence are somewhat less acute, he may grow into a 'soft heterosexual' like his father. But where the gender roles are more extremely polarized, and a greater degree of self-repression is needed, the outcome is as likely to be not the soft heterosexual but rather the queer-basher.

Biological sex divides all of us virtually without exception into female or male, in a manner that leaves no room for ambiguity. The gender system is a human invention that defines certain norms appropriate for female and male individuals, and seeks to force everyone into these. Its success, however, is only relative, and none of the aspects of gay oppression and liberation can be understood if this is not borne in mind.

First of all, there is no rigid demarcation between 'masculine' and 'feminine' individuals. Gay people have suffered in the past from ideologies that seek to compress us into one or other of these categories, and we are by no means free of this today. For the crudely reductionist psychologists, the 'psychonazis', gay men are seen as essentially feminine, women trapped in male bodies. But then there are inevitably very many gay men whom they simply can't squeeze into this box and must accordingly define as 'masculine'. Why a 'masculine' man should seek another male partner, however, boggles their heterosexist imagination. As Robert Stoller, a Los Angeles psychiatrist, immortally put it: 'Masculine homosexual men are an exception that I cannot discuss because I do not yet(!) understand them.'[31]

More recently, however, a new reductionist ideology has gained currency, which denies that there is anything effeminate about gay men at all. Our homosexuality is seen simply as 'something that men do', and those phenomena of the traditional gay subculture that seem to challenge the boundaries of gender — drag, camp, etc. — are explained as a now outdated way of coping with our oppressed situation. Gender deviance is viewed as an insubstantial by-product of deviance in sexual orientation, not as its underlying cause.

The popularity of this theory, like the popularity of the old heterosexist reductionism, derives from ideological adaptation rather than scientific inquiry. In the past, it suited not only psychologists to see gay men as a special kind of 'woman'; it also suited the mainstream of the gay community itself, giving us a certain kind of legitimacy on the grounds that we were 'born that way'. Today, however, given a somewhat greater social tolerance of homosexuality, the new tendency in the gay community is to see ourselves as essentially men just like any other.

It is only possible to understand the gay phenomenon, i.e. ourselves and all that we do, if we are prepared to accept that gayness precisely does break down boundaries, and to jettison once and for all any attempt to present ourselves either as basically 'all woman' or 'all man'. Gay men are unquestionably biologically male, and accept ourselves as such, and on the strength of this fact society has also treated us as boys and subsequently as men, no matter how untypical our experience in the family may have been. But compared with the masculine norm, we are all unquestionably effeminate. Just as the (male) schoolteacher is traditionally described as 'a man among boys, a boy among men', so the gay man who likes to distinguish himself from the blatantly effeminate queens still appears effeminate in the eyes of straight men, who have no difficulty in seeing that he has not repressed the maternal culture as he was supposed to do. The self-deception that the 'butch' gay man is really just a 'man who likes men' is particularly pathetic in that 'femme' gay men themselves have no illusions on the subject whatsoever. They know that underneath the facade, he's really more of a 'Miss Butch' than a true 'Mister'.[32]

But if there is no rigid boundary line between 'masculine' and 'feminine' individuals, whether coinciding or not with the division of biological sex, it is also impossible to reduce the division between gay and straight to one of effeminacy and non-effeminacy. Gay men are not the only category of effeminates, even if we are certainly the most visible. On the heterosexual side, there are a minority of soft heterosexuals, and a possibly larger minority of 'over-compensators', who play such an important part in our oppression as queer-bashers. These are the unofficial shock troops of the gender system, compelled to project outward, onto the visibly effeminate gay minority, the aggression they have mobilized to keep down their own effeminacy, and who are doubly dangerous when they can act out their psychological needs within the uniform of a policeman, a judge, a psychiatrist, a priest, a schoolteacher, a journalist, etc.[33]

The queer-bashing mentality based on the denial of effeminacy is even at work in our own ranks. For the 'butch' gay man who insists he is as good a man as any other not only represses himself, he can also be seen to externalize his aggression against his effeminacy onto the more blatant queens, causing them a further oppression and harmfully dividing our movement.

The male-to-'female' transsexual, paradoxically, is a further case of an effeminacy that will not recognize itself as such. If the traditional queen's self-image as a 'woman trapped in a man's body' always has a certain inescapable element of camp to it, invariably falling short of absolute conviction, the transsexual, who has generally developed a cross-gender identity at a very early age, really does have this conviction, to the point that he seeks to live as a woman, nowadays often seeking surgery to acquire the right external characteristics, and will unflinchingly sacrifice sexual satisfaction to his search for acceptance. The transsexual and the queer-basher might appear poles apart, yet both of them have their lives distorted by the rigid barriers that the gender system strives to impose, and the transsexual represses with equal violence the idea that he might actually be queer.

Finally, the division between gay and straight, even as arising from a conscious choice, should not be seen as absolute, nor simply reduced to that between heterosexuality and a deviant homosexuality. Just as there are forms of homosexuality that are consonant with the gender system, so there can be forms of heterosexuality that reject the barriers of gender. In the milieu of the gay liberation movement, lesbians and gay men have found the possibility of relationships with one another that are possible precisely because neither party is a 'proper' woman or man. Such relationships show how, with the breakdown of the gender system, heterosexuality too can become a relationship between equal and similar individuals, rather than between oppressor and oppressed.[34]

## 5. *Gay Relationships and the Gay Subculture*

Gay shows the way. In some ways we are *already* more advanced than straight people. We are already outside the family and we have already, in part at least, rejected the 'masculine' or 'feminine' roles society has designed for us. In a society dominated by the sexist culture it is very difficult, if not impossible, for heterosexual men and women to escape their rigid gender-role structuring and the roles of oppressor and oppressed. But gay men don't need to oppress women in order to fulfil their own psycho-sexual needs, and gay women don't have to relate sexually to the male oppressor, so that at this moment in time, the freest and most equal relationships are most likely to be between homosexuals.[35]

Relationships between gay men are marked by four basic characteristics that distinguish them from the norms of heterosexuality.

1) They are relationships between individuals who are biologically alike.

2) They are relationships between individuals whom society does not differentiate into a dominant and a subordinate gender.

3) They are relationships between individuals who are emotionally more alike, as relatively effeminate men, than are a normal heterosexual couple.

4) They have a transitive character, i.e. if A and B are lovers, and so are B and C, it is possible for C and A to be lovers as well.

No two individuals are alike in every way. Gay men, too, as I showed in the previous section, are differentiated in their relationship to the gender division, some being more deviant than others. Differences between the individuals involved, at many levels, undoubtedly play a fertilizing and stimulating role in gay relationships as well as in straight. Yet while heterosexuality is constructed around the gender difference (its very slogan being *'vive la différence'*), and a difference moreover that involves an aspect of domination and oppression as well as a purely functional aspect, gayness – precisely as opposed to those forms of homosexuality consonant with the gender system – is constructed around similarity. Reactionary psychologists, unable to think except in heterosexist categories, sometimes waste their time, among other ways, in wondering how on earth genuine sexual attraction between two gay men is possible. But in human relationships, unlike electromagnetism, it is just as possible for like poles to attract one another as it is for unlike poles. In the long run, indeed, this proves the stronger attraction.[36]

This crucial contrast between gayness and heterosexuality is immediately highlighted by the fact that if two gay men are both lovers of a third, this does not prevent these two from themselves becoming lovers, either simultaneously or at a later date. This possibility may be cancelled by a number of factors, one of which is indeed the persistence of the gender influence even within the gay subculture. Yet this transitiveness is possible in the gay situation, to the extent of being by no means uncommon, whereas heterosexuality rules it out a priori. For in heterosexuality, the two lovers of the third person are automatically of the same sex, so a relationship between them would be homosexual.

A potential rivalry is involved in any sexual relationship that is more than casual. Yet the exclusion of homosexuality rules out any element of mediation such as a transitive network of relationships provides. Even when straight men are allied by common work, kinship or belief, they are still underneath it all enemy brothers, and it is legendary how competition over women turns brotherhood into hate. Even when not immediately realized, this potential always lurks just beneath the surface, dividing men from one another and thus helping to perpetuate the law of violence — indeed it is the first precondition for masculine hierarchy. If men are to love one another, as all great religions have taught, it must be possible for us to love one another in the full, sexual sense; so long as this is tabooed, inter-male competition can never be dissolved.

What establishes this vicious competition, of course, is not the practice of heterosexuality, but the non-practice of homosexuality. It would disappear if the gender system were abolished, and human beings could relate to one another irrespective of biological sex, i.e. both homosexually and heterosexually, with the family accordingly replaced by a form of commune. But in this case, the resultant 'bisexuality' would be clearly established on the terms of homosexuality, or rather gayness. It would be a sexuality between essentially similar individuals, rather than essentially dissimilar, thus 'homo-sexual' rather than 'hetero-sexual'. Gay relationships today, therefore, for all their distortion by the gender system around us, can in the best of cases prefigure the communist sexuality of the future, an order in which love does not automatically establish alongside itself a relation of rivalry and hate, but can assume an altogether more inclusive form.

This striking contrast between gayness and heterosexuality refutes the attempt by the 'psychonazis' to understand the dynamics of gay relationships in terms of an attraction between the 'feminine' gay man who is really a woman, and

the 'masculine' gay man who (despite their failure to understand him) is really a man. Even assuming that the two contrasting routes to gayness outlined in the previous section
did divide gay men rigidly into two categories (and they do
not), it would still be quite false to equate the sexuality of
the more effeminate gay man with that of a heterosexual
woman, or that of the less effeminate (but still far from
'masculine') gay man with that of a heterosexual man. Even
when there is a real difference between two gay men in their
degree of deviance from the masculine norm, they can attract one another perfectly well without either of them cultivating the illusion that one partner is really a woman and
the other a 'proper' man. But equally, it is possible for two
gay men to attract one another just as much when they
share the same degree of effeminacy, and as I shall go on to
show, the tendency in the gay subculture today is very definitely away from the role division that was cultivated in
the past, and towards a more radical equality than before: in
fact, towards 'being what gay is'.[37]

The attraction of 'like poles' that is the essence of the gay
relationship involves the several levels at which gay men
are qualitatively more similar than are a heterosexual
couple. At the psychosexual level, both categories of gay
man have internalized their mother to a significant extent;
both are accordingly able to care for one another in a way
that in normal heterosexuality is the unreciprocated province of the woman. (Though even in the heterosexual context, it is a sorry relationship in which the man has not
maintained at least a vestige of the tenderness he imbibed
from his mother; what woman really wants as her lover the
101 per cent superman divested of the last remaining shred
of maternal softness?) At the biological level, there is a
unique kind of intimacy to be gained from sexual relations
with someone whose physiology is the same as your own.[38]
In fact, this gives homosexuality a specific pleasure that
heterosexuality can never have, which is not to say that sex
between female and male may not also have a joy unique to
itself. Finally, there is also the level of companionship, at
which the shared sensitivity that gay men have by virtue of
our deviance from the gender system (reinforced by the similar way that each partner is viewed by the heterosexist soci-

ety) provides a very deep channel of communication, as indeed it does among all gay people, whereas it is only too typical for a heterosexual couple to fail to understand one another.

There is thus simply no problem as to what attracts gay men to one another. And according to personal compatibility and the general social situation, gay relationships, just like heterosexual, can vary from the most casual anonymous encounter through to the life-long partnership, as well as in many other dimensions. There is absolutely no shortage of cement; this is a pseudo-problem generated from trying to understand gay relationships in terms of heterosexual categories, and the narrowest categories of gender at that.

The dominant and distinctive characteristic of the gay relationship is its radical equality. But within this context, there are certain counter-tendencies, of which two need particular mention here.

Firstly, the 'father' is not completely absent from the gay situation, intervening in particular through the less effeminate gay man who has significantly internalized something of both parents. In the great majority of gay relationships, this does not give rise to a gender structuring even remotely equivalent to heterosexuality. The father, in this case, is a 'soft heterosexual', and it may be that both parties in a relationship share this internalization, in which case any tendency to a masculine domination is cancelled out. But even in a relationship between two gay men differing in their deviance from the masculine norm, the more effeminate partner, as I have shown, is by no means necessarily looking for a substitute father; in general, what he wants is simply a male person who is attracted to him. That said, there are a minority of gay men who do seek a 'big daddy', and there are a further minority who are not unhappy to play that role. In this case, mere difference in emotional make-up is not usually enough for such a relationship; other factors are required, such as significant difference in age, and very often also the older man's possession of certain class privileges that are a further source of power.

This involves the second major factor of inequality in the gay situation. Difference in age alone does not necessarily involve inequality. An older man may be just as dependent in a relationship as a younger man. But when the younger partner is still an adolescent who has not yet found his footing in the adult world, and the older man is a strong personality, the relationship can certainly not be described as egalitarian. An element of parenting is involved. This in itself should not necessarily be seen as harmful. Young people genuinely do need the help of adults, and young gay people in particular, who are so often rejected by their parents (and in the best case these can't offer much help in establishing a gay identity!),[39] can undoubtedly benefit in many cases from a relationship with a mature adult. From the adult's point of view, moreover, the motivation is by no means necessarily just wanting to play the dominant father. Indeed, in seeking to explain male homosexual relations of a paedophile kind, Freud himself adduced the older man's mother-identification as cause, rather than any father-identification:

> A young man has been unusually long and intensely fixated upon his mother in the sense of the Oedipus complex. But at last, after the end of puberty, the time comes for exchanging his mother for some other sexual object. Things take a sudden turn: the young man does not abandon his mother, but identifies himself with her; he transforms himself into her, and now looks about for objects which can replace his ego for him, and on which he can bestow such love and care as he has experienced from his mother.[40]

Undoubtedly, Freud's analysis is much too facile. And yet the parenting factor involved in paedophilia certainly includes an aspect of mothering just as it does fathering. The young man, in any case, has not grown up with the abject father fixation that the gender system strives to impress on women. And he is a man himself, free of responsibility for children, and with access to the privileges that the masculine world offers. In the vast majority of cases, therefore, relationships between adult and adolescent men are genuinely *gay*, quite unlike anything among the Siwans or Keraki. The good side of parenting thus outweighs the aspect of paternal domination, and this is certainly the criterion by which such relationships should be judged.

This is a good place to contrast the further development of the less effeminate gay man with that of the soft heterosexual, whose path was very similar until adolescence. Involvement in a gay relationship, even with a more effeminate and possibly younger man, does not reinforce his masculinity; quite the contrary. From the standpoint of the society around, he has defined himself as effeminate. And within the relationship, he can in no way treat his partner like an oppressed woman and get away with it. Both these factors have the opposite effect for the soft heterosexual. His relationship is defined by the society around as normal, and he is legitimized in acting the dominant partner. Thus while the gay man undergoes a certain 'de-masculinization' after establishing his gay identity, the soft heterosexual continues forward on the path of masculinization — at least until 'his' woman discovers feminism, and forces him into a men-against-sexism group!

In the gay subculture at large, the tendency for relationships to be squeezed into heterosexist categories is a product of our oppression by the environing society, rather than something generated by the inherent dynamic of the gay relationship itself. This becomes clear if we consider how the gay subculture has developed over the years.

The berdache phenomenon, however different from anything we can recognize as gay, does show that gender deviance is manifested by a certain number of individuals in many societies; a minority of boys do not grow up as they are supposed to, for the family situation is always bound to deviate to a certain extent from the social norm. (Some mothers, in particular, always find a way to resist their sons being taken away from them and made into 'men'.)

Yet even if there are always individuals who are inwardly deviant, who do not feel the things they are supposed to, and find themselves feeling things they are supposed not to, it is only relatively recently that a space has arisen for the existence of a definite subculture based around this deviance, i.e. for effeminate men to develop an identity as *gay*, rather

than being faced with the stark alternative of either struggling along in the masculine role, or perhaps a radical rever-
sal into the feminine. This could only come about when
family and kinship ties broke down sufficiently to allow
individuals (at least men) to live an atomized existence in
relative anonymity. The commercial city is its precondition. I don't know whether there was already a gay community in imperial Rome or Baghdad. But we can certainly
trace its origin and development in 16th century London, as
Alan Bray has done in his pioneering work *Male Homosexuality and Society in England 1550-1700*.[41] Once the preconditions exist, gay men begin to congregate together,
needing contact and communication with one another not
just for sex, but even more so as to develop an identity and
awareness of self that the surrounding society denies and
suppresses.

Across wide differences of culture, gays are able to recognize one another. Yet the form taken by the gay subculture,
and the ideology through which gay men view themselves,
varies according to the specific modalities of the gender system. The more rigid and extreme the gender polarity, the
more viciously it imposes its oppressive dualism on the gay
subculture as well.

In the extreme situation, as displayed for example in the
Arab world, only the man who gets fucked is stigmatized as
'queer'; the man who fucks is perfectly normal, no matter
that it's another man he's fucking rather than a woman.
(There's scarcely room in this system for any sexual practice
besides anal intercourse.) In a similar vein, an ostensibly
heterosexual man can fuck a transvestite who acts the
woman, though is visibly not so, as is still common in the
Latin countries.

The traditional ghetto situation in Britain or America,
with its 'butch' and 'femme' role-playing, reflects a gender
system that is one degree more flexible. Here, the gay subculture is that much less gender-bound that it recognizes
the existence of 'masculine' homosexuals as well as 'feminine'. The converse of this, of course, is that the outside
world is quite sure that anyone involved in homosexual
relations must be 'queer', i.e. effeminate, less than a proper
man. And yet the gender system is still so strong, even in its

effects on those it excludes from its definition of normal, that it is still very common for gay men to conceive of themselves as 'really a woman', or alternatively 'a man who likes other men'.

Against this dismal background, we can see how the theory of the 'third' or 'intermediate' sex, which seems so ridiculous to gay liberationists today, initially had a progressive aspect to it. It also had a very clear instrumental use. It was no coincidence that its most vigorous proponent was Magnus Hirschfeld, leader of the German homosexual rights movement of the early 1900s, who waged a thirty-years war against Freud and all his works for suggesting that sexual orientation was acquired rather than innate. For if it was acquired, then it could presumably be disacquired, and the door was open for legal and medical sanctions to force gay people back into the straight world. It was only in the 1970s that the gay movement was able to face the truth about its own gayness, once it set its sights on abolishing the gender system as such.

In this perspective, we no longer need strive to squeeze ourselves into oppressive heterosexist categories. We are neither 'proper' men nor any kind of woman, nor are we a new intermediate sex. The concept of a 'gay man' belongs to a time when the rigid and inflexible character of the gender system is already fraying at the edges, particularly due to the advance of feminism, and when it is generally recognized that homosexuality and heterosexuality are not born but made. In the early days of gay liberation, we often used drag and make-up to bring home to people that the gender system, however deep-rooted, was a cultural artifice, and that 'boys can be girls'. However challenging this was at the time, from today's hindsight it seems still far too marked by the ideology of the ghetto. Gay men have never been women, and never will be. It is understandable how many feminists, initially sympathetic to the gay movement, were put off by the insistence that the position and interests of women and gay men were simply identical. We are differentiated from women not just by our biology and our economic position in the present society, but by our position in the gender system as well. We are effeminate men; as such our interests are ultimately convergent with women's liberation, in that they both require the breakdown of the gender system; but they converge from very different starting-points. After ten years of the new gay movement, it is certainly far more acceptable for male human beings to be openly effeminate than it was a decade ago. This is the fundamental direction in which human society is moving, however much of a struggle still lies ahead.

There is a further change, too, that takes place as the extreme forms of the gender system begin to soften. In the earlier and most rigid forms, it is that much more difficult to come out as gay (even in the most limited traditional sense, i.e. into the gay ghetto), and those brave enough to do so were likely to be the most effeminate gay men who had greatest difficulty in concealing themselves. Naturally, this situation encouraged them to define themselves as 'really women', to adopt transvestism and even seek to 'pass', particularly as prostitutes, etc. As the repression begins to subside and the gender system slowly but inexorably softens, particularly with the rise of the women's and gay liberation movements, the gay ghetto broadens out into a less rigidly confined gay community, and it is that much easier for those gay men who could pass as straight, if need be, to come out as well — today in a fuller sense. Combined with the softening of the masculine stereotype for straight men, one would therefore expect gay men and straight to appear somewhat less different than in the past (not to mention the rise of 'bisexuality' in various modes).[42] In this situation, the balance between the contrasting routes to gayness steadily shifts. More gay men, in other words, tend to come from families where the father is himself relatively effeminate, and there is no basic conflict between the parents, and fewer from families in which the father is a 'proper' man, and the son becomes gay by being sheltered from his masculinizing intervention by the mother.

Yet this is not sufficient to explain the pronounced 'butch shift' that has taken place in the gay subculture in the last few years, the emergence of the clone look, the denim and leather cult, even the rise of sadomasochism. From the standpoint of the early gay liberation movement, this might seem disturbing indeed. In one theory put about by the ex-

treme 'effeminist' tendency in the early 1970s, male homosexuality was seen as becoming a reactionary force in comparison with heterosexuality; heterosexual men were at
least changing in response to the rise of feminism, whereas
gay men increasingly appeared as the minority who refused
to relate to the women's movement, and abandoned heterosexuality for the joys of an all-male environment.

This theory, fortunately, is altogether misguided. It is indeed sad, and more than a little ridiculous, that large numbers of gay men feel the need to adopt the external signs of
masculine toughness, to dress as cowboys, policemen, soldiers, even Nazis. This is sad not just for what it betokens
about our psychology, but from a political standpoint too, in
that it makes it more difficult for the objective convergence
of the gay and feminist struggles to be made conscious and
deliberate. Yet the 'butch shift' does not signify, except for
perhaps a tiny minority of gay men, any serious attempt to
repress their effeminacy and rejoin the male club on the
most traditional of terms. The fact that in San Francisco, for
example, where this tendency is most extreme, you can generally tell a gay man from a straight man by the gay man's
more 'masculine' appearance, should precisely be taken for
the surface appearance that it is. Scratch almost any of these
superbutches, and you'll still find an effeminate gay man
underneath. Even in the S & M scene, the great majority of
those involved participate essentially at the level of a
manipulation of symbols, and are wary of the tiny minority
who take their activity with too deadly a seriousness.[43]

The 'butch shift', then, is simply a ploy designed to
heighten sexual tension among gay men by presenting an
image of masculinity designed to fit the fantasy of a 'man'. It
characteristically goes hand in hand with regular reliance on
drugs such as amyl nitrate, also designed to enhance the in-
tensity of the sexual encounter. Between two gay men, each
of whom may look 'clonically' similar, and be similarly a
queen underneath, the other's butch image is taken at face
value. The ploy, however, can only function within certain
very particular limits. It evidently can't survive closer ac-
quaintance with the person behind the image. Indeed,
having become a general custom, everyone knows the game
in advance, and can simply not have any illusions of finding

a real he-man. The terrain on which the game is played, however, is precisely not that of courtship for any protracted mating, but rather the one-off performance of recreational sex. At the level of a casual pick-up, it is only the surface appearance which you need to relate to. Two effeminate men can thus have sex with one another that is heightened by their symmetrical fantasies that the other is as real a man as his denim, leather, chains or whatever try to suggest. This is particularly the case when consummation takes place in bars, saunas, toilets, parks, disused warehouses, etc. — often without a word being spoken. A minute's conversation or a glance round his apartment would immediately belie the butch image, but it need never come to that.

If even those involved in the 'butch shift' are not really taken in by the appearances they create, it would be foolish indeed to allow these to distort an objective understanding of the phenomenon. Denim or leather queens are precisely that, i.e. queens: effeminate men who are oppressed as such by the gender system and whose fundamental interests lie in its erosion. Even if their responses are misguided, there should be no doubt as to which side they are on. Feminists should therefore seek to relate to them for what they really are, and not fall into the trap of focussing the attack against male domination on that very group of males who need to be won as an important ally. Only the most superficial view of things can see leather queens as doing harm to the feminist cause by their use of this masculine image as a fetish. The only real harm they are likely to do is to themselves, with the mental and physical damage to which their extreme forms of masochism can sometimes lead.

The disease of which the 'butch shift' is really a symptom is something else, a disease that is inflicted on us as part of our oppression. The gay ghetto, even if it has greened somewhat in the post-Stonewall era, and now prefers to be referred to as a 'gay community', still suffers abysmally from the marginalization of gay people, the way we are expelled from our communities of origin and driven to seek refuge in the anonymity of the big city. Relatively free from the crassest expressions of gender in our own personalities, we are nevertheless trapped quite involuntarily in the masculine role in as much as we are excluded from the vital social function of childcare. Indeed, we are even more excluded from this than are heterosexual men, who, with the gradual erosion of the gender system, are beginning to play a more active role in tending for the infants they help to produce. This is not to say that all gay men would necessarily want to become parents, any more than all heterosexual women or men do today. But our forcible exclusion from parenthood is an aspect of our oppression the importance of which is often underrated.

In a notable display of false consciousness, it has become popular in the gay community, especially in the United States, to define our marginalized existence as a 'lifestyle', implying that it is essentially freely chosen rather than an adaptation to oppression. And part of what the gay male 'lifestyle' involves is not breeding. (Heterosexual couples, by contrast, are referred to pejoratively as 'breeders'.) In an extreme form of this, certain sections of the gay movement have even joined forces with other representatives of the 'single' population to demand reductions in the tax concessions for dependent children. 'We've decided not to have children. Why should we pay for other people's?'

But children are not 'ours' or 'theirs'; they are their own. They are the next generation of our society, indispensable to its continuation. We all have an obligation to contribute towards their upkeep; rather than seek to contract out of this, our demand should be to play our part in caring for them. In this way, we can help the erosion of the gender system.

Our exclusion from childcare, moreover, also has a vicious effect on our 'lifestyle' here and now. Bringing children up is a form of activity that binds those involved together in a peculiarly intimate way. It is responsible, far more than any other factor, for making at least the more successful heterosexual marriages evolve in the long run into a more equal and quite unbreakable companionship. While the majority of people in our society take part in bringing up children, there are relatively few opportunities for other activities that have a comparable bonding effect. (For example, the joint participation of a couple in politics, a particular artistic or sporting activity, etc.) The difficulty of finding an important common activity is the main reason why gay relationships are often short-lived and unsuccessful.

This is in no way to maintain that the monogamous couple is the only route to happiness. There are other ways, too, in which sexual energies can be sublimated and channeled into paths that provide a more lasting and ultimately higher form of fulfilment than sex itself ever can. Larger groups than the couple living together, sharing sexuality and the raising of children, would certainly be an advance from the over-intense and neurotic atmosphere of the nuclear family household. The Gay Liberation Front accordingly proclaimed its aim of the replacement of the family by the commune.[44] Yet in the gay subculture of today it can be very difficult to establish any lasting relationships, based on a love fed by the sublimation of sexuality into affection for which our species has a peculiar disposition.

Without this sublimation, our sexuality simply follows the ever-changing flux of desire, seizing on partial objects, surface appearances, rather than being used to form genuine interpersonal bonds. This has actually been glorified by certain theorists of sexual promiscuity, ranging from the pragmatic John Rechy through to the more highbrow approach of Guy Hocquenghem.[45] The experience of the gay subculture, however, is that this is a destructive dead end. The drive behind so much gay promiscuity is not that this is more satisfying than the cultivation of 'deep meaningful relationships' (not that these cannot also leave a certain room for casual, purely recreational sex as well). It is rather as a resigned second-best, if not actually a desperate quest for a 'Mr Right' who, almost by definition, will not be found by this route. We have successfully disentangled sexual pleasure from the constraints of religion, marriage, enforced heterosexuality, etc. that oppressed it in the past, and it is entirely a good thing that sex can be sought and enjoyed for its own sake. Yet we still have great difficulty in linking our sexuality in a non-oppressive way with other dimensions of life, and it is unquestionably a symptom of some very deep malaise that gay men so often find it hard to form ties of solidarity, and live so individualistic an existence.

In all this, the gay subculture of today simply shares the problems of our society as a whole, often in the most glaring degree. It is the system of class and gender that tosses us around in this way, preventing us from collectively determining a way of life designed to meet our real needs. The gay subculture is essentially an adaptation to the present society, making the best of a bad situation just as oppressed groups necessarily do so long as it is still possible to go on in the old way, and it should be criticized from this point of view. The problem for gay liberationists today is how to act against this distortion of our lives, how to consciously take up the common maternal culture that is at the heart of our being, and direct this energy into a better life for ourselves, and for our whole society and planet.

## 6. *Sexual Liberation and Gender Liberation*

In the previous sections of this chapter I have examined the ways in which the gender system structures sexuality, and the various parameters that define the existence of a deviant gay minority. Focussing on the specific forms of our oppression, there are three particular enemies that can be singled out.

First, there is the system of social control, which forces us to behave in ways foreign to our own desires.

Second, there are the queer-bashers of all kinds, who act out against us the aggression they mobilize to keep down their own effeminacy and homosexual desire.

Third, there is the oppression in our own heads, the distortion of our lives so as to minimize friction with the straight world.

The most immediate demand of the gay movement, as this first found a voice at the beginning of the century, was for our right to exist, i.e. to express our sexuality without falling foul of the law, and to have the same protection as any other citizens from abuse and assault. But even in the new wave of the gay liberation movement, which sought a more radical solution to our oppression, this was not necessarily seen in terms of the abolition of gender. An alternative perspective, not altogether contradictory but conflicting on certain important points, located the struggle for gay liberation as part of a struggle for sexual liberation.

In many ways this perspective extrapolates from a valid insight into the development that has made possible the undoubted advances already achieved, i.e. the relative relaxation of our persecution by the system of social control. Past history is certainly marked by quite major swings between a very severe repression against all non-procreative forms of sexuality, and a relative relaxation. Even if the Judeo-Christian religious tradition formally proscribes all forms of sex outside of marriage (and has sometimes even attempted to restrict sex between husband and wife to the task of pro-creation), there have been periods when this observance has been honoured more in the breach. A greater space then developed for unofficial forms of sexuality, even if these were still in theory capital crimes, and the supreme penalty never ceased to loom in the background.

These swings in sexual morality are associated above all with the ascent and decline of successive ruling classes. A tightening up on sexuality has been characteristic of the rise of a new and relatively progressive social class, which has needed not just to channel the energies of the masses into production, but also to discipline itself and accumulate rather than consume. In Britain, in common with most other Western countries, we had the period associated with the rise of merchant capitalism (the Reformation), and more recently that associated with the rise of industrial capitalism (the Victorian era). In those parts of the world which appear sexually repressive compared with our own region today, such as the 'socialist' countries, this is associated with the rise of a new type of managerial class, whether you like to call it capitalist or not. Before and after these periods of severe repression, there have been periods of relative relaxation, in which the ruling class is able to rest on its gains and cultivate the arts of leisure, including sexual pleasure.[46] For the champions of the moral order, gayness has always been peculiarly abhorrent, and especially associated with 'decadence'. For while pre-marital or extra-marital hetero-sexuality only gives unlicensed expression to a sexuality that is still socially normal, gayness is against the norms of the gender system as such. It raises the spectre of a whole society, a whole civilization, becoming effeminate and suc-cumbing to foreign conquest or internal revolution. (The working masses are always more tied to the gender system out of economic necessity.)

Gay people cannot but welcome any phase of relaxation. When we have been granted even the most minimal tolerance, on the margins of society, this has been in times of 'decadence'. And when we hear such 'decadence' under attack, as for example by the fascists of the 1920s and 1930s, who sought to gear their societies up to wrest world hegemony from the 'decadent' Western powers, we know immediately that we are in for a new round of vicious persecution. 'Decadence', however, is never a society's official self-description. In accepting a certain relaxation of sexual norms, our rulers have preferred the term 'liberalization'; even 'permissiveness' has a certain pejorative connotation. It is in the name of liberalization, then, that legislation against homosexuality has been repealed in the majority of Western countries, along with other laws that have sought to confine sexual expression to holy matrimony. And despite the very clear difference that exists between making something legal and accepting it as moral (the English courts, for example, still officially define homosexuality as 'immoral'), there can be no question that the liberalization of legal controls and the liberalization of moral controls proceed closely in parallel. It is simply that changes in the law can come about more quickly, just as they can be reversed more quickly if the pendulum swings the other way.

Until the rise of the Gay Liberation Front, the demands of the earlier homosexual movement, which suddenly seemed so meek in comparison with the radicalism of GLF, had not gone beyond the limits of liberalization. It is quite understandable how this had to be the first step. For with the very expression of our sexuality an offence punishable by years in prison, it was difficult indeed to form any cultural or political organizations which could formulate more ambitious goals and begin to struggle for them. Yet the limits of liberalization were immediately apparent to the new wave of gay liberationists. Liberalization, and its close associate 'tolerance', meant that we would still be classed as a deviant group on the margins of society. The heterosexual majority would allow us certain privileges, but what was granted in this way could just as readily be withdrawn, as the experience of fascism had shown.

In the advance from demanding civil rights or 'homosex-

ual equality' to the demand for gay liberation, our movement expressed an awareness, for the first time, that a defin-
itive solution to our oppression was possible, i.e. that its
underlying structures could be rooted out. There was no
immediate agreement as to what exactly these were, but
there were many signs around that the situation today was
different from anything known in the past, and that things
which had previously been taken for granted as a basic fact
of life were now open to question.

It had become clear, by the late 1960s, that the 'sex wave'
of the post-War period, as it came to be known in Germany,
went far beyond any past relaxation of sexual taboos. Those
who sought to stem the advancing tide in the name of traditional Christian morality found themselves fighting a desperate losing battle, and the church and other guardians of
the moral order were forced to make ever greater compro-
mises with the mass demand for freer sexual expression.
The underlying basis for this development lay in the unprecedented expansion of the productive forces under capitalism, and the consumerist adaptation that the capitalist system had stumbled upon in the interest of prolonging its own
survival. In the advanced capitalist countries, leisure, in the
sense of both free time and the material wherewithal to
enjoy it, was brought within reach of the majority of the
working population, in a way that has no historical parallel.
The same technology, moreover, that made this development possible, also came up with methods of birth control
of qualitatively superior efficacy to anything in the past,
while advances in nutrition, hygiene and medical care made
it possible to reproduce the human population with an average of only marginally more than two pregnancies per adult
woman, in a lifespan now approaching eighty years. Even
heterosex was effectively separated from procreation.

In this completely new historical situation, it was possible for the first time for the mass of people to develop a
culture of sexual enjoyment that had previously been confined simply to a small minority. Certainly, the sex-negative
attitudes instilled in the course of centuries take a couple of
generations to break down. But unlike the situation with
the rise of fascism half a century ago, it would be very difficult today for a would-be new ruling class to find mass sup-

port in the hostility or ambiguity of ordinary people towards the new sexual freedom, turning a revolt against 'decadence' to its repressive political aims. The 'sexual revolution' has gone too far to be reversed in this way.

But this does not mean there is no basis for a turn in the tide. As I shall go on to argue in the next chapter, the consumerist economy of contemporary capitalism is increasingly fragile. It is based not just on the monopolizing of resources by the privileged quarter of our planet, while the great majority of Earth's population still suffer absolute deprivation. It is also based on the breakneck depletion of limited raw materials in the most wasteful of ways, and the substantial deterioration of the planetary environment. Its life expectancy is limited indeed, and a radical change of course will have to come pretty soon, if our species is even to survive.

What this certainly does undermine is the argument that bases the possibility of a radical sexual liberation on the existence of a 'post-scarcity' economic situation that will remove any need for human energy to be channeled into labour. This is quite simply a ridiculous extrapolation of existing trends, which may even now have reached their limit and be going into reverse. As far as it is possible to foresee, the human race will face daunting tasks of survival, of radically reorganizing its social relations, and putting its ecology on a sound basis. We are possibly a thousand years from the point where we could simply lay back and eat the lotus. But even if we do solve the problem of meeting our material needs satisfactorily, a culture centred completely on bodily pleasure, as suggested in the writings of Norman O. Brown, is only one choice that our species can make. There are arguments against it, as well as arguments for. Only a society so stricken by sexual repression in the past could believe that the ending of this repression would mean – for better or worse – that sex, even in the widest Freudian sense, comes to dominate the whole of our life. The spirit has its claims to gratification too, claims which are likely to increase with the evolution of our species, rather than to decline.

Mario Mieli, in his *Homosexuality and Liberation*, falls into the trap of seeking to base gay liberation on sexual liberation in the sense of the 'Freudian left'. He starts off by assuming far too simplistically that the innate polymorphous potential of the human infant, which psychoanalysis has clearly demonstrated, can be equated with a bundle of ready-formed erotic trends, which fail to gain expression in adult life simply because they have been repressed. It is on this basis, for example, that Mario ends up with the thesis that all heterosexual men are really closet queens: a notable case of wish fulfilment.

Freudian theory has undoubtedly provided certain insights that help to explain the reproduction of masculinity and femininity, and the consequent repression of effeminacy and gayness. But in developing his theory, Freud precisely took for granted the sexual division of labour, and male domination, that requires girls and boys to grow up into these two contrasting variants of human being. Indeed, he has repeatedly been taken to task for this by contemporary feminists. Mario Mieli, however, though throughout his book he appeals to Marxism, never so much as mentions the sexual division of labour, i.e. the basis of the masculine/feminine dichotomy in society at large, and consequently has to try and explain this dichotomy purely in terms of sexual repression. According to him, it is only this negative force that prevents us from all being the same, i.e. polymorphously perverse. He ignores the fact that besides the undoubted reality of sexual repression, there is also a positive principle of differentiation: female and male children, placed in different social relations, actively learn to seek gratification in different ways, with the deviant categories such as ourselves exploring still other options.

Polymorphous perversity only describes the potential field of our sexuality. It can never describe adult sexuality, and we cannot grow up unstructured by gender and all that this involves unless the sexual division of labour in the wider society is eroded.[47] As long as this remains intact, then heterosexual primacy, for the man, is not simply or even primarily the result of the repression of his homosexuality; I have shown above how it is relatively easy for him to make a homosexual object-choice, for example in a prison situation. Male heterosexuality, in the gender system, is a very convenient arrangement for sexual gratification, and

until the gender system is done away with it would be foolish to expect the straight majority of men to have the same
interest in homosexuality as the gay minority.

There are three things in the concept of 'sexual liberation'
that are perfectly valid. First, the insistence that mere liberalization is not enough; the complex of sex-negative attitudes
must be completely overthrown, and sex must be seen clearly
for what it is, a source of tremendous pleasure and satisfaction that can validly be pursued for its own sake. Second,
the insight that sexual repression leads to repressive and
authoritarian attitudes in other fields as well, and generally
makes it far more difficult for people to formulate their
interests and needs in a rational way. And thirdly, that with
the separation of heterosex from procreation, there is no
reason whatsoever why homosexuality should not be as universal and acceptable as heterosexuality. (A conclusion not
generally drawn by theorists of 'sexual liberation' before the
rise of the gay liberation movement, Wilhelm Reich being
the most notoriously anti-homosexual of these.)

Yet the preconditions of gay liberation go far beyond this.
Not in the false sense of making sex the be-all and end-all
of human existence; but in the sense that there can be no
true solution to the problem of the subordinate status of
homosexuality and the oppressed position of the gay minority
until the gender system is completely done away with. For
as I have argued, it is not simply sexual activity with other
men that the gender system suppresses, but more fundamentally our characteristic effeminacy. As long as masculinization is the rule, then the ideology of the gender system
will torture gay men with our failure to live up to its norm,
as will the queer-bashers who are straining every nerve in
their determination to be 'proper' men. (It is important to
note that queer-bashing has not undergone any significant
decline in the last three decades of the 'sex wave'. Nor do
more enlightened policies of containment on the part of the
legal and moral order seem to have had much effect on this
gut-level hostility towards the effeminate.)

The greatest achievement of gay liberation, therefore, has
been its recognition that our oppression can only be brought
to an end by the abolition of the gender system, in convergence with the women's liberation movement. As I ex-

plained in Chapter One, this goal is not only possible today, because childcare no longer need be ascribed solely to women; it is also essential, as the masculine specialization in violence must be eliminated if we are not going to use the high-technology weapons that our science has developed in a cataclysmic spiral of destruction. This crucial link with the feminist movement, and through it with the movement for communism in general, was first made in the early days of GLF, and marks a qualitative transformation in the signif-icance of the gay movement.

Of course, it is only a minority, even among those actively engaged in the gay movement, who have a clear under-standing of this goal. This is a problem encountered by all movements against oppression, and indeed a radical formu-lation of the requirements of liberation can rarely obtain a mass audience, except at those times of crisis when political consciousness is heightened, and momentous decisions have to be made. The same problem is certainly shared by the women's movement, by the movement of the working class, and others. But the crisis is already looming, and the time is rapidly coming when the illusion of the eternal character of the present social order will be most rudely shattered. If even a minority have some notion in advance of the direction to take for survival, this may prove a great asset for our society as a whole.

# Chapter Three:
## The Crisis of Humanity

## 1. *The Concept of Crisis*

What does the concept of crisis mean, when applied to the development of human society? Above all, a crisis is a fork in the road, a point at which development can proceed along either of two divergent lines, whereas in non-critical times social development, like the evolution of a biological species or the life of an individual, remains stuck fairly firmly in an entrenched pattern.

Very rarely does a crisis pose a choice between two roads of development that are equally satisfactory. Indeed, the heightened urgency that is characteristic of any crisis in human affairs precisely suggests that one possible outcome is significantly better, the other significantly worse. In the medical model from which the concept of crisis is derived, a crisis in an illness is a point from which the patient may proceed either to recover or to die. It would over-dramatize the situation facing the human race today to claim that the immediate crisis is quite as absolute as this. The choice is probably more like rejuvenation versus chronic disability, and that is quite fateful enough. In the social situation, however, it is generally more difficult than in medicine to perceive the outcomes of alternative decisions. Doctors, too, can make mistakes, but in politics above all, the very task of diagnosis is often vitiated by the complexity of the factors involved and the struggle of conflicting interests.

In times of crisis, the concern that people show for politics is greatly increased. If decisions are going to be made that are completely non-routine, and may tip the balance between a good and a bad resolution, then it is far more worthwhile taking the trouble to read the newspapers, discuss with fellow-citizens, form an opinion, join an organization, and so on. Radical political parties, almost by definition, owe their existence to a situation of crisis; for if there is no crisis, even looming on the horizon, then there is nothing to be radical about. In this case, it may well be possible to put forward utopian alternatives to the status quo, but there is no viable way of furthering their achievement.

Marx himself chose a medical metaphor to explain the role of the 'subjective factor' in social transformation, the metaphor of the midwife. While he believed he had demonstrated the inevitable development through crisis from capitalism to communism, this development still required conscious struggle to achieve, and if the working class gained an adequate understanding of the process, it would be possible to 'shorten and lessen the birth pangs' of the new society.[1]

Today, the seeming unilinearity of the orthodox Marxist conception is out of fashion. The argument that communism is inevitable strikes a false and hollow note. But the triumphalist interpretation of orthodox Marxism that is nowadays associated above all with Soviet imperialism is not the only possible reading of Marx's metaphor. The birth of a baby may well be inevitable, but its birth alive and well is certainly not so. The midwife in fact does more than simply decrease the birth pangs; she helps determine the baby's life or death (not to mention that of the mother). In the evolution of species, too, the outcome of a crisis is far from certain. We are today beginning to understand more precisely how living matter evolves higher forms of organization, to adapt to and eventually control its environment. Yet at so many points along the way the process of evolution could have been cut short. The geological changes that overwhelmed the dinosaurs, for example, might possibly have killed off our own ancestors as well, had they been a degree or two more acute. There must be many planets where life has begun to evolve, but never reached the stage of multicelled organisms, of a central nervous system, or of rational intelligence.

In reacting against the triumphalist doctrine of inevitability, then, it would be foolish to abandon the tremendous insight of Marx that there is an objective dynamic to social evolution, following on from the biological evolution that provided its preconditions, and that this dynamic does push in the direction of communism — a society where human beings consciously and collectively control their patterns of life in the common interest. The evidence for this is before our very eyes, in the thousands of organized efforts, from the gay liberation movement through to the struggle of the South of our planet for a new economic order, that are all ultimately convergent. The question is not whether this new society is waiting to be born, but rather whether it will be born alive, i.e. whether the development that is already in progress can successfully continue to fruition, or whether it will be cut short by disaster.

In the midst of the First World War, more than sixty years ago, Rosa Luxemburg already saw the choice facing Western civilization as that between 'socialism or barbarism'. Though the questions facing us today are different in particulars, the basic form of this dilemma is absolutely correct. The choice facing our planet is indeed between advance to a superior social organization, or a regression that may make future progress impossible for all time. It is highly unlikely that we would, in even the worst case, destroy our species in one fell swoop. But it is completely within the realm of possibility that, by taking a wrong course in the crisis now facing us, we could set in motion a spiral of decline. Either we make the leap forward to communism, using the vast potentials our intelligence has discovered in a constructive way; or else we fail to master these forces, and they will be our destruction.

Our planet is not yet a single society, even a single society still riven by internal contradictions. If we had indeed reached that stage, we would most likely be already over the hump, with only minor hurdles still ahead. Yet the process of integration is under way, as it has been ever since the European discoveries of the 16th century first established global routes of communication, and global relations of economic exchange and political power. This integration is just one aspect of what Marxism calls the development of the productive forces. In the widest sense, the concept of productive forces includes all those cultural elements that enable human beings to manipulate the material world. It is common knowledge today how the progress of material technique has followed an exponential curve, with a qualitative leap forward occurring with the development of scientific technology.

In the first flush of intoxication with the fruits of technological innovation, humankind was depicted as having finally 'conquered' nature, a dangerous myth that unfortunately dies hard, and has penetrated deep into the dogmas of orthodox Marxism.[2] Nature does not confront us as an enemy to be conquered; this attitude leads to a contempt for the biosphere of which we are part that is potentially disastrous. What the advance of scientific technology allows is rather a steady process of rolling back the natural boundary. But firstly, this process is never ending; we shall always find new areas where nature, i.e. the way things have proceeded spontaneously, can be replaced by culture, i.e. the way we decide things should proceed. Secondly, of all the possible areas of this kind, only a certain proportion are beneficial. We never have more than partial knowledge of the implications of our actions, and it is unwise to replace nature by culture until we have established that the cultural alternative is better than the natural. (For example, the ability to transport ourselves mechanically from city to city at 100 or 1000 kph. is a great advance. But the replacement of human muscle-power for transport within the city is not just a cause of pollution, but also of the many diseases due to lack of exercise.) Thirdly, there is a definite value in deliberately maintaining certain elements of the natural environment in their pristine state, e.g. reserves where wild animals can live in their natural habitat.

Scientific technology as such is not the problem; on the contrary, it is an indispensable part of the solution. The problem is the uses that we make of our power, still increasing so incredibly from one generation to the next. But bad and destructive applications of our science are not just unavoidable or accidental, nor do they proceed from some twist in our vision of our relationship to the universe, like the mass human sacrifices of the Aztecs. If the concepts of nuclear physics were used to build the atom bomb, this was a decision made in a rational way, in pursuit of a clearly defined goal. And there is no doubt that the bombing of Hiroshima and Nagasaki achieved that goal, i.e. the immediate surrender of Japan. The trouble here is simply that this is only a partial rationality, the pursuit of the interest of one particular group of people − it matters little whether you define it as the American nation or the American ruling class − in a situation of conflict with another group. Human reason is completely capable, at its present level of development, of choosing how to pursue its goals. The trouble in the world today is simply that the human species does not have commonly agreed goals, but is still divided between competing societies, and by various relations of oppressor and oppressed. This is of course nothing new. It is simply that the advance of scientific technology has made it insupportable, by amplifying so enormously the effects of our actions, and above all the violence deployed by one human group against another.

## 2. *The Symptoms of Crisis*

In discussing the gender system in Chapter One, I argued that the development of scientific technology has brought this oldest of all social divisions to a critical point. On the one hand, there is the possibility, for the first time in human history, of abolishing altogether the sexual division of labour, and ultimately making propagation of our species itself a branch of conscious production. On the other hand, if we allow the gender system to continue unchecked, then the masculine specialization in violence threatens to provoke a cataclysmic spiral of destruction.

Masculine violence may be the most basic precondition leading to war, but it is so only in the context of a complex pattern of social divisions, in particular the class system, the division of humanity into competing states, and imperialism. I shall come on in the next section to analyze this interlocking pattern of contradictions, which our species has to find a way out of if we are to survive. First, however,

it will be useful to examine the symptoms that this structure generates, of which the danger of nuclear war is only
one.

## War and Pollution

There have been many wars in the past, and above all the
two world wars that are still within living memory. Each of
these brought death and destruction on a completely unprecedented scale, with mass extermination being practised
with all the refinements of modern science. If the Nazi holocaust was unrivalled in its systematic annihilation of groups
that did not fit in with its political ambitions, on the Allied
side, too, the practice of strategic bombing was heedless of
any distinction between soldier and civilian. The atom
bombs dropped on Japan were simply a development of a
policy of 'psychological' warfare already practised with conventional weapons against Hamburg and Dresden on a hardly less massive scale.

Yet it is recognized on all sides that the development of
nuclear weapons has brought warfare to a qualitative turning-point. The power unleashed for destructive purposes,
which in a single hydrogen bomb can be a thousand times
greater than the bombs dropped on Hiroshima and Nagasaki, makes all-out war between the nuclear powers a completely irrational undertaking, the risks involved for the
aggressor making nonsense of Clausewitz's classical dictum
that 'war is the continuation of politics by other means'.
Irrational, but unfortunately not impossible, for there is still
a certain logic in the deployment of nuclear weapons to deter
conventional attack, and the whole pyramid of weapons systems based on this has so far proved resistant to all attempts
at negotiated disarmament. In a conflict situation between
the superpowers, there can be no guarantee that escalation
will stop short of the nuclear threshold. The atomic stock-
piles of the Soviet Union and the USA are a sword of Damo-
cles poised over our heads, and the longer nuclear weapons
are still around, the greater the chance that in some contin-
gency or other, however unintentional, they will actually be
used. The proliferation of nuclear weapons to the turbulent

societies of the third world, which is increasingly moving from possibility to established fact, will multiply the chances of nuclear war many times over.

Any nuclear war, however 'limited', would be unprecedentedly devastating of human life and equipment. Yet however frightful it is to contemplate the destruction of ten, twenty or a hundred of the world's great cities, including our own, this immediate loss would by no means bring 'the end of civilization as we know it'. Gigantic as the work of reconstruction would be, and having for shortage of resources to take forms very different from the old ones, it is highly unlikely that any major elements of culture would be lost. Today, the 'noosphere', i.e. the web of information existing both in the minds of human beings, and in books, films, data banks, computers, etc. is so dense that the knowledge needed for reconstruction would survive almost any holocaust.

The worst effect of a nuclear war would be the uncontrolled pollution of the environment by radioactive isotopes, both directly from atomic bombs, and indirectly from the destruction of nuclear power stations (even if effected by conventional weapons). In this way, we would not simply be killing off millions of human beings of the present generation, but poisoning the air, land and water on which future generations are equally dependent, as well as causing harmful mutations in the gene pool.

The wholesale pollution that would result from a nuclear war, however, would be simply an acceleration of the degradation of the environment that is being wreaked every moment of the present peacetime economy in the name of production. In all the advanced industrial countries, and increasingly also in those developing countries that are striving to modernize as rapidly as possible, the productive process releases into the environment noxious Atomic, Biological and Chemical substances, precisely corresponding to the three types of weapon that are deemed most repugnant, and which international negotiations strive to ban.

The rapid ecocide of nuclear war, and the more gradual ecocide through the present economic process, are thus two convergent results. Each of these threats has different roots in the present pattern of social organization, and appears as a distinct symptom of the present crisis. Yet in their ultimate effects, they are one and the same.

At the present time, it is by no means accidental that the movement against nuclear weapons, and the movement against nuclear power, are beginning to recognize each other as essential allies, indeed as two strands in the same movement, whereas not so many years ago the slogan of 'atoms for peace' still suggested that nuclear power was a benign use of the energy discovered at the very heart of matter. The nuclear fuel cycle, in fact, links both uses of atomic energy together in an integral way, as the dynamic of proliferation is making ever more clear.[3] Those people whose awareness starts with horror at the prospect of nuclear war are understanding that its worst effects would be the uncontrolled release of radioactivity·into the environment, while those initially aware of environmental pollution can see that the worst form of pollution we can imagine is that which would result from a nuclear war. In this way, a more powerful movement against both applications of nuclear energy is gathering steam, with a correspondingly greater chance of success on both fronts

Yet even today, radioactive waste is only one of many death-dealing substances being leaked into our air, water and land. At the moment, there are still more deaths attributable to the heavy metals such as mercury, cadmium and lead, than there are to radioactivity. 500,000 tons of lead, for example, are spewed out into the environment every year, in forms that, just like radioactivity, can never be totally cleared up. It is a proven fact that children who grow up close to major traffic routes suffer permanent brain damage from the lead they breathe in. And what is most atrocious is that this lead is not even a necessary additive to petrol, but simply put in to create a smoother burning mixture. If this massive blighting of children's lives is tolerated by their parents for one moment, it can only be because of their own furtive awareness, in the more shaded corners of their minds, that they are themselves in collusion with the process of environmental pollution, through their addiction to the consumerist lifestyle (not to mention their direct intake of nicotine and other poisons that they inflict on their children).

It is easy to see the problem of pollution as simply a negative side-effect of an effort that is in itself commendable — the great leap forward by the forces of economic production, which has finally brought working people in the advanced countries a decent material existence, for the first time in the history of class society. In this interpretation, the problem is simply to reduce this side-effect to a minimum, by stricter controls on the release of toxic wastes and on the use of pesticides, food additives and drugs, while leaving the essential productive processes of our society unaffected. Undoubtedly this attack on specific symptoms is possible and very necessary; the more progressive sectors of the advanced industrial world, such as Oregon or Sweden, show that a lot can be done to decrease pollution in these immediate forms. But this is a losing battle, not just because ever new pollutants are constantly being introduced, but more fundamentally, because it does not call into question the basic dynamic of consumerism that generates the problem of pollution.

The capitalist system of production for profit is essentially unconcerned with the social costs incurred by the productive process, in particular the social costs involved in the degradation of the environment. At its laissez-faire origins, capitalist production was conceived, even by its theorists, as a purely linear process from input to output, and it was one of Marx's great advances to have understood production as actually a circular process of metabolism between the human species and its environment, and to have pointed out the missing links that the ideologists of capitalism had omitted.[4] For a long time now, of course, the capitalist state has had to intervene against at least some of the environmental costs, just as it has had to enforce a certain measure of protection for industrial workers. And in its present consumerist adaptation, the role of the state is far greater than ever before, designed to sustain an economic growth geared to the satisfaction of the mass consumption market. Yet production is still assessed in the linear terms of output, rather than by any criterion of the total effects on social well-being of the metabolic process as a whole, and the situation in the 'socialist' countries of the Soviet bloc is in no way different. Controls on pollution, therefore, necessarily appear as a brake on 'economic growth', a negative quantity rather than a positive one.

Above all, 'economic growth' as defined in this linear sense is dependent on a constant increase in energy consumption. There are three basic sources of energy human society can draw on for its various requirements: income energy from the sun; a certain fraction of past income energy stored up in fossil fuel; and nuclear power. Everyone now knows that fossil fuel is a one-off bonus, a 'special introductory offer' we gave ourselves in the first flush of industrialization, and which we are now rapidly using up. The only long-term choice in energy policy is between nuclear power and solar power (including its indirect forms of hydroelectricity, wind and wave power, biomass, etc.).

From the standpoint of consumerism, income energy is immediately less attractive. It is not just a question of comparative costs, for if anything like as much research effort had gone into solar power as into nuclear power, the unit cost of electricity generation (very difficult to assess on a long-term basis) might be no higher. What jars against the capitalist and consumerist perspective is rather the philosophical connotation of solar power, the implication that humanity must live off a fixed energy resource, rather than one that is, at least in theory, limitless.

The ultimate limit to the use of solar energy is in fact a very high one. Our planet receives from the sun, and radiates out again as a 'black body', approximately 20,000 times the amount of energy presently generated by human activity.[5] Even with present techniques, it would be possible to use completely desert land in the oil-producing countries of the Middle East alone to generate several hundred times as much energy as their oil is contributing at its present rate of extraction. Technologies are already being developed that enable income energy to be tapped, in a whole variety of ways, virtually anywhere in the world. In north-west Europe, where sunshine is unfortunately on the low side, we are amply supplied with rough seas and strong tides,[6] not to mention the possible application of wind generation and biomass. A University of Sussex study concluded in 1977 that a global programme of conversion to income energy, phased over 75 years, could easily satisfy the estimated energy requirements of the mid 21st century, without any major new technological breakthroughs.[7]

Yet a policy based on income energy means seeing production as a circular, metabolic process, dependent on the Earth's own natural energy metabolism, in a way that is fundamentally alien to the linear concept of production which ends with the finished consumer good and treats the social costs of its production (and consumption, i.e. conversion into waste) as purely incidental. Nuclear power, on the other hand, promises a limitless expansion of output, i.e. 'economic growth'. If fusion power should ultimately be harnessed, using heavy water as fuel, it would be possible, if required, to cover the whole surface of the globe with electricity generating stations. Yet the dream of unlimited growth is ultimately a mirage, precisely because our planetary environment is a limited one. If a policy of nuclear power came to generate 100 times as much energy as we use today (and this is certainly well within the predictions of its more extreme exponents), then it would have a significant effect on the Earth's climate, raising the surface temperature by almost 1 degree F. Any increase much beyond this would rapidly make our planet quite uninhabitable. Solar power, on the other hand, simply intercepts the Earth's natural energy metabolism, and has no net heating effect whatsoever.

There are certainly more specific reasons why governments both East and West have opted for nuclear power, ranging from its connections with nuclear weapons production to the desire to keep energy generation under firmly centralized control, as a possible instrument of political discipline. Ultimately, however, the issue of nuclear versus solar power is an issue of which path humanity is to take, a path governed by 'economic growth', or by a far more comprehensive conception of human needs. This can explain why even those planners and politicians who are wary of fission and its obvious dangers look forward to the clean nuclear power they hope fusion will eventually provide. It can also explain why, against the very few who reject fission power on grounds of human safety, there are far more 'experts' of all kinds who are prepared to run the dreadful risks of fission as a temporary step on the way to fusion. For them, the overriding commitment is to perpetuate the existing system of social relations. And while nuclear power in its present fission form is so deadly a threat to the human species, it is precisely the least threatening to the present class system, proposing an indefinite expanded reproduction of the consumer economy.

As of today, the threat of a new world war and the threat of drastic environmental pollution are the two most immediate and terrible problems of human survival, and they are linked by the application, for both destructive and productive purposes, of atomic energy. Yet even so, it should not be ruled out that nuclear power, at least in its clean, fusion variant, might ultimately have a productive use. Even here, it is ultimately not the technology itself that is the problem, but rather the social relations within which it is deployed. When we genuinely do understand the operation of the Earth's meteorological system rather better, then the concentration of vast amounts of energy for highly specific purposes such as the diversion of rivers, for example, might be worthwhile. And in space travel, where the effects of an accident would be strictly confined to a small number of people, nuclear power might indeed come into its own.

## Genetic Engineering and Artificial Intelligence

This same contradiction between scientific technology and our present pattern of social organization also promises to generate equally dangerous symptoms in the future, as new productive forces come into play. Two great innovations, each already in preparation, seem set to dominate human existence in the 21st century: genetic engineering and artificial intelligence. Both of these, in their very different ways, are going to transform our conception of what it is to be human. Indeed they are already doing so for those prepared to grapple in thought with their possible implications. Both appear to have uses that can tremendously enhance the life of our species. Yet what might be a force for good, if harnessed to the needs of a unified human society, can still be a tremendous force for harm, if used in the interest of one section of humanity against another.

Genetic engineering brings into the realm of conscious decision our biological material itself. The positive opportunities that it presents are tremendous, even within the present horizon of possibility. First, as a preliminary, the removal of gestation from the human body into the laboratory, which is the precondition for any eugenic policy not based on the crude oppression of women. Second, the filtering of the gene pool to prevent the birth of individuals with severe physical or mental handicap. Third, the gradual elimination of at least phenotype differences between female and male, even if the principle of sexual reproduction at the chromosome level still remains necessary for a while. And fourth, a positive programme of improvement of our biological material, so that we shall at last begin to *produce* ourselves as human beings rather than continue conservatively to hang on to the half-evolved bodies we have now, still all too similar to our animal forebears, let alone place our trust in the blind, wasteful and slow process of random mutation.

Yet there is no guarantee that the opportunities opened up by genetic engineering will be used in this liberating way. The negative 'brave new world' imagined by Aldous Huxley has become a universal point of reference in our debates. From the traditional Marxist standpoint, the danger is one of a particularly desperate ruling class making use of genetic engineering to give the division of labour that biological anchoring which its apologists have fantasized since the dawn of class society (e.g. Plato's souls of iron, bronze and gold). In the perspective of contemporary feminism, the danger is also seen in terms of men responding to the feminist challenge by seeking to perpetuate their domination via a male parthenogenesis. It is easy to dismiss these nightmares out of hand because of their undoubtable paranoic aspects. To effect the first, a form of fascism far more rigorous than that of the Nazis would be needed, while the second implies an even more total and unlikely breakdown of human solidarity. Either variant of an embryonic super-race would appear an abomination to those it was designed to oppress. If the test-tube were indeed used to produce such monsters, then the great majority of us would surely join in seizing every chance that came our way to destroy them. Yet however extreme these scenarios, though well worth exploration in science-fiction form, there is no doubt that the distortion of medical technology by both the class and gender systems is with us even now. This can be seen in a particularly vicious form in South Africa, for example, where white expectant mothers have access to the most advanced techniques designed to ensure the optimal development of their foetus, including oxygen therapy to increase its brain activity in the womb, while in the same society black mothers suffer third-world conditions of deprivation, with a consequently high level of genetic disorders. In the United States, techniques to choose a male or female infant are already being pioneered, and likely to be used to increase still further the proportion of boys.[8]

The precise extent that this distortion may reach is hard to assess; it will obviously depend, among other things, on the pace of technological advance in relation to social change. But until the human species can control its technology as a single society free from structured conflicts of interest, there can be no guarantee that genetic engineering, any more than any other new technology, will be used for liberation, rather than to perpetuate enslavement. And in this case, as with the nuclear question, what is at stake is the destiny of our species itself.

The same applies, in a rather different way, to artificial intelligence. If genetic engineering transforms our definition as human beings by bringing the evolution of our biological material into the realm of conscious decision, artificial intelligence does so by forcing a rethinking of the relationship between mind and matter. Our Western civilization, in particular, has tended in recent centuries to define the specificity of the human species in terms of our unique intelligence. In doing so, we both expressed a correct realization of what it was that had constituted our peculiar adaptation, and a commitment to taking this key differentiation, the big brain, as a deliberate basis for future development. The definition of our species as 'intelligent life' thus corresponds to the rise of modern science.

The thinking machines we have built so far, from Babbage's first calculator in the 1860s through to the electronic computers of today, still have a considerable way to go before they match the human brain in sophistication. They are built, in fact, on quite different structural principles, though there is no reason why these could not eventually be made closer to those of human intelligence. What has become clear beyond doubt, however, in the last decade or so, is that it is perfectly possible, and may well be realized less than thirty years from now, to build computers, using new techniques of switching based on molecular processes, that can outstrip the human brain not just in speed, as is already the case, but in complexity as well. The intelligence on which we have prided ourselves so highly proves to be merely a mechanical function after all, not really that different from the use of the arms and legs, hands and fingers.

Thinking machines, it may be said, can ultimately do only what they are programmed to do. True, but the human brain can itself do no more. It is logically possible, and will undoubtedly become technologically so as well, to programme computers to design future generations of computers, each of increasing capacity, and to harness this entire system to such a general goal as — for example — improving the human environment.

We can always pull the plug, or take a machine-gun and blow the central computer system to bits. Of course. But who is this 'we'? There may be certain machine-wreckers, luddites or vandals, but surely the great majority of human beings will become ever more dependent on computers as an essential part of their life-support system.

A human environment that includes super-intelligent computers of this kind will be qualitatively different from anything we have known. It would be pathetic to take pride merely in the fact that it was we who initiated this development, for the point will be reached where the processes at work are far more complex than any individual human being can follow. We shall only be able to understand what is going on in terms of what computers tell us. Is the answer then for human beings to retreat from the stage altogether, leaving the world to this silicon species? Would resistance merely be trying to put the clock of evolution back, a struggle like that of Australopithecus against homo sapiens?

I believe, like the great majority of people, that there is a crucial difference between a living human being and the most super-intelligent of computers. A living being *feels*, a machine has no equivalent to sentience whatsoever. Feeling is something we share with our animal relatives; it seems to depend on having a central nervous system, yet it is something qualitatively distinct, even ontologically distinct, from information-processing. Besides thinking (i.e. processing information), we *feel* our thoughts. This is the specificity of consciousness, that it is a state of feeling, not just an arrangement of data. Living beings, i.e. certainly all mammals and birds, as well as reptiles, amphibians and fishes to a decreasing degree, possibly in a minimal sense even crustaceans and insects, have this 'inside' to them, such that, even when everything about their physical being has been described, including the state of their nervous system and brain, there is something else that has not even been mentioned, i.e. what this particular state of being feels like. But that which is 'only in the mind' is in fact the only thing that matters. Mere matter, on the other hand, no matter how complex its arrangement, does not at all mind what happens to it. A computer simply doesn't care whether you rip its innards out, disconnect its fuel supply, or cannibalize it for spare parts.

Some people argue that machines, if complex enough, can and will be truly conscious, in the sense of feeling. After all, we human beings are only made up of macromolecules, why should the carbon base have this unique ontological property that silicon doesn't? I wish I could find a convincing reason why this is not the case, why there is something about biological life and life alone that should give it this unique property. But I can't, any more than any convincing reason can be given to the contrary. And not only does this question seem to be almost beyond rational debate; it is certainly beyond empirical experiment.

How would you set about discovering whether a computer could feel? Obviously, you have to speak to it. Assuming that it understands the English language, it is familiar with statements of feeling, from the simplest 'I feel cold' through to the most complex statements of philosophical consciousness. If the computer can feel, then it will join in our discourse about feelings and express its own. If the computer cannot feel, though, then it will have no access whatsoever

to this dimension of existence, and will interpret statements such as 'I feel cold' as simply expressing a physical
state. (Not meaning the same as 'I am cold', but something
more like 'My blood — or my electricity — isn't circulating
very well'.) It will thus use the language of feeling, but
merely to refer to what in our case are the physical corre-
lates of sentient states. And if you tried to have the present
kind of philosophical discussion with the computer, about
whether machines could feel or not, the computer could
only interpret this as a similar kind of discourse to that
which human beings used to have about gods and demons,
the soul and immortality, etc. in the pre-scientific age. It
would naturally agree that it did feel, as from its standpoint
there is indeed nothing to distinguish it from human beings,
but its own understanding of sentience would be a purely
metaphoric one, the same as our own use of the outmoded
concepts of idealist ontology.

The amazing thing about this cyborg philosophy is that it
doesn't sound completely unfamiliar. It is the way that
many people who specialize in the physical sciences talk
today, particularly those who have a lot to do with computers. It isn't as if they no longer feel pain when they cut themselves shaving or go to the dentist, or even that they deny
the phenomenon of this internal dimension if you discuss it
with them. But the existence of feeling, of sentience, simply
does not fit into their vulgar-materialist philosophy, and so
they suppress questions of this kind. Feeling may be something that you share with your wife and kids, but it's not
part of the Real World, the world of science and gleaming
machines.

It would be a regression to primitive thought-modes of
magic to make computers responsible for this peculiar
mentality on the part of those who work with them. The
mentality comes first, i.e. a certain kind of scientist credits
computers as being potentially 'just like us' because science,
as he knows it, is encased in a vulgar-materialist philosophy. But the denial of feeling, far more common as an implicit assumption among scientists and technologists than
as an explicit confession of faith, ultimately reflects the particular position of these workers in the division of labour.
They are employed by governments or corporations whose

object, in the majority of fields, is ultimately geared to manipulating ordinary people as passive objects. The extreme case is how this mentality actually affects many medical doctors, supposedly working in the most caring of professions, tending sick human beings. The patient is so frequently dehumanized and treated simply as an object, even though this invariably has a negative effect on her/his recovery. And for the great majority of medical researchers involved in vivisection, the feelings of the animals experimented on are as non-existent as the feelings of their human objects were for the medical criminals of Auschwitz.

It is quite undeniable that women as well as men can be guilty of this attitude. In her very pertinent exposure of the ethics of the American medical profession, Mary Daly, for example, who ascribes the contradiction between women and men to a difference in chromosomes, has a very real difficulty in dealing with this fact. Ultimately, for her, such women are 'fembots', mere tokens whom the male masters have manipulated into taking part in their world.[9] I see any difference in this respect as deriving from the sexual division of labour, with regard to which scientific work falls in the 'secondary' penumbra, structured to some extent by the gender system, but not in an absolute or rigid way.[10] Yet the 'scientific attitude' of dismissing feeling as irrelevant, epiphenomenal or even non-existent certainly does tie in with the masculine gender role, in which boys are brought up to suppress their feelings, to regard the internal dimension as unimportant, the better to participate in the ultimate dehumanization involved in killing their fellow human beings.

'Capitulation to the computer', then, as this tendency might possibly be called, follows not from the abstract characteristics of the human-computer interface as such, but rather from the hierarchical system of domination and oppression under which we live, with its interlinked dimensions of gender and class. Seen in the perspective of the masculine culture of violence, the computer is a human being freed from the inevitable imperfections of human existence, this irrational bit called feeling. Seen instead from the perspective of the maternal culture, the computer is merely a machine which may be highly useful, but which it would be simply ridiculous to confuse with a living being.

The field of artificial intelligence is an area where the scientific technology developed by class society is rapidly proving a productive force of incredible power. But this force can be used either to serve and promote human life, or to degrade it. Under the present social system, the basic relationship that human beings maintain towards their super-intelligent but absolutely non-sentient machines is in danger of being distorted by the class/gender system of domination. Only if social contradictions are resolved, and the system of domination broken down, can we ensure that the prodigious transformations that artificial intelligence will bring about in the human world will be a force for good, not for ill.

## The Persistence of Destitution

It is impossible to discuss the global crisis facing humanity without focussing on the atrocious scandal of the billion or more human beings who still suffer the full ravages of primary poverty and deprivation. Every day, young and old, women and men, die by the thousand from hunger, malnutrition and easily preventable diseases, while we make ourselves ill from overeating, throw away a quantity of food that would abolish hunger in the whole of the Indian sub-continent, and pour our tax revenues into a never-ending arms race. If this monstrous situation is not the starting-point of the present argument, it is because it cannot unfortunately be the starting-point of political mobilization. For that we have still to depend on those perils that directly hang over the peoples of the advanced industrial countries, as discussed above.

Yet the destitution of whole nations in the South of the planet does exercise an increasing hold on the consciences of sensitive people in our part of the world. For if the phenomenon is in no way new, it is certainly far more visible to the rich countries today, thanks to mass communications. Even more, it is visible in a new way as a problem because the conditions exist for its solution.

For at least the last thirty years, hunger has been totally unnecessary, and a small proportion of the surplus produced in the rich countries could also provide at least basic hygiene, health care and education for people who lack all these things. There is one level at which the poverty of the South is a directly material question of survival for us in the North. As polluting industrial techniques and nuclear weapons begin to proliferate in the developing countries, we shall indeed be forced to meet their demand for a new international economic order, if we want these countries to join with us in saving our common environment. Yet aid that is grudging and purely self-interested will not be nearly enough to carry the poor countries with us on the journey to communism; there are some countries, indeed, so destitute that their leverage on us in this way is minimal. The choice facing the advanced countries of the North is ultimately between a new conception of our species as genuinely a single society, in which each inhabitant of Indonesia or Somalia has the same claim on the material wherewithal for a truly human life as the inhabitants of Sweden or Japan, or a situation in which the divergence between North and South, which has been escalating steadily through four hundred years of imperialism, will lead to a qualitative break between two virtually different species, as the societies of the North apply the fruits of 21st century technology to transforming the basic parameters of human existence.

This second path, the 'lifeboat' solution, might seem the easier one, yet its cost would be a hardening of our hearts, a new degree of masculinization, that could not but recoil disastrously on our own way of life, in a permanent state of war against the barbarians outside our gates. The alternative we are posed is a long overdue blossoming of maternal empathy, as demonstrated by the Buddhist saint Kuan Yin, by Jesus of Nazareth, and in modern times by Mother Theresa and Albert Schweitzer. If the awareness of suffering humanity that is so far shown by a relative few in our rich societies can spread to take hold on a really massive scale, then this will also have radical effects, in this case positive ones, on our own way of life, and speed our own transition to communism.

## The Extinction of Species

In this final symptom, the empathy for other living beings that is so important in resolving the problem of human destitution comes fully into its own. There is no way that the jeopardized species, even those closest to us such as the gorillas and whales, can help themselves. They are entirely dependent on us, the populations of the 'have' countries, for their survival.

To some people it might still seem a sacrilege to recognize our animal cousins as having a claim to our empathy comparable to other human beings. And indeed, the needs of humans and animals are different, increasingly so, and these differences should not be forgotten. Yet what is at stake today is not the suffering of a certain number of individuals, but the survival of entire species. Here again, it is we who are being tested. Human life could certainly continue and go forward with the destruction of very many of the million or so species of animal with whom we share our planet. Yet if we demonstrate a contemptuous attitude towards the biosphere of which we are inescapably part, then this cannot but recoil also on the way we handle our own biological material. Having reached the point at which it is becoming possible for us to plot our own forward evolution, how can we decide which path to take unless we have a deep feeling for the path that has led to where we are today? Once again, the choice is between the application of the powers of science in the genuine interest of human progress, or an application distorted by a narrow and sectional definition of our interest.

In all these fields, nuclear weapons and nuclear power, genetic engineering and artificial intelligence, the destitution of the South and the extinction of animal species, the direction of human evolution is at stake. Either the new productive forces will be used in a destructive fashion, for all the apparent privilege they bestow on a minority, or they will be used to usher in an age of unprecedented and scarcely imaginable improvement, the take-off into a truly human existence. One thing we cannot do is pretend that the old parameters of human life are constant and unchanging. Limitations that were previously seen as simply 'natural' are now dissolving into thin air, disclosing whole new fields to be explored and paths to be chosen. There can be no putting the lid back on the Pandora's box that science has opened, today less than at any time in the past. The powers that humanity has accumulated, for good and for ill, are so awesome that we might well wish them away. But the choice is unavoidable. And in this supreme crisis, the greatest determinant of a successful outcome is the realization of the stake involved.

## 3. *The Pattern of Contradictions*

In the final section of Chapter One, I argued that the abolition of gender should be seen as one element, however crucial, of a basic change in the human relationship to our environment. The masculine specialization in warfare that led the sexual division of labour to develop into the gender system as we know it was concomitant with the reorganization of social relations on the basis of violence: systematic conflict between rival societies led to the subordination of some peoples to others, and led within each society to the class system and state. All this corresponded to the development of humanity from its original gathering/hunting adaptation to the new adaptation of agriculture. Just as it was the crisis of the gathering/hunting adaptation that made this new development necessary, so today the transition to communism, the establishment of a new harmony based on the abolition of gender and social conflict, is made necessary by the crisis of the present system. And the new relationship with our environment that makes a communist society possible is scientific technology.

The rise of scientific technology is the first sign of the radical change impending, and it is this that makes a reordering necessary. This relationship was first grasped by Marx with his concepts of the forces and relations of production. It has suffered, like so many elements of Marxism, from an ossification into dogma, in particular the tenet that it is only possible to begin the reordering of society, which today means the construction of communism, when all the productive forces which the old society has room for have already been developed.[11] In a period of transition, the precise order in which the various elements of the new social pattern will fit together is dependent on many factors, and will evidently vary from one region of the world to another. But in the broader sweep of human development, we can indeed see scientific technology as the new productive force that makes a radical change essential in the way that human society organizes the basic processes of its life.

If scientific technology first appears in the era of capitalism, i.e. still within the framework of class society, the relationship between these two things is a contradictory one. Ultimately, scientific technology is radically incompatible with the relations of violent conflict, based on the gender system, that structure the world of class society. Yet the symptoms of this incompatibility, as I showed in the last section, are many and varied, and it is this that makes the transition from class society to communism an intricate and complex one.

The aspect of class society on which Marx focussed, in his mid 19th century analysis of the contradiction between forces and relations of production, was the conflict between competing private capitals, which he called the anarchy of production. The greatest symptom of this anarchy, of the system of production for private profit rather than social use, he saw as the commercial crisis, the modern form of which we are once again experiencing today, now known as a recession. Yet however wretched the effects of this anarchy of production, they pale before the far worse symptoms of the underlying contradiction between scientific technology and the existing system of social relations that I surveyed in the previous section. The capitalist system of individual private property may well have played a central role in the development of scientific technology, but in no way can the threats to our existence posed by nuclear weapons and nuclear power, by genetic engineering and artificial intelligence, by the destitution of the South of the planet and the extinction of animal species, be ascribed to the competition between private capitals. As is shown most clearly by the example of the Soviet Union, it is quite possible for the anarchy of production in the form analyzed by Marx to be abolished, while leaving intact not only the gender division, but also the basic class relationship between mental and manual labour, those who give orders and those who take orders, which is institutionalized above all in the state, with all its devastating effects both in international relations and in the relationship between human society and its environment.[12]

I have already discussed in Chapter One the particular contribution that the gender system makes to the pattern of social contradictions, by providing the violent masculine personality that is the prerequisite for the class system, the domination of the state over society and warfare between states. The question now is to investigate these other contradictions in somewhat more detail, in order to see how they fit together in the present situation. This is an essential condition for any subjective intervention into the historical process to help 'shorten and lessen the birth pangs'.


*Consumerism*

The starting-point of this analysis must be the development of the capitalist economic system in its heartlands of the West. For it was the expansionist drive of Western capitalism that established an imperialist relationship with the rest of the world, and it is in reaction to this system that both the Soviet Union and the struggle of the third world have been shaped.

I mentioned in Chapter One, section 3, how Marx's analysis of the capitalist mode of production exaggerated the extent to which the class system could be interpreted as a function of private property. This was an understandable focussing of attention in a situation where other forms of class organization were relatively subordinate, but even in Marx's own writings it becomes a virtual reduction of class to private property, in a way that has had very bad effects on orthodox Marxism, narrowing the scope of its critique in an age when the more basic form of the class system, i.e. the mental/manual division and the state that enshrines this, is again overwhelmingly dominant.

In Marx's day, the vast majority of wage-earners were

simply 'labour-power', hired by capital to perform menial tasks over which they had no control. And in so far as the concentration of capital brought with it the development of a particular section of salaried managers, Marx and Engels saw this as confirming their view that the capitalist mode of production was becoming redundant. If even this necessary function of management was performed on the basis of wage-labour, then the capitalist, who had previously justified himself by his entrepreneurial function, now became quite superfluous. To the anarchy of production that marked capitalist industry from its very beginnings there was now added a parasitism of finance capital, particularly isolated from any productive role, and hence a more ready target for attack by the producers.

The development of this 'leisure class', as Veblen termed it, was certainly a reality in the late 19th and early 20th centuries. At the very least, what happened in this period was that a specifically capitalist leisure class increasingly displaced the traditional leisure class of landowners. The finance capital that provided their incomes, moreover, expanded not just on the basis of domestic investment, but also and above all of investment abroad. In 1914, the British ruling class had a foreign investment stock of some $18,000 million. No wonder the most parasitic sections of the privileged class today still look back to the Edwardian era as their golden age.

Faced with the steady rise of the workers' movement, which had developed into a mass political party before the First World War in all capitalist countries outside of North America, it was by no means fantastic to expect the parasitic finance capitalists, with their close connections in the state apparatus, to meet the challenge to their privilege by naked repression, as Jack London predicted in *The Iron Heel* (1907). When fascism did arise in Europe, in the 1920s and 1930s, the Comintern still analyzed it, in far too simplistic a fashion, as the rule of the most reactionary and parasitic sectors of finance capital. Yet the development of the capitalist West has been distinctly away from parasitism of this kind, ever since the First World War. The tremendous rise in state expenditure, which took a particular leap forward in wartime, but never fell back to its previous level, required progressive taxation and death duties which bit into the luxury consumption of the rich. An increasing share of this went to finance the welfare measures that the bourgeois parties adopted, following the model of Bismarck's Germany, to defuse the threat from the workers' movement. The Depression of the inter-War years began to instil the lesson, associated especially with the name of Keynes, that prosperity depended on the working class being able to consume a larger share of the social product. And finally, the new class compromise that came out of the Second World War established the 'welfare state' and a reorientation of industrial effort towards the mass consumption market.

One result of this adjustment is the virtual disappearance of the parasitic rentiers or coupon-clippers who were so prominent in Western society even in the inter-War period. But this process was only possible because there were other classes in capitalist society besides the finance capitalists on the one hand and the working class on the other. In particular, the hierarchies of managers and experts of all kinds, who had been only marginal in the competitive capitalism of Marx's day, came into their own as the size of the capitalist enterprise vastly expanded in an incessant process of concentration. In name, even a general manager in one of the giant private corporations of today is simply a servant of the shareholders. In fact, the hierarchy of management, precisely because of its more necessary role in production, is able to insist on a hierarchy of salaries and other benefits that generally takes a greater share of the social product than is paid to the shareholders. Unearned income in the form of rent, interest and profit (the 'trinity of greed' in traditional socialist rhetoric) is absolutely marginal in Britain today, accounting for only some 3 per cent of the consumption fund. Even the top 1 per cent of income recipients, who have at their disposal about 6 per cent of the consumption fund (adjusted for household size), obtain some three-quarters of this in the form of 'earned income'. If the transition from 'monopoly capitalism' to 'state monopoly capitalism', and increasingly today in the further direction of 'state capitalism', has not involved any violent conflict, it is because this development only threatens that small minority of the privileged class who depend in particular on income from ownership of property, and would not threaten the majority of privileged even if no compensation were paid to individual shareholders whose assets were nationalized.

The welfare state, and the reorientation of production to the mass consumption market, means that the capitalist economies of today display considerably less inequality of income than was the case before the last War. Standardizing for household size (i.e. numbers of economically active members and dependants), the top 10 per cent of households in Britain today consume just about 20 per cent of the consumption fund, the second decile just over 14 per cent and the third decile just over 12 per cent. This inequality that is strictly a function of class (rather than age, sex, family size, etc.) is still very significant, the lowest decile, for example, with 4½ per cent of the consumption fund, having a share that is less than a quarter that of the top decile. Yet an absolute equalization would not improve the living standard of skilled manual workers, and an upper limit set at 1½ times the national average, which is very much more egalitarian than any industrial society today, would release no more than 5 per cent of the total consumption fund for redistribution to the poorest households. If this income structure is highly resistant to further change, it would seem to be because it is a function no longer of private property, but essentially of the division of labour, the hierarchy of skill and competence, that enables those with most education to insist on a significant differential.

The inequality of income distribution in the advanced capitalist societies of today is above all a function of the mental/manual labour division. But in a society where the top 10 per cent of households have a living standard 'only' twice the average, and the bottom 10 per cent a living standard 'as much as' half the average, this hierarchical division of labour is far more pernicious as a form of inequality than is the inequality of consumption to which it gives rise. Even if the cultural gap between workers and managers has been markedly reduced compared with the 19th century, the majority of people still have to work harder and longer, and in worse conditions,[13] at jobs which have virtually no inherent satisfaction and in no way aid their development as human beings. The minority of experts, on the other hand, work less hard, less long, in better conditions, and at jobs which are relatively satisfying in themselves and contribute to their all-round development. There is no real common standard by which these two types of inequality can be measured. But if jobs and rewards were distributed from scratch between individuals in a collective, it would certainly be necessary to pay those condemned to work on a factory assembly-line, for example, at least twice as much as those privileged to become journalists or doctors, rather than the other way round as at present. Of course, the first concern of a society governed by such a principle would be to erode as rapidly as possible this division of labour itself, enabling everyone to work in a field that genuinely developed their talents, and requiring everyone also to take part in the routine and menial tasks, which the whole society would now have an interest in reducing to a minimum.

In the present system, however, people seek the privilege of education as much as they seek the material rewards that it brings. And disparities of cultural level are handed down from one generation to the next just as much as are material assets. A child from a professional family in Britain today has nine times more chance of going to university than a child from a manual worker's family (the difference is somewhat less for boys, very much greater for girls; scarcely 1 per cent of girls from manual working families reach university). Unlike the parasitic wealth of finance capital, however, the cultural capital that is stored up in the human brain is both necessary to society, and inaccessible to an expropriation that would bring about equality by a political act. As the division of labour and education has come to take over from ownership of property as the dominant form of class inequality, so the working-class political movement has in fact declined. However militant trade-union struggle might be today, we no longer have in Britain that proletarian socialism which found expression in both the Labour and Communist parties until the 1940s, and even in the more traditional societies in France and Italy the mass Communist parties are now in the painful throes of adjustment to this new situation.

As I shall go on to argue in the final chapter, a different approach to radical change is required today. But this will certainly have to involve the working class, the majority of people who are still relegated to menial jobs, and in particular those specially underprivileged by their low pay, and dangerous and dirty work. If it proves so difficult to interest working-class people today in the ideas of socialism, this is not just because a struggle against the division of labour is more daunting than one of expropriation. It is equally a function of the consumerist culture that marks the capitalist economic system in its latest ('last'?) stage.

At an earlier and more parasitic stage of capitalist development, there was a clear division between 'necessaries' that were produced for the working-class market, and luxuries produced for the rich. Of course, there are signs of this division still today, just as there are signs of still earlier forms of privilege, e.g. the hereditary monarchy and peerage. Yet the dominant tendency today is towards a single consumer market, within which there may well be gradations of quality, but where very few of the better quality goods are completely unavailable to the average consumer. The modern supermarkets for food, clothing and other daily necessities display an increasingly cross-class character, typified in Britain by Sainsbury's, Marks and Spencer or Boots, in each of which the wife of a senior executive might well rub shoulders with her cleaning lady.

In setting the tone of mass consumption, however, the rich still play a crucial role (another parallel with the essentially ideological function of the royal family), even if today these are less coupon-clippers than show-business personalities. The mass of people can't go on holiday to the Bahamas. But this is the dream they go in search of on the Costa Brava. The man in the street can't drive a Rolls-Royce. But the range of mass-produced cars are all designed from the top down — each substituting for the more expensive one above it.

Like any major historical trend, the roots of this can be traced back a long way indeed. A perceptive observer such as Frederick Engels could write as far back as 1858 (!) that 'the English proletariat is actually becoming more and more bourgeois, so that this most bourgeois of all nations is apparently aiming at the possession of a bourgeois aristocracy and a bourgeois proletariat *alongside* the bourgeoisie.'[14] The context of this comment was the political turn by the former Chartist Ernest Jones towards the middle-class parliamentary Reform movement, this reflecting the position of the minority of skilled workers, the 'aristocracy of labour'. The incorporation of the working class en masse into bourgeois society took the best part of a century. But by the 1930s, even during the Depression, the new pattern was clearly coming into its own, one major element of this being the move of the better-off industrial workers of the South of England into home ownership in the spreading suburbs.[15]

Today, those nostalgic for the good old days can still find residues of the more authentically proletarian conditions of the past: the plight of the homeless, houses still without a bath, unemployed families having to cut out meat, and so on. But it is simply ridiculous, in the 1980s, to seek to rebuild a radical movement for communism on the basis of material deprivation of this kind, and it is not insignificant that those who cling most lovingly to the dogmas of orthodox Marxism are not manual workers, but middle-class intellectuals.

The 'bourgeois proletariat' exists *'alongside* the bourgeoisie'. For all the inadequacy of these categories, as categories of possession/non-possession of property rather than of functions in the division of labour, the crucial point is that the working class has been integrated, in a subordinate position, into a pattern of consumption that is still defined by those at the top. The economic mechanism is fuelled by the quest for material comforts, not as a means to an end, but precisely as an end in themselves. It would be inadequate to reduce this motivation simply to the drive for status, though this undoubtedly plays a part. There is a genuine enjoyment to be gained from driving a fast car, watching colour television or holidaying in the Mediterranean, which is not reducible to status. The point is that a class society, one still based fair and square on the division of labour, for all the relative reduction in consumption inequality, cannot set itself any higher goals than merely material ones. The old spiritual values of Christianity have broken down, precisely because they assumed a fixed hierarchical ordering of society in which high and low had their respective obligations to one another. Everyone today is aware that no hierarchy is natural and eternal; we've at least got that far towards communism![16] Yet the dissolution of the old order of class society, which is already well under way, is not the same as the positive establishment of a new order. This can only come about on the basis of a new spiritual principle. Consumerism, this crass materialism that is common to both Western and Soviet societies alike, is a desperate attempt to prolong the class system after this has already served its purpose and is holding back human progress.[17]

'Economic growth' has become the touchstone of legitimation for any government of an advanced industrial country, whether conservative, liberal, social-democrat or 'communist'. In an era when the state has long since assumed ultimate responsibility for economic performance, the goal of production is no longer, as it was (spontaneously) in Marx's day, the maximization of surplus-value. As long as industrial profit is sufficient for the purposes of new investment, an increase in 'economic growth' always takes priority. Even in Mrs Thatcher's Britain, the reactionary policies of monetarism must ultimately stand or fall by whether they lead to a higher rate of growth, a bigger cake and more for all. The balance of social forces is not one in which a backward shift in favour of privilege can be brought about for its own sake. Yet a forward shift in favour of the working class will only be possible on the basis of quite different policies than further nationalization.

## Imperialism

'Economic growth', in the sense of capitalist consumerism, means the production of ever more material use-values, the consumption of ever more resources. There are only two sources on which this can draw, the South of the planet, where consumerism is non-existent, and the planetary future, in the form of a depletion of scarce raw materials and a degradation of the environment, leaving the mess to future generations to clean up, or to survive in as best they can.

The above quote from Engels on the 'bourgeois proletariat'

already located this development in a global context. 'For a nation that exploits the whole world this is of course to a certain extent justifiable' (ibid.). The imperialist relationship between the capitalist metropolises and the dependent countries, what we see today as a relationship between North and South, has undergone many changes over the past century and more. The term 'imperialism' was in fact only given its present sense in Marxist vocabulary when the European great powers divided the world between them in the late 19th century.[18] This was certainly the peak of the imperialist relationship, when Britain, France and the others, even little Belgium and Holland, could use direct military force in their colonies so as best to serve their needs for raw materials. And undoubtedly it had a profound effect on relations between the classes in the capitalist metropolises themselves, giving the working class at least a partial common interest with their rulers in exploiting the colonies. Thus if Lenin extended the classical Marxist slogan 'Workers of all countries, unite' into 'Workers of all countries, and all oppressed peoples, unite' (on the foundation of the Communist International in 1919), he was also quite clear about the corresponding weakening of the revolutionary front in the capitalist heartlands.

At this time, when Europe was certainly as near as it ever came to proletarian revolution, Lenin saw this weakening as expressed in the division of the working class between a 'labour aristocracy' who supported the reformist parties of the Second International, and the genuinely proletarian masses who (potentially at least) supported the new Communist parties.[19] Today, of course, this division is quite untenable. The fruits of imperialism do not differentiate the working class in this way, but enable the working class as a whole to enjoy an enhanced level of consumption. Indeed, Lenin seemed himself to be coming round to this idea in his last writings, particularly the 1923 article 'Better Fewer, but Better', where, already perceiving the defeat of the revolution in Europe, he wrote that the Western states were able to make certain concessions to the working classes which, 'insignificant though they are, nevertheless retard the revolutionary movement in those countries and create some semblance of "class truce"'. On the other hand:

> In the last analysis, the outcome of the struggle will be
> determined by the fact that Russia, India, China, etc.
> account for the overwhelming majority of the globe...
> In this sense, the complete victory of socialism is
> assured.[20]

As so often, Lenin clearly saw which way the wind was
blowing. In the West, the 'class truce' has become a permanent fixture. While the revolutionary movement against
Western capitalism came in the next few decades to be
located above all in the dependent countries, the adaptation
of Marxism to this new situation being indelibly associated
with the name of Mao Zedong.[21]

After the Second World War, it was no longer possible for
the capitalist metropolises to keep down the dependent
countries by brute force. The withdrawal from empire was
rapid, even if for a couple of decades there was a flourishing
of a subtler neo-colonialism, particularly on the part of the
'non-imperialist' United States. But even this now survives
only in a few isolated instances. The great majority of
nations of the South are genuinely independent states, with
governments that, whatever their political complexion, are
set on pursuing a national interest of their own, and not the
interest of any foreign power.

In this situation, the fundamental relationship of
economic dependence is extremely clear. Just as was the
case in 1858, when Engels wrote that Britain 'exploits the
whole world', the dependent countries are held in thrall
today by the monopoly of advanced technology in the hands
of the developed countries. It is this that forces the unequal
exchange on the world market, so that Ghana, for example,
can only obtain a tractor representing one thousand hours of
British labour in return for a quantity of cocoa that repre-
sents several thousand hours of Ghanaian labour. No matter
how anti-imperialist a third-world government, if it wants
the fruits of Western technology, it can obtain them only at
this exploitative price. It goes without saying that trade
between the 'socialist' Soviet bloc and the third world is
similarly conducted on the basis of the world market. And,
under greater pressure to satisfy their own unmet consumer
needs, these countries are today far less willing to give even

a minimal aid, without strings attached, than are the Western states.

In a few cases, of which oil is the most notable example, a producers' cartel has been able to charge a monopoly price for their commodity that is considerably higher than its cost of production. In many others, however, this attempt has been tried, and has failed. If the struggle for a new international economic order does finally make real progress, it will only be because the advanced countries themselves come finally to recognize the necessity for changing this crucial dimension of class society: whether they do so out of a genuine blossoming of the humanitarian (maternal) impulse, or from the purely instrumental need to involve the South of the planet in a common struggle against war and ecological disaster. As explained in section 2, only the former can bring about a really radical change.

Little need be said here about the other source on which consumerism draws, the wasteful depletion of resources that are the common heritage of humanity, and which we should accordingly cherish for our descendants, as well as the degradation of the planetary environment in the process. I have already discussed the symptoms of this in section 2, and far more detailed treatments can readily be found elsewhere. There is however one aspect of the connection between consumerism and the search for an infinite supply of cheap energy that still needs to be traced. Energy is not simply one resource among others. It is in a way the universal equivalent of other resources. There is no raw material that has absolutely no substitute. And there is no raw material that cannot be obtained, if sufficient energy is put into obtaining it. Just as the impoverishment of the soil due to bad farming methods is made up for by the application of artificial fertilizers (a very high-energy product), so the depletion of mineral ores can be made up for by mining poorer and less accessible deposits, provided energy is available. This is already a pressing problem in the processing of aluminum, which takes a vast amount of electric power. Given an unlimited supply of cheap energy, virtually everything is possible, and no raw material need ever absolutely run out. And this is why, in the dynamic of consumerism, nuclear power is such an attractive — indeed, an inevitable — option; the clean power of fusion when and if possible, the dirty power of fission in the meantime.

## The East-West Conflict

There is still one central element of the pattern of global contradictions to be introduced: the Soviet Union, as an alternative model of development to the West, and as contender with its rival superpower, the United States, for world leadership.

More than six decades after the October revolution of 1917, it is quite anachronistic to try and grasp the basic nature of the Soviet system by starting from the original aspirations of Lenin and the Bolsheviks and seeing how these have 'degenerated'. At most, these aspirations, in their 'degenerated' form, play a certain role in the superstructure. In the Soviet Union and the other countries following its road, a new social formation has developed that is different from Western capitalism yet in no way progressing towards a classless society. The most striking difference about this 'socialist' formation is the monopoly ownership of means of production by the state — and a state that is authoritarian and hierarchical, showing no signs whatsoever of even wanting to 'wither away'. This was a necessary precondition, if the Soviet Union and its imitators (voluntary and involuntary) were to develop into advanced industrial societies without falling into dependence on the capitalist heartlands of the West. Yet through the technologies they took over, and the industrial organization that went with them, the Soviet countries very definitely reproduced the mental/manual division and the hierarchy of competence that characterizes modern capitalism. Indeed, this was never even seriously challenged. It is this that makes it quite unfeasible to understand Soviet social relations in terms of a (genuinely) socialist economic base distorted by a political dictatorship. If the dictatorship were overthrown, as began to happen in Czechoslovakia in 1968, then the underlying class structure would very definitely persist, if possibly complicated by the re-emergence of small-scale private property alongside the nationalized 'commanding heights'.[22]

When the Soviet economic system is viewed from the standpoint of the working class, then the most obvious fact is the hierarchical division of labour which it shares with Western capitalism. The curve of income inequality is well within the spectrum of Western societies, reflecting the hierarchy of skill and competence. As in the West, a certain basic level of welfare is guaranteed, and − despite the special shops where party officials can buy foreign goods otherwise unobtainable − there is a single mass consumption market. The goal of production, and the overriding social goal in general, is 'economic growth', to produce a bigger cake of the same recipe and to be shared out in the same way, even if the satisfaction of consumer demand is inherently more fraught than in the West, the Soviet system still being too inflexible even to meet many basic consumption needs.[23] Among the effects of this essential similarity, the Soviet countries have moved away from the autarchy of Stalin's time to develop their trade with the South on the exploitative terms of the world market, while their contribution to the depletion of resources and the deterioration of the environment is also of a piece with that of the West.

The major differences of class structure between East and West are the absence, in the Soviet societies, of independent small businesses, and of the tiny minority who in the West draw their income from equities. The Soviet Union, however, does have the more modern kind of rich, in the form of millionaire writers, artists and musicians and their dependants, also the children − and grandchildren? − of top party bosses, etc. The remaining very substantial differences of economic organization are not vertical but horizontal, i.e. the way that enterprises are connected via the plan rather than via the market.

What is quite distinctive about the Soviet Union is its political system. The Soviet state is, above all, a totalitarian dictatorship, in which power is transmitted from the summit down without any checks and balances from below. No opposition parties are allowed, and there is no effective parliament; there is a rigorous censorship of all information;

trade-union organization is banned; the mass media serve a unitary function of indoctrination; an extensive secret police clamps down on all criticism, and is little fettered by law or public opinion in its exercise of repression. All these things it shares with other dictatorships of the 20th century, notably the fascist ones.

It is the totalitarian form of state, in particular, that is responsible for a more rigorous form of the gender system than that in the West today. Despite certain advances that Soviet women made in the early post-revolutionary years, particularly in the 'secondary' penumbra of the sexual division of labour (see Chapter One, pp. 54-55), the primary division between the feminine specialization in childcare and the masculine specialization in violence remains rigidly upheld, as does its psychological anchoring. The intense repression of gayness is particularly associated with the militaristic cast of Soviet society, which seems to have become permanent in the context of the Second World War. A policy statement of 1943, for example, stated that 'the task is to strengthen our primary social unit, the socialist family, on the basis of the full development of the characteristics of masculinity and femininity in the father and mother, as heads of the family with equal rights'; co-education was abolished at this time so that 'the school develops boys who will be good fathers and manly fighters for the socialist homeland and girls who will be intelligent mothers competent to rear the next generation'.[24]

Yet the ruling party in the Soviet Union is a 'communist' party, with its social origins in a radical popular revolution, and its ideological origins in the theory of Marxism. While the fascist dictatorships used their power to defend the traditional rights of property, and only improved the position of the working class, if at all, through an intensified practice of imperialism, the Soviet regime has always recognized the right of the mass of the people to a guaranteed level of welfare, and to a living standard rising in line with economic growth. At its inception, to be sure, the development of the productive forces was seen simply as a means to an end, i.e. communism, but under threat of Western attack, and having failed to win the support of the peasants who made up four-fifths of the Soviet population, the spiritual dimension of Soviet communism fell by the wayside — for good and all in the 1950s, after being rekindled at least in a fashion with the national defence against Nazi Germany. The Soviet Union and the West approached consumerism from different starting-points, but it is here that they have converged. Particularly when looked at from the South of the planet, the Soviet East and the capitalist West appear to have far more features in common than those that divide them. And this is the perspective of the majority of human beings.

Between competing imperialisms, however, even minor differences are sufficient to prevent a genuine understanding, and a united and 'peaceful' approach to their business of exploitation. There was certainly as much in common between Edwardian Britain and Wilhelmine Germany, possibly even between Britain under Chamberlain and Germany under Hitler, as there is today between the United States and the Soviet Union, or between the respective camps that each superpower leads. It would certainly have been rational for Britain and Germany to have halted the First World War and come to terms, in an ultra-imperialism such as Kautsky thought possible. And in the early stages of the Second World War, Hitler himself believed that peace with Britain still lay within his grasp. Today again, despite the far greater perils a new world war would bring, the concrete fact is that both sides are once again locked into a struggle for dominance from which they seem quite unable to disentangle themselves. The SALT agreements only legitimize a nuclear arms race already under way, while the Mutual and Balanced Force Reduction talks in Vienna have long reached an absolute stalemate.

In the nuclear age, it would be far too risky for the Soviet leadership to pursue their ambitions in the reckless fashion of previous challengers to Western world leadership. Where they have made adventurist mistakes, as with the Cuba crisis of 1962, they backed down so as to avoid escalation towards nuclear war. And where the Soviet Union has sent armies across its frontiers, this has so far been within carefully defined political parameters. The invasions of Czechoslovakia in 1968, Hungary and Poland in 1956, were within its accepted sphere of influence.[25] In Afghanistan, which bids fair to become the Soviet Vietnam, the intervention was again in a state that was both immediately adjacent, and which the United States had explicitly not sought to incorporate in any of the security treaties of the Cold War. In Angola and Kampuchea, it has found the Cubans and Vietnamese to do its fighting for it, and in each case in a situation where at least the pretext of a progressive cause could be found. Even in Eritrea, where Soviet and East German 'advisers', together with Cuban combat troops, are treacherously engaged in repressing the liberation struggle they used to support (given that they now have 'their' government in Addis Ababa), the Organization of African Unity's policy of accepting all inherited colonial frontiers provides a certain political cover, by defining Eritrea as a province of Ethiopia.[26]

In Africa and Asia, where the Soviet Union particularly seeks to present itself as an alternative model of development to Western capitalism, its increased military capacity allows it to follow a far more active policy, and it seeks to step in wherever Western influence has been expelled. Yet it has come on the scene too late to build up a world empire on this basis. The tide has already turned against imperialism, and many nations of the South even have a substantial military force of their own. For all its efforts to identify itself with the have-nots, the Soviet Union is clearly seen by the great majority of third-world countries today as part of the problem. And in some cases, notably Egypt, it has burnt its fingers very badly from trying to meddle in another country's internal affairs in the guise of 'anti-imperialist' aid.

For all these difficulties, however, the Soviet rulers still believe they have a just claim to displace the 'decadent' West. In their case, this claim is strengthened by an element of universalism that the German and Japanese fascists could never draw on. Moscow may be the historical centre, the Rome,[27] from which the Soviet system expands, even the gendarme of what Mao Zedong used to call the 'barbed-wire socialist community'. Yet the men in the Kremlin feel themselves borne forward by the movement of humanity as a whole, the representatives of a social system that will ultimately give decisive proof of its superiority, for all its present problems in meeting consumer demand, in beating the Americans in space exploration, or even in gaining military superiority, despite its gigantic efforts in this direction for almost twenty years.

Rudolf Bahro can be quoted here again, as he has a certain knowledge of the working of the East European Communist parties from the inside:

> In all our parties holding state power, there are still people, right up to the very top, who are tied to the Marxist idea at least by their bad conscience. Even in the Soviet Union, where the revolution is already so far in the past that the leaders of today have scarcely learned anything from it but Stalinist bureaucracy, the communist tradition still bequeathes a certain uncomfortable inheritance. If they publicly renounced the idea, they would immediately be swept away. Pursued by an inescapable legitimacy complex, they need a distorted Marxism as their daily bread, and they must even believe in it themselves, at least in certain honest moments, for the sake of their own psychological survival.[28]

It is this that explains the peculiar intractability of the Soviet leadership, their inability to abandon their pretensions of hegemony and seek to modify the policies of their rivals (the West and China) by cooperation rather than conflict. At the political level, at least, Soviet policy cannot be called anything but expansionist. The Soviet rulers are quite determined to see their social system exported to other countries, an expansion that is certainly promising for their own influence over those countries' affairs, even if not strictly coterminous with this. To achieve this goal, they will use any means short of deliberately starting a major war; and the presence of superior military force has always been a very important lever in diplomacy. Unfortunately, however, it is not possible to eliminate the possibility of war without a genuine disarmament.

For all the conflicts of interest between the West and the Soviet Union in the third world, it is in Europe that the contention between the two social systems is ultimately centred. It is the European situation that led to the 'exterm-inist' logic of the nuclear arms race, which Edward Thompson very plausibly argues has now become rooted in the social structures of both superpowers.[29] The precon-dition for working to unravel this terrible knot is to under-stand how it came to be tied, which means rejecting not only the Soviet mythology of 'imperialist aggression', but also the similar mythology of our own ruling classes.

There is, to be sure, a fundamental asymmetry in the European situation as this came into being in 1945. The Soviet Union, as was bound to happen sooner or later, emerged from the War as the dominant military power in Europe. It had industrialized at a breakneck pace in the 1930s, and then thrown all national resources into a life-and-death struggle against Hitler. It was determined to ensure its future security by a buffer zone in Eastern Europe, which had been such a powder-keg for generations past. Stalin had no difficulty in obtaining from his allies, Roose-velt and Churchill, Western acceptance of a Soviet sphere of influence east of the Elbe, on top of a substantial expansion of Soviet frontiers on the Baltic, with Poland and with Romania. Yet even in those countries which had been wartime allies, such as Poland and Czechoslovakia, the Soviets were not content with imposing conditions of perpet-ual friendship, but moved within a couple of years to extend the Soviet economic system and the dictatorship of the Communist party. At the same time, they maintained in Eastern Europe an army that was more than required to meet any possible needs of defence, including defence against the peoples forced into 'socialism' against their will.

In Eastern Europe, as increasingly in the Soviet Union itself, there is a massive popular resistance to the Soviet system and an unquenchable desire for Westernization, which is held in check only by armed force. The Western system is spontaneously attractive to the peoples held down by the Soviet military machine, in a way that goes far beyond those Western efforts of subversion which Soviet propaganda exaggerates out of all proportion. Recent efforts to copy Western consumerism have done nothing to allay the attraction of the West. What the peoples of Eastern Europe yearn for above all is the civil and political liberty, necessarily founded on national independence, that no literate nation can feel happy without. This is something which the gay minority in our own countries should be particularly able to appreciate. However inadequate our democracy, it at least enables us to organize and struggle for changes that steadily increase our freedom, in a way that dictatorship makes impossible.

NATO was formed in 1949, and the American nuclear umbrella erected over Western Europe, as a response by the ruling classes to the enforced Sovietization of Eastern Europe. Despite the Berlin blockade of the previous year, the idea that the Soviet Union was set on a war of blatant aggression was never seriously credible. The deployment of nuclear weapons to deter Soviet expansionism was a criminal act by the Western ruling classes, even if the speed with which the Soviet Union rushed to follow suit shows how its rulers already shared a complete lack of concern for the peoples of the countries supposedly languishing under American imperialism.

To understand Western resort to nuclear deterrence, however, it is necessary to appreciate the particular threat that our ruling classes perceived. For against the economic lure of the United States to the peoples of Europe (the Marshall plan, etc.), Stalin had mounted a fresh political assault with the creation in 1947 of Cominform (the integration of the French and Italian Communist parties into a joint body with the East European, replacing the Communist International that had been finally dissolved in 1943). And in the context of a prospective revolutionary struggle in Western Europe, Soviet intervention was a factor that the Western Communist parties were themselves far from ruling out. In February 1949, for example, Maurice Thorez, leader of the Communist Party of France, could speak of the welcome that the French people would allegedly give the Soviet army were it to 'liberate' France in the course of new hostilities in Europe. From the ruling-class standpoint, therefore, the threat was one of a possible alliance between the Soviet Union and the West European working class against the capitalist system. That was why the defence of the West could not be strengthened by popular mobilization, so that the American nuclear strike force was called in.[30] Once the dreadful logic of nuclear deterrence had been set in motion, it continued in an ascending spiral until the two superpowers now have between them a stockpile of some 20,000 warheads, for the whole range of contingencies from theatre use through to doomsday.

Over the last thirty years, the appeal of Soviet 'socialism' to the working classes of Western Europe has drastically declined. With the further development of democracy, consumerism and the welfare state, the West European Communist parties are either breaking their Soviet connections, like the Italian and Spanish, or they are maintaining these only at the cost of a steady decline, like the French. Yet the Soviet leaders cannot give up their doctrine of an inevitable revolutionary transition from capitalism to 'socialism' without thereby sacrificing their own legitimacy — particularly because it is only by westward expansion in Europe that they might hope to wrest world leadership from the United States. Certain signs, even now, may actually give them encouragement, for instance the current recession, or the support given by large sections of the 'new left' to their invasion of Afghanistan.[31] They take the long view of history, so they are not easily put off by temporary setbacks; and they are far indeed from abandoning hope.

Even if the two superpowers managed a negotiated process of nuclear disarmament, there would still be a situation in Europe where the existence of a powerful and anti-democratic empire on our borders required strong military defence (which is certainly possible without posing any threat in return). This is the key reason why these negotiations have been so unsuccessful, putting the Left in countries like Britain in a strong position to contest the very idea of reliance on nuclear weapons. At the level of morality, our case is certainly a strong one. Yet if we are to win over a majority, in a situation where every year brings a continuing risk of nuclear holocaust (even 'by accident'), we need to further strengthen our case by proposing a viable positive alternative to the present suicidal policy that passes as 'defence'. This is a theme I'll take up again in the next chapter.

In this section I have tried to explain the main lines of

division in the world today, which hold us back from an advance to communism. There is the division between the rich North and the poor South; there is the class division between mental and manual labour within the rich countries themselves, enshrined in both economy and state; and there is the conflict between the Soviet East and the capitalist West. This model allows us to see the symptoms of the crisis of humanity in perspective, as generated by the basic structure of our present pattern of social organization. Each line of division, however, has a particular form, which has come into being and is still undergoing change. And in studying the relationships between these three divisions, and the possibilities of abolishing them, their particular forms must necessarily be taken into account. It is apparent to anyone that the ecological problem, for example, results from the present economic process in the rich countries of the North, and that the danger of nuclear war arises above all from the East-West conflict. But we can only work out a way of averting these perils by understanding the particular forms assumed by the class system, imperialism and the East-West conflict, and consequently the dynamic that lies behind them.

# Chapter Four:
# The Way Ahead

## 1. *Communism and Class Struggle*

In discussing the idea of crisis in the previous chapter, I referred to Marx's metaphor of the midwife, who 'shortens and lessens the birth pangs' of the new society. This expresses very well the relationship that exists in history and politics between the objective course of development, which proceeds independent of human will, and the conscious intervention into this process that is indispensable if the potential objectively present is to be concretely realized.

It was in this sense that Marx classically defined the tasks of the communists in the *Communist Manifesto* of 1848, against the background of the anticipated proletarian revolution. The communists were defined, in the first place, by their understanding of the historical process in which they were themselves involved: 'They have over the great mass of the proletariat the advantage of clearly understanding the line of march, the conditions, and the ultimate general results of the proletarian movement'. Naturally, therefore, they were also in their practical activity 'the most advanced and resolute section of the working-class parties of every country, that section which pushes forward all others'. And in particular, Marx stressed that the communists sought to 'point out and bring to the front the common interests of the entire proletariat, independently of all nationality'.[1]

This conception of the relationship between objective and subjective led to orthodox Marxism distinguishing between *theory* and *tactics*. Theory was the analysis of the objective historical process, in particular the 'laws of motion' of capitalist society and its developing contradictions that would give rise to proletarian revolution. Tactics was the subjective intervention by the body of organized communists. Yet though this intervention was absolutely essential, if the revolution was to succeed, it was clearly circumscribed by the objective development as understood by Marxist theory. Thus even for Lenin, whose tactical flexibility was so rich and innovative that he was accused by fellow-Marxists of 'voluntarism', such major questions as whether to take part in parliament, the organization of revolutionary armed forces, etc. were viewed within the perspective of an objectively determined development. Whether the Russian revolution would have a definite 'democratic stage' of development prior to the stage of proletarian revolution, i.e. whether the peasant masses would be able to overthrow tsarism and take back the land before the industrial workers could expropriate the bourgeoisie, was even for Lenin not a question of subjective tactics, but rather part of the objective process to which tactics had to be geared.

If the orthodox Marxist conception of proletarian revolution has been so influential, over the last century and more, among people committed to the communist goal, this is because it succeeded in grasping certain fundamental contradictions of capitalist society that pointed in the direction of a communist resolution. The best way to approach the possibilities and problems of an advance towards communism today, accordingly, is to examine the elements out of which Marx and Engels constructed their model of the communist transition, and see what change is needed in order to bring them up to date.

For orthodox Marxism, the crisis that brings the contradictory development of capitalism to a head, and forces its transformation into a very different social system, is a double one. There is firstly the contradiction between the characteristic capitalist relations of production and the productive forces that these engender:

> Modern bourgeois society with its relations of production, of exchange and of property, a society that has conjured up such gigantic means of production and of exchange, is like the sorcerer, who is no longer able to

control the powers of the nether world whom he has
called up by his spells...It is enough to mention the
commercial crises that by their periodical return put
on trial, each time more threateningly, the existence of
the entire bourgeois society.[2]

This contradiction was referred to by orthodox Marxism as
the anarchy of production. The productive process of
capitalist society was ever more a social one, with each
particular factory, etc. depending for its inputs and outputs
on a large number of others. Yet the 'hidden hand' that
Adam Smith had seen as harmoniously coordinating the
productive effort proved increasingly shaky, from 1830
onwards, and if the capitalist system has survived through
to today, it is only because the state has increasingly inter-
vened to regulate this anarchy and introduce at least a
certain element of planning.

Secondly, there is the struggle of the working class:

But not only has the bourgeoisie forged the weapons
that bring death to itself; it has also called into
existence the men who are to wield those weapons —
the modern working class — the proletarians.

Wage labour rests exclusively on competition between
the labourers. The advance of industry, whose involuntary promoter is the bourgeoisie, replaces the isolation of the labourers, due to competition, by their
revolutionary combination, due to association. The
development of modern industry, therefore, cuts from
under its feet the very foundation on which the bourgeoisie produces and appropriates products. What the
bourgeoisie therefore produces, above all, are its own
grave-diggers. Its fall and the victory of the proletariat
are equally inevitable.[3]

This is Marx's theory of the revolutionary transition from
capitalism to communism, in his own summary presentation. And those dogmatists who even today prefer the letter
of Marx's teaching to the marvellous liberating spirit behind
it, still latch on to every conceivable straw in the wind as a
sign of the impending proletarian revolution. Yet in the
hundred and thirty years since the *Communist Manifesto*

there has been only one successful revolution that could by any stretch be squeezed into the classical pattern, the Russian revolution of 1917, and today the revolutionary overthrow of capitalism in its heartlands looks further away than ever. The advance of capitalism has certainly led in every country without exception to the 'association' of the working class in mass trade unions and reforming political parties. But at this stage, the proletarian movement seems to have got stuck, essentially failing, despite the ripples sent out by the Russian revolution, to wage a revolutionary struggle against the capitalist system as such.

I examined in section 3 of the previous chapter the main lines of capitalist development that have undermined the prospect of proletarian revolution: the rise of a hierarchy of salaried experts and managers, the intervention of the state to bridle the anarchy of production, the decline of the parasitic leisure class, and the reorientation of production towards mass consumption. Yet far from this change having stabilized the capitalist class system, it has simply altered the form of its contradictions. The crisis we are facing today, still essentially a crisis between the relations and forces of production, is indeed far deeper and more threatening than the orthodox Marxist anarchy of production. The question is, if the resolution of the crisis is not impending in the classical form of proletarian revolution, how is it going to come?

The decline of the revolutionary workers' movement in the capitalist heartlands was already visible in the 1920s, the first decade following the foundation of the Communist International. What made it possible to evade this problem for a while was the anti-communist reaction of fascism and the Second World War, when the particular needs of the working class were merged into the general needs of the anti-fascist struggle. By the 1950s, however, those communists less inhibited by the binds of dogma were forced to admit that it was no longer possible to look to the industrial working class as a revolutionary force. One possible alternative was suggested by Khrushchev: the 'socialist camp' would overtake the capitalist world economically, and the force of its example would induce a 'peaceful transition' to the Soviet system. Since most countries not held down by Soviet military force show no desire to remain in the 'socialist camp', this model of the transition must ring hollow today even for those who still accept the Soviet system as at least the embryo of the new society.

Another alternative, certainly far more in the liberating tradition of Marxism, came to see a new proletariat in the peoples of the third world, which is after all where revolutionary struggle has been concentrated for the last half century and more. Yet however imperative it was for communists in our countries to support the struggles of the Indians, Chinese, Algerians, Vietnamese, etc., the effect that their victories have had on the capitalist heartlands is inevitably limited, for the reasons explained above (Chapter 3, pp. 145-146). Ironically, the 1974 'oil revolution' of the Arabian sheiks had a far greater effect on the world economy than the liberation of the greatest third-world country, China, and yet even OPEC has done no more than intensify the current recession.[4]

The *Internationale* proclaims that 'no saviours from on high deliver', and no saviours from outside can deliver either. Our salvation can only come from our own efforts, from within our own society. And yet nowhere in this society, the society of consumerism and the hierarchical division of labour, is there to be found a class or group who can fill the role of the proletariat, who, again in the words of the *Internationale*, 'are naught but shall be all'.[5] The search for a new proletariat has not been abandoned. In the 1960s, Herbert Marcuse made a valiant effort to locate this in the marginal minority groups of blacks, students and hippies. In the 1970s, some theorists, particularly in Italy, sought to cast women and gay men in this role.[6] But to most people, even those who are themselves members of these oppressed groups not accounted for in the traditional Marxist model, the idea that any such combination can fill the role of proletariat seems extremely far-fetched. I believe it stems ultimately from the false assumption that radical change is dependent on a pure and uncorrupted subject, and from underestimating the dire straits in which our whole society finds itself today, giving even those who are very much corrupted and privileged in the present social system an interest in finding an alternative that will enable us all to survive.

The linkage in the original Marxist model between the crisis of relations and forces of production, and the struggle of the industrial working class, is not an absolutely rigid one. The capitalist anarchy of production is ultimately an irrational form of social organization, as was recognized before Marx by Saint-Simon, in his case without any commitment to radical social equality. (Saint-Simon did not even look to the state to reorder the system of production, rather to the bankers, even if his true heirs today are the state socialists of all kinds.) On the other hand, the anarchy of production expressed in periodic commercial crises was only one factor that fostered working-class association into trade unions and political parties, the more basic factor being the exploitation of the working class by capital and its opportunity of organizing against this.[7] What was completely original in the *Communist Manifesto* was the thesis that the rational reordering of production would be achieved by the revolutionary workers' movement, and this is what history has since disproved.

It is not, therefore, as if the element of revolutionary conflict was the only motor of radical change for Marx, even if he begins the *Manifesto* with the polemical assertion that 'the history of all hitherto existing societies is the history of class struggles'.[8] There is always a sense in which the crisis is a crisis for the whole of society, and this is reflected in the *Manifesto* itself when Marx refers to the role of the radical intelligentsia:

> Finally, in times when the class struggle nears the decisive hour, the process of dissolution going on within the ruling class, in fact within the whole range of old society, assumes such a violent, glaring character, that a small section of the ruling class sets itself adrift, and joins the revolutionary class, the class that holds the future in its hands. Just as, therefore, at an earlier period, a section of the nobility went over to the bourgeoisie, so now a portion of the bourgeoisie goes over to the proletariat, and in particular, a portion of the bourgeois ideologists, who have raised themselves to

the level of comprehending theoretically the historical movement as a whole.[9]

This was of course the experience of Marx and Engels themselves.

Even in the orthodox Marxist scenario, therefore, the division of society into two hostile camps is never quite complete. Besides the zero-sum distribution of interest between the privileged bourgeoisie and the oppressed proletariat, there is also a certain positive interest that the whole society has in resolving social contradictions and evolving a higher level of social organization. It is simply that, in the form of crisis which Marx and Engels defined in the *Communist Manifesto*, this latter interest was relatively subordinate, so that only a small section of the privileged class, 'in particular, a portion of the bourgeois ideologists', was prepared to forfeit its material privilege for the sake of aligning itself with the future.

The situation today is very different. On the one hand, the degree of class privilege and oppression has been significantly reduced, and its predominant form today is the hierarchical division of labour, which is peculiarly unsusceptible to resolution by the violent struggle of the oppressed against the privileged. On the other hand, the interest that the whole society has in the resolution of its contradictions is incomparably greater. In Marx's writings, the bad side of the status quo, as far as the privileged class were concerned, lay simply in the irrational behaviour of the productive system with its periodic commercial crises. Today, what is at stake, if we fail to move forward to communism, is the very future of our species and our planet.

In this situation, the dominant motor of social change is the interest that the whole society has in survival. It is not that the class division no longer exists; it all too evidently does. And as long as there is class division there will be class conflict. Those privileged by the present social system, moreover, have correspondingly less interest in its replacement, and those oppressed by the present social system correspondingly more interest. It may even be that the class division is still the most prominent form of privilege and oppression in the advanced capitalist countries today, though this cannot just be assumed a priori.[10] Yet this class division and class conflict does not contain a revolutionary potential. Indeed it can only contribute to the process of radical transformation, of transition to communism, if the oppressed class, i.e. the menial workers of all kinds, guide their struggles by the needs of society as a whole, rather than waging them simply in terms of the present society's zero-sum distribution of privilege. In the Gramscian vocabulary the working-class struggle has to be 'hegemonic' rather than 'corporate', yet even so, in today's conditions it can be no more than one strand in the communist transformation.

Orthodox Marxism, from Marx himself down to the present day, has championed a particular theory of the bourgeois state. The rule of law, parliamentary government and universal suffrage may be forms that this state can assume. But when the capitalist class faces a threat of expropriation the essence of the state is revealed as one of dictatorship; in the last instance, the special forces of armed men are designed to uphold the rights of property.

Even this orthodox position, however, is less simple than it appears. In the French Second Republic of 1848-51, Marx saw the extension of suffrage to the exploited classes as temporary and unstable, which indeed it proved to be: 'It gives political power to the classes whose social slavery it is intended to perpetuate: proletariat, peasants and petty bourgeoisie. And it deprives the bourgeoisie, the class whose old social power it sanctions, of the political guarantees of this power.'[11] Yet before the end of Marx's life a more stable form of universal suffrage was developing, and this has since become the general norm for advanced capitalism.

Marx's response in the 1870s, when at least most male skilled workers in Britain already had the vote, was to grant the possibility of a peaceful 'evolution' to communism via parliamentary majority in countries lacking a large bureaucratic and military state apparatus; he particularly referred to Britain, the United States and Holland in this connection.[12] Yet Lenin, commenting on Marx in *The State and Revolution*, saw this situation as altogether exceptional. Writing in the midst of the First World War, Lenin claimed that 'England and America...have completely sunk into the all-European filthy, bloody morass of bureaucratic-military institutions which subordinate everything to themselves and trample everything underfoot'.[13] Every bourgeois state, therefore, should be seen as essentially a 'cudgel' in the hands of the capitalist ruling class, and this is a recurrent theme in all Lenin's subsequent writings on the state.[14]

It is clear, of course, that if the state apparatus is ultimately a cudgel, then it is impossible for the working class to make any decisive advance by constitutional means, and violent revolution is the only way forward. Indeed, Leninists in a bourgeois democracy must struggle within the workers' movement against the illusions of constitutional advance, and prepare the working class to meet the eventual necessity of armed struggle. If the German Communist Party contributed to bringing down the Weimar republic in the early 1930s, and thus unwittingly helped Hitler to power, this came precisely from its pursual of tactics learned from the Bolsheviks. And if there are few Leninists today who have not learned to appreciate the distinction between bourgeois democracy and fascism, their doctrine still requires them to contest the substantiality of democratic forms. In fighting fascism, for example, the police who protect the fascists' demonstrations are seen as an equal part of the enemy, even if they are only upholding a law that might also protect the Left from fascist assault.

In support of the 'cudgel' theory Leninists will point to the examples of Italy or Germany between the wars, to Chile only a few years ago, even to the Special Patrol Group and other paramilitary bodies that the British state is deploying to deal with violent political agitation. And there can be no doubt whatsoever that where the capitalist class has perceived a threat of proletarian revolution, as it did in so many European countries after the Bolshevik victory of 1917, then it has shown itself perfectly prepared to resort to whatever form of dictatorship was practicable in the circumstances.[15] The fundamental error of the 'cudgel' theory, however, is that it hypostasizes the social relation of the state and makes it into a thing, thus short-circuiting an understanding of the dialectic of class struggle which can lead to such a situation of violent conflict. The capitalist class will resort to dictatorship when faced with a threat of revolution, but it does not follow that working-class advance on the constitutional road will at some point meet with an insurmountable barrier: the cudgel is not there ready and waiting.

Bourgeois democracy is possible, as a stable constitutional form, precisely because the working class does not present a revolutionary threat. It was out of this confidence that the British bourgeoisie felt able to concede working-class suffrage step by step, from 1867 onwards. After the Russian revolution, and faced with a strong socialist movement at home, there were voices heard even in Britain for a fascist solution. The more parasitic elements of the privileged class, from the then Prince of Wales downwards, were full of admiration for Mussolini, who made the trains run on time by knocking the engine-drivers over the head. Yet the majority of the privileged class in inter-War Britain, for all their conservatism, never showed the same fear of working people as the minority of parasitic idlers. They already felt the security of a competence and expertise that would always be in demand and could insist on its 'due reward'. This being the case, bourgeois democracy was a far preferable option than resort to brute force in holding back the working-class tide. For the violence of the oppressors can only breed violence on the side of the oppressed. And whatever damage might from time to time be inflicted on the privileged sections of society by working-class advance in the struggle of opinion is very much less than they might expect to suffer under a proletarian dictatorship.

By holding out to the workers' movement the prospect of forming a government, the privileged class in fact still further reduces the chance of this government being unacceptably radical. As the parties of the Second International discovered at the turn of the century, it is a slow process to build up a radical majority for socialism, and long before this is achieved, there will be a potential majority for more limited programmes of reform. A 'possibilist' wing is bound to emerge in the workers' movement, appealing both to non-socialist workers who see no further than the next round of reforms, and to those socialists who, in the circumstances, opt for a gradualist tactic rather than wait for the distant radical majority. As the reformist option is seen to deliver at least some of the goods, in the way that the Labour government of 1945 very clearly did in Britain, and on a lesser scale the Wilson governments of the 1960s and 1970s, this gradualist course becomes steadily more entrenched in working-class mentality and institutions. It is significant that those socialists in the advanced capitalist countries today who stand out against gradualism do so by arguing that somehow or other, in the context of economic crisis, bourgeois democracy will collapse and the working class will have to turn to a Leninist path.[16] But no one seriously maintains, as did the Marxist parties of the Second International, and the Independent Labour Party in Britain through till the 1930s, that a radical change in social system could be brought into being at one stroke by a parliamentary majority. (This is the position of that 'monument' from another age, the Socialist Party of Great Britain.)

The state in the advanced capitalist countries today is certainly very far from perfectly democratic. The mass media are distorted by monied interests, working-class MPs are corrupted by exposure to a bourgeois lifestyle, the various state apparatuses seek to protect their operations from public scrutiny, and so on. But the only viable ground on which Leninists can argue that all this cannot gradually be reformed, and that the state is ultimately a cudgel in the hands of the ruling class, is that they still anticipate a proletarian revolution à la 1917, even though this becomes ever more remote as the gradualist course that working-class struggle has actually taken in our part of the world makes its slow but steady progress.

Consumerism and parliamentary democracy fit together as the core economic and political structures of the present social order. Consumerism integrates the working class into the bourgeois mode of consumption, parliamentary democracy integrates the working class into the bourgeois political arena, in both cases ascribing it a subordinate role. But this subordination can no longer be attributed, as it is by orthodox Marxists, to the persistence of a minority of capitalists on the one hand and a majority of proletarians with nothing to sell but their labour-power on the other. As I argued in Chapter Three, section 3, even privilege of the crudest economic kind is now derived far more from the hierarchical division of labour than from ownership of capital; and on top of this, the 'meritocrats' who preside over our society today derive a still more important privilege from the very nature of their work and the education that enables them to perform it.

There was a time, still within living memory, when political expropriation of capitalist wealth appeared the royal road towards the liberation of the working class. But if nationalization could still make a real difference for the coal-miners in the 1940s, to pretend there is any noticeable advantage in nationalization for the workers at British Steel or British Leyland today is simply laughable. The Socialist Workers Party can still put forward the slogan: 'We don't want another slice, we want the whole bakery', but the rank-and-file workers to whom this is designed to appeal are well aware that things are a lot more complicated. Private bosses can easily be replaced by state bosses, even bosses claiming to represent a workers' state. But the underprivileged of our society, those relegated to menial tasks, will only make genuine progress towards liberation to the extent that they manage to gain an increased control of their immediate work situation and to erode the hierarchical division of labour itself. This is a long and arduous business, a process of education in every sense of the term. There is little mileage for them in lightning strokes of expropriation — especially when you can hardly wipe out the savings of several million people by refusing compensation to shareholders — and they basically understand this very well.

This is at the root of what Barry Hindess has called 'the decline of working-class politics'[17] since the peak years of the 1940s. For though trade-union struggle is as militant as ever, and indeed has to be simply to keep pace with inflation, working-class participation in the political parties of the Left has been steadily on the wane for the last thirty years. In the British Labour party menial workers have been replaced ever more by teachers, social workers and other 'lower professionals', and the groups of the revolutionary Left, purest in their Marxist doctrines, are also purest in the virtual absence of any working-class members. Any broad historical movement like that of the modern working class necessarily has its ups and downs. The Labour party was adapted to the immediate needs of the working class in the first half of this century — the struggle for social welfare — just as the Chartist party was adapted to the needs of the working class a century before — the struggle for suffrage. It will inevitably take time for the workers' movement to reconstitute itself, both ideologically and organizationally, in the ways needed to challenge the hierarchical division of labour that is the very root of the class division in East and West alike. But we can be confident that the first shoots in this direction, such as the workers' control movement, the alternative production plans of the workers of Vickers and Lucas Aerospace, and producers' cooperatives as attempted at Triumph Meriden, will sooner or later blossom into a genuine mass movement — provided our industrial society survives long enough to see it.

The working-class struggle in the capitalist heartlands has thus taken a form very different from the 'ascent to extremes' that Marx originally anticipated, that Lenin insisted upon, and that was the concrete reality at a few great historical moments: Paris 1871, Petrograd 1917, Barcelona 1936. The bourgeois ruling classes gradually came to realize that 'if you do not give the people social reform, they are going to give you revolution', as Quintin Hogg (now Lord Hailsham) classically put it in the House of Commons in 1943.[18] Even such characteristic scions of the richest and most traditional landed families as Lord Home accept with remarkably good grace the repeated loss of half their kingdom with each succeeding generation,[19] realizing that the alternative would have been far worse. For those of us impatient to see the advance to communism, the sluggishness of the gradualist path is agonizing. Yet it is not a question of subjective preference, even the 'preference' of the working class, but of what is objectively inscribed in a nation's history. Nor is it as if the revolutionary road, when this is so inscribed, does not have its particular problems too.

We have no choice but to build on the foundations already laid. And once we accept this necessity, it becomes possible to see a positive side to bourgeois democracy which orthodox Marxism has understandably overlooked. In the zone of democracy that is roughly coterminous with a certain maturity of industrial capitalism, mechanisms have been developed that allow social conflicts to be handled, both within and between nations, in ways that stop short of armed struggle. It is salutary to recall that there has never been a war between two bourgeois democracies, while there have been armed conflicts both between fascist states and between states describing themselves as proletarian dictatorships.

The zone of democracy, for all its terrible faults, displays two interrelated aspects that prefigure an achieved communist society, and on which communists in this zone must build if our work is to be at all effective. On the one hand, a degree of social solidarity across national, class and other divisions that prefigures the greater solidarity of communism. Orthodox Marxism sees this simply as an ideology that ties the oppressed classes to their oppressors, but it works the other way around as well; whenever the workers' movement has built up a sufficient head of steam behind its current demands, then the ruling class has chosen to surrender a slice of privilege and compromise, rather than dig in its heels and abandon the ground of democracy. On the other hand, the bourgeois democracies provide for an intellectual freedom that is far more than simply a freedom for intellectuals, being in fact the very precondition of social progress. The word 'dialectic', which we Marxists are so fond of, is directly derived from 'dialogue', a form of discourse in which no single viewpoint claims a monopoly of the truth, and any statement, no matter how firmly believed, is open to even the most subversive challenge.

When a people's revolution overthrows a reactionary dictatorship, it may be possible for the communist vanguard to establish a revolutionary dictatorship. In this case, power becomes centralized in the hands of a single party and its leading core, in the interest of preventing the return of the dispossessed privileged class and transforming social structures according to Marxist theory. The idea of the dictatorship of the proletariat as a multi-party system, as the Trotskyists for example propose, is a contradiction in terms. It is said that only the bourgeois parties will be proscribed; but in this case, as happened in Russia in 1918, opposition to the revolutionary dictatorship will focus in the professedly socialist parties and they will each be proscribed in turn. A revolutionary dictatorship can certainly advance the interest of the people very greatly, as the examples of Soviet Russia, China, Cuba and others have shown. But with the passage of time the negative side of any such dictatorship comes increasingly to the fore. The state defines a certain group within society as an enemy, and although this enemy may have its roots in a specific social class, it necessarily manifests itself in the ideological field in a way that is far from simply coterminous with class origin. Given that the enemy is there somewhere, anyone can potentially be classed as the enemy. It is impossible to have the broadest possible democracy among the people, as Lenin intended, while at the same time exercising dictatorship over the bourgeoisie. In the same way, it is impermissible that all ideas should be voiced. And if certain ideas are denied a hearing on the grounds that they are bourgeois, then any ideas can find themselves classed as bourgeois and suppressed.

The example of the gay minority and the cause of gay liberation is a particularly apt one here. We know how the gender system has defined us as deviant, and how this negative description has never been disavowed by orthodox Marxism, even when it has rejected the categories of religion (it's a sin) and law (it's a crime) to speak in the more modern vocabulary of medicine (it's a sickness) or politics (it's bourgeois). In the countries of proletarian dictatorship, this backwardness in the understanding of gender leads to gayness being branded as anti-socialist, with those who persist in their deviance being refused all social solidarity. The existence of an official ideology, moreover, even that of Marxism, makes it impossible to challenge traditional ideas and struggle for a change. In the zone of democracy, on the other hand, uphill as our struggle undoubtedly is, we do have on our side the benefits of social solidarity and intellectual freedom. The fact of our difference is no longer sufficient, as it was in the past, for the straight majority to treat us as pariahs, and we are able just like any other pressure group to come together, discuss among ourselves and propagate our ideas to others, no matter how heretical, subversive or ridiculous these might seem to majority opinion.[20]

Marx was himself absolutely clear on the value of civil and political liberty, describing the French state apparatus under Louis Bonaparte as 'a frightful parasitic body, which surrounds the body of French society like a caul and stops up all its pores'.[21] He also crossed swords with Andreas Gottschalk in the German revolution of 1848, and Ferdinand Lassalle in the 1860s, for their subordination of the struggle for democracy to the immediate economic interests of the working class.[22] It is an impossible question to ask what position Marx would have taken in the great split that divided the workers' movement after 1917, the side of Lenin or the side of Kautsky. Precisely because he was Marx and died in 1883, he never had to confront this issue. But no matter how necessary the path of violent revolution in Russia, China and elsewhere, there can be no doubt from the experience of the 20th century that dictatorship, however revolutionary, always has a very definite negative side to it as well, and that democracy, however bourgeois, also has a very definite positive side to it: positive precisely from the standpoint of the liberation of the oppressed, and the struggle for communism in general.

Given that we have in the zone of democracy both a certain degree of social solidarity and intellectual freedom, our efforts should be bent towards building on the gains already made. Rather than criticizing the defects of the present society in a destructive way, merely to mobilize feeling against the present order in the interest of a struggle for power, we should criticize these defects in a constructive way, in support of positive alternatives. An example of what should not be done is the response of so much of the British Left to the Bullock report of 1977, which proposed far-reaching measures of workers' participation in management; in their view, this was simply a ploy by the capitalists to divert the workers from the *real* struggle to seize power. As an example of the path on which the class struggle can advance, I have already cited the various new attempts at self-management that groups of British workers have pioneered in recent years. At the theoretical level, too, there are signs now that at least some British Marxists are striving to redirect themselves to the real requirements of popular advance in the present situation, like their Eurocommunist counterparts in Italy and Spain.[23]

## 2. *The Communist Utopia*

In 1884, when Marx was struggling towards the ideas of communism, he justified his political commitment by an ethical ideal: to abolish 'all conditions in which man is a despised, enslaved, neglected and contemptible being'.[24] In the light of the materialist conception of history that Marx and Engels were to formulate a year or so later, it is possible to explain the adoption of such an ideal by a section of the bourgeois intelligentsia in the way indicated by the *Communist Manifesto* (see above, p. 162). The point, however, is that Marx and Engels were communists, seeking a radical transformation of social relations, before they came to their characteristic understanding of the historical process.[25]

Any movement for communism requires its participants to rise above immediate interests and act in the interest of a general human liberation. If the conflict between immediate interest and ethical ideal is more acute for intellectuals from the privileged class, the two things are never identical even for the working class. This is precisely the basis of Lenin's antithesis between mere 'trade-union politics' and genuinely 'social-democratic [i.e. communist] politics', as made in *What is To be Done?* The same thing is involved again in Gramsci's distinction between 'corporate' and 'hegemonic' working-class struggle.

No matter how much the particular support for communism shown by the working class is a function of its objective situation as a 'class with radical chains', the fact is that the ethical ideal of communism is a principle by which large numbers of women and men have necessarily acted in those historical instances where even the most orthodox of Marxist movements have flourished. This ethical ideal is a most wonderful thing, the vision of a global human society free from privilege and oppression, a planetary harmony that will raise our species a decisive step above the animal world from which we have sprung; not for nothing did Marx see communism as the beginning of a truly human existence, rather than the end.

Yet in orthodox Marxism there has always been a certain unavoidable contradiction, which undoubtedly had a dampening effect on the capacity of this ethical ideal to mobilize people for political struggle. The path from capitalism to communism had to pass through the stage of intensifying class conflict and forcible revolution. The task of communists, therefore, was destructive before it could be constructive. The ethical ideal makes its appeal to the empathy which spontaneously grows between rational sentient beings, and which no class society, however brutal, has managed completely to suppress. The path of revolution, however, demands that empathy should be restricted to one's class comrades (solidarity), and that towards the adversary it is the opposite sentiment of hatred that must be fostered, the better to precipitate the revolutionary explosion.

What made the conflict between the ultimate goal and the means to achieve it particularly sharp was that, of the various attempted modalities of a revolutionary Marxist tactic, the only variant that proved in any way successful was that of Lenin. For Leninism, the concrete form in which the revolutionary shift in power is envisaged is not simply a parliamentary majority for the Marxist party, nor even the setting up of a higher form of democracy against the bourgeois-parliamentary state (workers' councils), but the de facto dictatorship of a 'Bolshevik nucleus'. This is formed and built up not just by treating the privileged class as a dehumanized enemy, but also by treating in a highly instrumental manner, as objects to be manipulated in whatever way best serves the capture of power by the nucleus, the broad mass of workers themselves. In this sense, the foundations for the worst excesses of Stalinism were already laid by Lenin himself, however much he might personally have recoiled at his progeny.

The Leninist machine may well have been necessary to bring at least the first step of liberation for the toiling masses of Russia, China, Yugoslavia, Vietnam, etc. For them, the immediate goal of revolutionary dictatorship already spelled such an advance towards freedom that all means that promoted it could easily be justified. In the process, however, the ethical ideal was negated and its actualization as the 'higher stage of communism' postponed into the indefinite future, serving no practical purpose except, eventually, as a myth to persuade people that the present task of 'building socialism' was indeed preparing the ground for further liberation.[26]

This can explain why, while on the one hand Marxism has looked forward to a qualitatively different society from that of capitalism, a genuine new civilization, it has always remained hostile to what Marx liked to dismiss as 'recipes for the cookshops of the future.' It is true that what Marx and Engels reacted against in the early utopians such as Fourier and Owen was indeed a mechanical and ahistorical attempt to lay down in advance the organization of the new social order. Yet as is vividly shown by the relationship between Engels and William Morris in the 1880s, orthodox Marxism could not appreciate that perfectly valid aspect of utopian thought which a French writer on Morris has called the 'education of desire', i.e. the challenge to the basic values of capitalist civilization that Morris believed necessary in advance of the revolution to ensure that the new social order was not just a refurbishment of the old.[27] This aspect of utopianism is precisely the anticipated application of the communist ethical ideal, as this will have to be applied concretely in ordering the new society. And utopias of this kind have a tremendous capacity to move people to struggle for a better world.

I believe that the fundamental refusal of orthodox Marxism to acknowledge the utopian dimension of communist thought derives from the contradiction between the ethical ideal at work in utopianism and the needs of violent revolution. Marx and Engels, having taken part in the German revolution of 1848, and having followed so closely the struggles of the working class in 19th century France, had a far clearer understanding than any British socialists that revolution, if this was indeed the way forward, would be in no way a tea party, but a bitter, protracted and violent struggle, from which the new society would emerge badly scarred. This was indeed what was to happen in Russia in

1917, and in all Marxist-led revolutions in the third world. On the other hand, if the way forward was an essentially peaceful 'evolution', as they thought might be possible in Britain, then it would be similarly impossible, if for quite different reasons, to inaugurate a new communist civilization by an act of political will. Either way, the communist society that '*emerges* from capitalist society' would be 'in every respect, economically, morally, intellectually...still stamped with the birth-marks of the old society from whose womb it has emerged'.[28]

The political tactic in the socialist movement with which utopianism has been most closely associated is that of 'majority revolution', which unlike both the 'minority revolution' of Leninism and the reformism of social democracy, seems to offer the promise of a new society at least relatively free from the 'birth-marks of the old'.[29] Yet this was precisely the tactic that did not work, for the reasons given above (pp. 166-167), and whose adherents had sooner or later either to regress to reformist gradualism, or to opt for Leninism. Neither of these could accomodate the utopian dimension, which was consequently relegated to the margins of socialist thought.[30]

Today, however, the situation has radically changed, since the present contradiction between scientific technology and the class/gender system gives our whole society a vital interest in overcoming its disharmonies, if it is to survive and go forward. There is accordingly no longer any need for the utopian dimension to be sacrificed on the altar of *Realpolitik*. On the contrary. The political tactic indicated today is a new kind of 'majority revolution', this time one in which everyone who is not blinded by immediate privilege has a material interest, because the side of the future is today the side of survival. And this being so, the utopian dimension, and the ethical goal it embodies, has a vital part to play in inspiring people to struggle for radical change.

In Britain we have a great tradition of utopian communism, its roots stretching back to the revolution of the 17th century. In the writings of William Morris, this was linked to the specific needs of the modern working-class movement. Morris' writings can still serve as radical political tracts today, and in Edward Carpenter this utopianism broadens out into the fields of sexuality and gender. For half a century or more, these ideas have been virtually banished from the communist movement, but the time is now ripe for them to return at a new and higher level. The first shoots of this are already to be seen, for example in the writings and practice of the 'alternative society', even if this is still held back by a certain elitism that turns its back on the needs of the masses, by a tendency to reject scientific technology and large-scale organization, and by a continuing male supremacism. The women's movement, too, has generated its own utopianism, particularly in the United States, and indeed the book that is presently head and shoulders above all others for its integration of a utopianism that is feminist, socialist and ecological is Marge Piercy's *Woman on the Edge of Time*.[31]

I believe very strongly that we should build on this tradition. For if in the past the exploration of utopia diverted energy from the tactical task of lining up as many bodies as possible in front of polling booth or barricade, creating the 'broadest possible united front', today it is necessary not to reduce our appeal to the lowest common denominator, but precisely to radicalize it, in order to show that an alternative way of life is possible, and 'educate the desire' for a communist transformation.

The ultimate sentiment behind the communist ethical ideal is that of love,[32] the same love that all great religious teachers have put forward as the principle by which human beings should live. Rather more frequently, and at a slightly more concrete level, this has been expressed in political discourse as 'brotherhood'. It might be tempting, with our present anti-sexist sensitivity to language, to interpret this as simply a solecism analogous to that which uses 'man' for human, really meaning siblinghood even if it doesn't say it. But there is another side to it as well. The concept of brotherhood is always associated with a certain recognition, however limited and contradictory, that the lack of siblinghood in the world today is particularly a problem between males, i.e. that the struggle for dominance is a masculine problem, and that, in this respect at least, men are the problem. There is already here a certain rejection of the masculine specialization in warfare (utopian communism is very often associated with moral pacifism), an implicit agreement with the critique that feminists would not formulate with full clarity until getting on for two centuries after the first French Republic established *'fraternité'* as the third term in its motto (if nowhere else).

Brotherhood can be given a muscular enough connotation, and by no means need imply support for women's liberation.[33] Yet even in Robbie Burns' vigorous lines, that 'man to man the warld o'er, shall brithers be for a' that', there is something just slightly embarrassing, so that the song might have to be sung extra loud, even, to prevent anyone from hearing between the lines. This is also the case, of course, with the message of Jesus: 'Love one another'. Even though the address is to human beings in general, the specific idea that men should love other men is very definitely included.[34]

It is not surprising that the utopian strand in the communist movement has always provided a somewhat more favourable environment for gay men. And if this is above all in the sense that we can feel more at home where masculine violence is not cultivated but at least partially criticized, the erotic undertone of love between men has certainly played a part as well. Yet it is not as if gay men were able actually to come out in this milieu, before the advent of gay liberation, in any but the most exceptional circumstances. (Edward Carpenter, in his day, was certainly exceptional in every way.) And the basic gender division already involved in the institutionalizing of heterosexuality accordingly remained essentially unquestioned.

The concept of brotherhood, therefore, has certain very definite limits. Men are told that they should 'study war no more', and yet children are still brought up to be 'proper' girls and boys, with at most a somewhat softened model of masculinity. Among other things, as I argued in Chapter Two (p. 93), the institutionalization of heterosexuality already sets men in an objective position of unmediated rivalry with one another. And the annals of the communist movement are replete with examples of even the most 'fraternal' of men exploding with a very masculine rage as soon as there is any suggestion that 'his' woman might be stolen by another man.[35]

This weakness of the utopian tradition was clearly to be seen in the counterculture of the 1960s, and is still perpetuated today in the 'alternative society'. At its worst it can take the most extreme and grotesque forms, and these were actually given a boost for a while by the 1960s celebration of 'sexual liberation'. In 1972, Aubrey Walter and I documented how 'the cultural radicals have not been forced to question the single greatest mainstay of individualistic psychology — *masculinity*', in an article reviewing a collection of countercultural manifestos and ephemera.[36]

Although these all came from the late 1960s counterculture, it would be unfair to lump them all together. Yet what we saw as a 'bare-faced sexual fascism' pervades even many tendencies that presented themselves as authentically political and claimed a certain communist consciousness. Thus the Dutch Provos, pacifist libertarians, extended their White Bicycle Plan, aimed against motor-car congestion in Amsterdam, into a 'White Wife Plan', 'directed towards the emancipation of women' (!). The American Yippies, at the 1968 Democratic convention in Chicago, announced: '230 rebel cocksmen under secret vows are on 24-hour alert to get into the pants of the daughters and wives of the convention delegates'. The American White Panthers wrote: 'Fuck your woman until she can't get up'. While the Berlin Kommune I [= First Commune], with greater sophistication, charged against the state authorities: 'We bugger you in the ass when you shake your bureaucratic cocks'. Women who came into the feminist movement with experience of the counterculture have amply documented how the gender system remained essentially unchallenged in even the most 'gentle' of countercultural milieus.

Whether it expressly sees it as 'natural' or merely fails to question received ideology, even utopian communism has up till now taken heterosexuality for granted. It would be wrong to say that the ideas of feminism have made no impact; there has been change, just as in the society around. And yet this change is secondary, still well within the parameters of the gender system, and can only be so as long as heterosexuality is institutionalized in this way. As the new feminist movement rapidly discovered, in order even to begin to struggle effectively against male supremacy, it is necessary to stop defining oneself as heterosexual. For women, the permanent option of lesbianism, preferably backed up by some practical experience of lesbian relationships, has proved essential, if they are not to get constantly pulled back into precisely what they are struggling against.

As long as heterosexuality is accepted as the norm, and homosexuality admitted only for the gay minority, any love between 'brothers' can only be secondary to the rivalry that divides them at a deeper level. As explained in Chapter Two, moreover, homosexuality, love between people who are *alike*, is decisively distinct from heterosexuality in its transitive character, i.e. the structural feature that two people who are lovers of a third can themselves also, in principle, be lovers. This provides an indispensable mediation, and is an absolute precondition if rivalry and hate are to be ended.[37]

It is not enough, then, for men to redefine themselves as non-violent and brothers. As long as the gender system is not abolished, and the heterosexual norm as part of it, they are only repressing the rival and the warrior within themselves, denying the existence of these, rather than even beginning to change their being. The only place where the brotherhood proclaimed by the communist utopia has begun to take root, therefore, is in the gay liberation movement, in parallel with the sisterhood in the women's movement which similarly acknowledges its erotic component. It is in this sense that 'the women's liberation movement and the gay liberation movement... have taken over and are developing the positive achievements of the counter-culture'.[38]

Today the struggle for communism requires not violent revolution, but a radical consensus to reorganize our society. There is therefore no basic conflict between the ultimate goal of the struggle and the means necessary to advance it. The communist society can accordingly be anticipated in a small way here and now, and indeed must be so, as a demonstration that human beings really can change, really can overcome the competition and struggle to dominate, the survival of the fittest, that reactionaries have always proclaimed is an eternal part of the human condition. But communism involves not just the abolition of class, but equally of the gender system that underlies this, with its masculine specialization in violence, domination of men over women, and institutionalized heterosexuality. And if the ideas of communism are to spread by force of example, then communists must show today how it is also possible to begin to live and relate in a way unstructured by gender. Until a decade or so ago, this might well have seemed outside the bounds of the possible. But the rise of the women's and gay liberation movements, for all their problems and contradictions, has clearly placed the abolition of gender alongside that of class as a goal, and has given a concrete example, through the sisterhood of the women's movement, and the genuine brotherhood between gay men, that the abolition of gender, too, is not just pie in the sky, but a principle that we can at least start to apply here and now.

The desperate need to abolish war shows in the most immediate and brutal way how the gender system has become intolerable. But the reassertion of the maternal culture of love is actually needed for the resolution of all social contradictions that divide the human race today and together generate the symptoms of destruction. It is needed in order to extricate our planet from the deadly rivalry of the two superpowers, and it must equally inspire our attitude towards the peoples of the South. The Brandt commission report[39] has documented very well how a massive expansion of what is quite inadequately called 'aid' to the developing countries is a question of self-interest for the advanced countries themselves. But the problem facing us today is precisely to induce people to pursue a genuinely enlightened self-interest, which on an increasingly small planet must in the last analysis be the well-being of humanity as a whole. Vis-à-vis the South of the planet, in particular, and even in handling the completely different contradiction that divides us from the Soviet Union, we need to cultivate a maternal care for those on the other side, if the barrier is really to be broken down.

The class division within our society may pale somewhat when compared with the East-West and North-South contradictions in the world today. But as I explained in Chapter Three, it is the consumerist dynamic of the present class system that leads us to continue the pillage of the South, in a way now joined by the Soviet countries. The division within our own society, not just or even mainly a function today of private property, but above all of the division of labour and education, must equally be radically challenged. The paradox here is that the new generation of Marxists in the West, i.e. the 'new left' of the 1960s and 1970s, while originally motivated by solidarity and love for the oppressed, have drawn a complete blank in attempting to rekindle the flames of proletarian revolution. If this had a certain (if minority) appeal to workers in Britain before the Second World War, today the base of orthodox Marxism is essentially confined to groups of intellectuals — thus refuting its own premises. It is no longer possible, in other words, to work for the abolition of the class division in advanced capitalist society simply by means of a revolt from below. The permanent state of struggle between privileged and oppressed in the class system today depends for its resolution on the privileged sections of society, i.e. the 'educated' classes, also feeling from their own standpoint the need to abolish the hierarchical division of labour.

Rudolf Bahro, in citing the Buddhist saint Kuan Yin (see above, p. 13), goes on to say that 'this metaphor may well be appropriate for that type of solidarity which needs to prevail in society when the focus of social inequality is shifted to the division of labour and education'.[40] This is completely true as far as it goes. But firstly, it must be stressed that there is no 'divinity' for the Kuan Yins of today, the privileged intellectuals, to attain, unless they carry the mass of the people with them. And secondly, the wonderful example of love shown by Kuan Yin requires, if it is to develop on any large scale in society, a process of de-masculinization, of reasserting the maternal culture, not as something ascribed solely to women, but as a quality that men must equally display.[41]

## 3. *A Radical Consensus*

The class and gender system that structures and distorts human life today is a unitary system, involving every human individual, and at several levels of social relation. People who become aware of one particular evil that the system generates are thus bound to stumble, as they struggle on this front, onto wider connections and deeper roots. We come into the movement from quite different points of entry, but the further we proceed, the more we converge, as we each increase our awareness of the system as a whole. When the point of entry is simply that of a symptom, whether nuclear weapons, queer-bashing, starvation in Africa or the extinction of the whale, it is not hard to work out that this symptom is part of a more systematic relationship, part of a social structure. Yet once the level of structure is reached, there are still very different perspectives, according to which aspect it is approached from, and these prove far tougher to integrate into a vision of the totality.

There are three such perspectives in particular. There is the perspective of socialism, by no means just confined to orthodox Marxism, that approaches the total structure from the aspect of economic organization and its class divisions. Then there is the ecological perspective, approaching the social totality from the aspect of the interface with our biological environment (including our own bodies). And thirdly, there is the feminist perspective, approaching the totality from the perspective of the contradiction between the sexes. Precisely because each of these three is aware that it has got down to the real nitty-gritty, to the structure, and is working for radical change at this level, it is the more difficult for it to appreciate how the structure can appear very different when approached from a different aspect; there is a spontaneous tendency to feel that the truth has finally been discovered, and that the other perspectives are merely stuck at the level of the symptom. Thus socialists believe the ecological problem and the gender system are simply functions of private property; feminists believe the ecological problem and the class system are simply forms of male supremacy; and ecologists believe both the class and sexual contradictions can be resolved by a more harmonious relationship with the biosphere.

It has been the particular object of this book to argue that each of these three basic perspectives has one side of the truth, but that none of them has more than one side. That if we really are to attain a radical resolution of social contradictions, and live harmoniously in the biosphere, then the premise of such a movement must be the fusion of these three perspectives together into a broader synthesis. Communism, in the fullest sense, equals socialism + feminism + ecology. There can be no question of ascribing an order of importance to these three things. Each has a unique and vital contribution to make, on the basis of its own partial truth. There is no division in human society more terrible than the economic one between North and South; there is no threat to our survival more dangerous than the degradation of the biosphere; and there is no division more deep-rooted and long-standing than the division of gender. But as soon as a partial truth is put forward as the whole truth, it becomes distorted even in terms of its own claims. In this way we get the metaphysical tendency in feminism that sees male domination as innate; the metaphysical tendency in the ecology movement that demands a 'return to nature'; and the metaphysical tendency in the socialist movement that looks to a 'pure' proletariat as subject of the revolution.

The total challenge to the present society, essential to cure the disease that generates such terrible symptoms, requires that all forces converge into a single radical movement. It follows from what has been said already that there can be no prospect of achieving this by one or other of the basic perspectives, the socialist, feminist or ecological, seeking hegemony over the others. Quite the contrary. This convergence requires each perspective to adopt a modest attitude, and seek to learn from the great insights achieved by the others. I believe that the movements of women and gay men are more ready to develop in this way and integrate into our own radicalism the radicalism of the socialist and ecological movements. But I would be only too happy if it turned out to be either of these that made the running. In a race to converge there are no losers, and we can only win together.

A convergent movement is essential, but this does not mean a monolithic party organized on the basis of so-called democratic centralism, and thus embodying precisely the division between rulers and ruled that it is imperative to break down. A revolutionary party of this kind is absolutely counter-productive, given that our aim is not to seize power, but rather to erode it. What we need is a convergence of ideas, so that groups specializing in different activities and campaigns can experiment and take initiatives with complete freedom, but inspired by a common understanding of the totality which leads them to spontaneously integrate their particular efforts into the common struggle. This conception of a convergent Movement is not brand new. It was pioneered in particular in the United States in the 1960s, and there have been echoes of it in Britain and other countries. The unresolved contradictions of the 'new left', however, led in the 1970s to a process of fragmentation, in particular with feminists and ecologists splitting away from a socialism that was unable to integrate the awareness they were seeking to express.[42] Ten years later, however, the feminist and ecological critiques are solidly established, as far as they go, while the pretensions of socialism to offer a comprehensive solution to the problems of our planet are ever less convincing. The stage is set for a dialogue on genuinely equal terms, and out of this there can come the building of a convergent and unprecedentedly radical movement.

Recognition that we share the common goal of communism does not require the separate movements to dissolve themselves in the wider unity. They remain its essential building-blocks, each struggling on one or other of the major fronts or frontiers of change. There will certainly be the need for these particular liberation movements to be complemented by certain organizational forms that represent the movement as a whole, for example in the arena of electoral politics. But this is not a question of a central leadership allowing the particular movements to keep their 'autonomy', as the more modern Marxist vanguards graciously yield to the 'autonomy' of the women's movement, for example, while in fact jealously seeking to control it by every means possible. The true locus of unity must rather be within each of the particular movements themselves, actively desiring to bring their efforts into a basic harmony for the sake of the common goal.

This harmony can never be absolute or devoid of contradictions. The convergence of efforts can only be a gradual and sometimes painful process. Above all, it is not just a question of harmonizing ideas in the abstract. The starting-points of the different movements are in many cases different social groups, for example women, gay men, industrial workers, and it would only be counter-productive to demand that they (we) should all at once accept a definition of tactics that was completely 'objective' and took no account of these divisions. The development of a common theory and convergent tactics can only come through the dialectical (in the literal sense of 'dialogue') exchange between the different particular movements. This is where experience is accumulated, and where understanding of the concrete contradictions begins to take shape. It is necessarily feminist theorists, i.e. women, who bring to awareness the relation between women and men, and even in those movements without such a clear constituency base, such as the movement against nuclear power, it is still those who specialize in this particular struggle that bring its problems to the general awareness. The same applies even to the struggle of the working class. For its needs, too, make themselves felt first of all, and most clearly, in the awareness of working-class individuals, not those of Marxist theorists, however orthodox. The attempt to 'understand the historical process as a whole' is certainly an essential task, but the subjective experience and consciousness of the practical movements struggling for liberation is an essential input in the elaboration of theory, and given the plurality of contradictions in our society, and the very separate starting-points of the particular movements, there is no way in which one will give priority to another simply because some theorist says so. The way to bring about a harmony of efforts is rather through the interest (in both senses) of each constituency and movement in learning the experience and awareness generated in the others. Anything more, i.e. a synoptic presentation of the historical process such as attempted in this book, remains merely a contribution to discussion, even if a discussion conducted in this way can legitimately hope to make genuine progress, ultimately expressed in the practical ability to change the world in a predetermined way.

A new advance towards communism will become possible, and necessary, when one or other of the symptoms generated by the underlying contradiction between scientific technology and the class/gender system comes to a head. It is to this conjuncture, accordingly, that we should orient our intervention to 'shorten and lessen the birth pangs' of the new society. But even if the socialist, feminist and ecological wings of the communist movement are integrated together in the way proposed above, it will still not be possible to make a decisive advance towards communism overnight, or even in the term of office of a radical government. Even as it becomes increasingly impossible for our society to stagger on in the old way, we cannot expect that more than a minority of people will come round to a communist conviction, even if we can legitimately expect this to be a growing minority. There is no need for us to tone down our radicalism in the interest of winning majority support; on the contrary, our communist message and its component parts are essential to the 'education of desire'. But we must be prepared, when the crisis becomes acute, to work together with other forces in society to resolve the most immediate and imperative problems, striking a compromise designed to maximize the advance in the communist direction. These other forces will include not just those single-issue campaigns that are not yet aware of their connection with the totality, but also sections of the existing political parties, and not necessarily just those parties that are generally considered of the Left. They will even include politicians with experience of government office, whom we could only dismiss as part of the Establishment at the price of our isolation. Past experience has shown that even some political figures whom the communist movement has perceived as reactionary can change and become allies in the event of a crisis situation.

The kind of programme around which such a compromise, a radical consensus, might be formed, will naturally depend on the particular conjuncture. But it will tend to have two parts to it. First, policies that are desired by both the communist movement and its allies in the established parties, as essential to national (and international) survival. These might include such things as increased aid to the South; unilateral nuclear disarmament and the expulsion of United States bases; the closing of fission power stations; increased agricultural production. Second, there would be policies that the established allies do not desire, but will acccept in the interest of national unity in meeting the essential tasks: for example increased workers' participation in management; a comprehensive system of socialized child care; a defence policy based on universal military training rather than an expanded regular army.

It is impossible to discuss a conjuncture of this kind without reference to that greatest of all crises in our national life, the Second World War, particularly the year from spring 1940 to spring 1941 when the threat of invasion confronted our people more seriously than for almost a thousand years. There is a deep generation gap between those old enough to remember the War, even as very young people, and those of us, like myself, whose earliest recollections begin with the first years of peace. But the effect of the War on British society, which is so strongly etched into the consciousness of the older generation, is well worth studying by us younger people too.[43]

If the biggest step forward by the working class this century is generally associated with the first majority Labour government of 1945, there can be no doubt that the new balance in class forces which this represented was in fact prepared already five years before. When the Churchill/Attlee Coalition took office in May 1940, the most reactionary elements of the ruling class who had dominated social and political life right through the inter-War period were sloughed off, especially those who, feeling threatened in their parasitic extremes of privilege, had flirted with fascism. The motto of the Coalition was: 'Everything necessary for the War, no matter how controversial' — even if this was qualified by 'nothing controversial, unless necessary for the War'.

The shift in class relations, as always, made certain old

enemies into friends, and certain old friends into enemies. Until 1937, at least, the Left had seen Churchill as an ultra-reactionary and warmonger, a figure on the far right of the Tory party. In May 1940, Churchill became Prime Minister rather than Lord Halifax (preferred replacement for Chamberlain by both the Tory party and the king) because he was the only Conservative leader under whom the Labour party would join the government. Churchill's first appearance in the House of Commons as Prime Minister, on the other hand, was met with stony silence from the Tory back-benches, and it was only after the Battle of Britain that he was able to take over the Tory leadership.

The spring and summer of 1940, in fact, was marked by an upsurge of democratic fervour and initiative in Britain that George Orwell, for example, hailed as 'revolutionary'.[44] (And he had seen revolution first hand in Spain, a few years before.) This unique period in our national life has all too often been brushed under the carpet. On the one hand, it is an obvious embarrassment to the ruling class. On the other hand, though, it is an equal embarrassment to the dominant representatives of the Left at that time, the Communist party, since after the Nazi-Soviet pact they were ordered to view the War as purely inter-imperialist, and actually worked to sabotage the defence effort. The most well-known mass initiative of the time was the Dunkirk evacuation, joined by several hundred civilian small craft and their crew. Yet the story of the Home Guard is equally striking, and involved far greater numbers; not without reason it is completely misrepresented today. It is quite false to see the Home Guard as simply a 'Dad's Army' of nostalgic veterans of the First World War, centred in the most benighted rural areas under the command of the local squirearchy. In actual fact the Home Guard started as a spontaneous mass movement, as news broke of the German invasion of the Netherlands. In the 24 hours after Anthony Eden, freshly appointed Minister of Defence, appealed on the radio for 'local defence volunteers' to combat possible German parachute landings, some 250,000 men (and unofficially a certain number of women; see below, p. 235) formed themselves into Home Guard units, and within a month this became a force of one million. The 'Home Guard spirit', as it was known, stood in complete contrast to the regular army, being from the start strongly democratic. The basis of Home Guard organization was the local community or workplace; it chose its own officers, and entire battalions were often formed on a factory basis. When the government failed to provide proper firearms, many Home Guard units improvised their own, and a favourite activity in the summer of 1940 was to set up road blocks and turn back the pleasure vehicles of the upper classes.

As a highpoint of this Home Guard spirit, an unauthorized Home Guard training school was set up in a West London suburb in direct opposition to War Office instructions, under the command of Tom Wintringham, who had led the British battalion of the International Brigade in Spain. In the political situation of the time, the Osterley Park school successfully resisted War Office orders for its closure, and taught weapons training and guerilla warfare to several thousand Home Guards, at which point the War Office had no option by to take the school over as a going concern, as the No. 1 School for Home Guard training.[45]

This is simply to illustrate how we have already experienced in Britain, once in the past, a shift in class relations within the framework of a radical consensus. In the face of the desperate crisis of those years, the privileged sections of British society were prepared, in their great majority, to accept substantial concessions to the working class so as to facilitate a united effort for national survival. The welfare state programme generally associated with the Labour government of 1945 was in fact mapped out already under the wartime Coalition, with the Beveridge report of 1943 and Butler's Education Act of 1944. William Beveridge, moreover, was a Liberal, and R.A. Butler a Conservative. The dynamic of this radical consensus can only be understood in terms of the location of class struggle within the wider context of a threat to the whole society. In no way was class struggle suspended for the duration of the War, as the Communist party wanted after Hitler's invasion of Russia. The Left could demand substantial reforms precisely because of the emergency situation, as these reforms were needed in the interest of a united national effort. And the ideas of socialism, which before 1940 had been confined to a relative minority, spread to a vastly increased audience in this political context.[46]

The radical consensus form of political change pioneered in the last War has been echoed more recently by those various movements of the post-War period that have sprung up in response to one or other symptom of the crisis of humanity. Among these, we can list the nuclear disarmament movement, a mass movement from 1957 to 1963, and becoming so again today; the movement in support of the South, which has been steadily growing from the early 1960s; the various environmentalist movements, each concerned with particular aspects of human ecology, but today increasingly dominated by the issue of nuclear power. In each of these cases, one of the most fundamental questions facing our planet is at issue. In each case, the problem and its solution do not divide our society into conflicting interests, but unite us by a common concern. And in each case, if the solution does require a tightening of belts, then those who have a higher material standard are prepared to make a correspondingly greater sacrifice.

This last fact is shown by the social base of these movements itself, which to date has been overwhelmingly middle-class. This fact, however, has precisely been used, in many quarters of the Left, to dismiss such movements as essentially marginal and irrelevant. But they are irrelevant only in terms of the orthodox Marxist paradigm of violent revolution; indeed, they get in the way by not taking a 'class stand' in defence of their particular privileges, thus muddying the waters and making proletarian mobilization more difficult. If the modality of change is that of radical consensus, however, then the strong middle-class involvement in these movements is precisely a healthy sign. Certainly no one can say that their concerns are irrelevant to the working class, who if anything have less compensation for the dangers of war, ecocide, etc. that threaten us all. Nor can the relatively weak participation of working-class people in the new movements be ascribed to the greater appeal of violent revolution, which seems to have just as predominant a middle-class base as do the new movements. A far better explanation, then, is that it is the middle classes, as always, who have more free time and energy to dwell on problems outside their immediate daily life, more 'surplus consciousness' in Rudolf Bahro's concept, and that this is why they are the first to respond to causes which involve the whole society in this way. But if this is the explanation, then the implication is that where the middle classes step today, the working class can tomorrow.

Tom Wintringham, a true pioneer in so many respects, also led the way in relating to middle-class radicalism of this kind as a Marxist. The political context of this was the Common Wealth movement, which sprang up as the major opposition force on the Left in the latter years of the War, i.e. after the Communist party had made a 180 degree turn following the Nazi invasion of Russia, and swung from 'all criticism, no unity' to 'all unity, no criticism' of the Churchill Coalition. The platform of Common Wealth centred on 'common ownership' of the means of production, the immediate implementation of the Beveridge report, and support for the resistance movements in Europe. It aroused considerable suspicion from the Communist party and Labour Left, being led by a baronet, Sir Richard Acland, and having a strong following in the Church of England (whose 1940 Malvern conference had also supported 'common ownership'). Acland's ideology was indeed eclectic and confused, and Wintringham, like other Marxists, recognized that Common Wealth was very much a middle-class movement. But by seeing it in the perspective of a radical consensus, his response was not to oppose it, but to work alongside Acland in order to guide Common Wealth into firm alliance with the working class. This effort culminated in the merger of the Common Wealth majority into the Labour Party in 1945.[47]

As I argued in Chapter Three, the crisis of humanity is manifested at the present time in two symptoms above all: the threat of nuclear war, and the expansion of nuclear energy production. The connections between the two, via the nuclear fuel cycle, are today blatantly apparent, as the efforts of increasing numbers of third-world governments to develop their own atomic weapons make nonsense of the former slogan of 'atoms for peace'. These are far from being the only symptoms of the crisis. The degradation of the biosphere in a number of ways, from pollution by heavy metals through to the extinction of rare (and even formerly common) species, is terrible enough; so, too, is the way that most people in the South have been left behind in the general progress of humanity. And in future, developments in genetic engineering and artificial intelligence may loom increasingly large as well. Yet the nuclear question today is *the* question of human survival. The risk here is not 'merely' the murder of some tens of millions of people, once again, to decide which form of class society will dominate the planet. It is that radioactive isotopes, indiscriminately scattered across the globe (whether as a by-product of bombs, or 'accidentally' in the course of energy production), may pollute the environment for thousands of years to come, as well as damaging our own gene pool, in a way that is virtually irreversible, and might, by preventing our species from further evolution, set in motion a downward spiral of decline.

The nuclear question is the hub of the matter, in the interconnected form of both nuclear weapons and nuclear power. The movements against its two aspects are today on the rise, and increasingly convergent. In its immediate appearance, the nuclear question is an environmental or ecological question. Yet through the connection of nuclear weapons with war in general, and of nuclear power with consumerism, the socialist and feminist perspectives can also find their way to link up with it. In the last analysis, it is only if the present system of class and gender is abolished on a planetary scale that the danger of radioactive pollution can be laid to rest, together with other symptoms of our crisis. For as long as war still exists, nuclear weapons might again be produced in the future. And as long as the class system still exists, there will still be the temptation to fob off the oppressed class with a 'rising standard of living' obtained at the price of environmental degradation, and nuclear power in particular. A communist movement that can integrate the socialist, feminist and ecological perspectives has therefore great potential for development, as public awareness of the nuclear danger grows.

When the crisis comes to a head, however, whether brought about by the imminent threat of war, or by a catastrophe in a nuclear power plant, this will find a small minority with an all-round communist consciousness, somewhat larger minorities with a radical socialist, feminist or ecological perspective, and a majority public opinion in favour of an immediate survival programme, which certain established politicians will support and articulate. This is the kind of conjuncture in which those of us who see ourselves as communists have to intervene, seeking to make as much progress as possible beyond the immediate needs of survival, precisely so that in dealing with the particular symptoms of crisis, we can also advance towards abolishing the system of class and gender that generates such symptoms.

If it is the issue of nuclear power that brings the crisis to a head, so that a survival programme starts from the phasing out of all fission power stations, then this will naturally have all kinds of implications. The total electrical energy generated in Britain would fall considerably, depending of course on the degree that reliance on nuclear power had reached. There would have to be a general tightening of belts; and even the most hidebound of socialists would demand that those with most inches of spare tyre should do the most tightening. A communist intervention, however, would seek to channel the anti-nuclear tide by further demands. This would be a most favourable conjuncture to press for the abandonment of nuclear weapons, and for stricter controls on conventional pollutants. And we might also demand that the sacrifice in living standards, which the working class will certainly have to share, should be compensated for by reforms of industrial organization that involved workers' participation in management, job rotation, provision of childcare facilities, etc., thus making life more pleasant in the workplace.

Abandonment of nuclear weapons and the American nuclear umbrella, which could be the starting-point of a survival programme to meet an imminent threat of war between the superpowers, might seem to have fewer repercussions on the general organization of our society; even if it would be a good time to remind people that catastrophe at a nuclear power station could be brought about in war purely by conventional bombardment.[48] However, the key reason why the Left has been so singularly unsuccessful in some twenty-five years of campaigning for nuclear disarmament is its reluctance to offer any constructive alternative defence policy to replace nuclear weapons. As I argued in Chapter Three, the ruling classes of Western Europe resorted to nuclear weapons, thirty years ago, at the price of putting themselves in thrall to the United States, because the Soviet threat had also an internal dimension, in the form of the pro-Soviet Communist parties, and they were reluctant to base national defence on a full popular mobilization.

Today, the situation has markedly changed. The appeal of the Soviet Union to the West European working class is greatly reduced, and yet the replacement of the nuclear deterrent by a more adequate conventional defence (necessarily a joint European one) would still involve a significant shift in social relations. Either it would require a larger regular army, inevitably a reactionary force in society as well as an economic burden; or else it would mean developing a territorial defence system such as is already practised in Sweden and Switzerland, with mass training in the use of arms.

Two things today hold the Left back from developing a positive alternative defence policy, even though this would greatly strengthen the movement against nuclear weapons and have a strongly democratizing effect on British society. One is the residual allegiance to the Soviet Union, still particularly strong in the generation who remember the War, and who are generally unable to accept that Soviet expansionism is anything other than defensive against the West. The other is the naive illusion that war is simply unthinkable today. This is particularly strong in the younger generation, those of us who have grown up under the shadow of the Bomb. But it is only nuclear weapons that make war unthinkable. Either you shelter behind the nuclear deterrent, thus actively contributing to the risk of ultimate calamity for humankind. Or you abandon nuclear weapons, and have to face the fact that we live in a world where armed invasion is still a real threat.

War cannot be abolished, unfortunately, simply by those opposed to it refusing to play. The lesson we learned from Hitler and his ilk was that failure to resist aggression only encourages aggression to spread, and in its wake the most hideously reactionary and repressive regimes. As long as there are states, such as the Soviet Union in Europe today, that are prepared to use machine-guns and tanks to hold down other nations, then those of us who want to protect such freedom as we have, and steadily expand this into the greater freedom of communism, must take the question of defence very seriously.

If we succeed in bringing about unilateral nuclear disarm-ament, and in replacing the American connection by a purely European defence cooperation, then we shall no longer present any conceivable military threat to the Soviet Union, and will be able to tell whether the Soviet rulers really do have no aggressive intentions towards the West. If they do not, it should at last be possible for a process of 'mutual and balanced force reduction' to get under way; we shall at least have done all we can do towards this on our side. If the Soviet Union does intend to maintain an offensive capacity, however, as a possible instrument of pressure on Western Europe, then we shall be forced to become a 'tough piece of meat', as the Chinese on the other frontier of the Soviet empire like to describe themselves.

At the present time, there is increasing realization in the nuclear disarmament movement that an alternative defence policy is needed if we are to win over majority opinion.[49] One possible option is that of non-violent resistance, as was practised to some effect by the Danes against the Nazi occupation of 1940-45. Denmark, however, is small and indefensible, and could rely on its much larger allies to do its fighting for it. My own belief is that resistance to aggres-sion generally involves less slaughter than the task of throwing off an invader who is already well entrenched, and as I shall argue in the next section, this is also quite compatible with the contribution that gay men and women must make to the abolition of war in general.

Socialists have always argued that, if the military func-tion is needed, it should be shared out in society as far as possible. This is the best way to ensure that the army is not used against the democratic process, or in aggression against another people.[50] If we are to abandon a 'defence' based on the threat to use weapons of mass destruction against the civilian population of Leningrad and Kiev, we should also demand that the forces which we must then rely on for the genuine defence of our country should be democratized, both in their internal organization and by combining a relatively small professional force with a very large territorial militia. The Swiss example shows the way here. Switzerland has only 3,500 professional soldiers for a population of 6½ million, yet the Swiss army's strength on mobilization is 625,000, and it has a fair reputation in military circles. This is achieved by compulsory basic training (for men only) of 17 weeks, followed by 3 weeks refresher training for 8 out of 12 subsequent years, and occasional reserve duty for some time beyond. If the armed forces were open to women on an equal basis, then it would be possible for the present regular army to be replaced by a territorial system basically along Swiss lines, while still providing full facilities for conscientious objection. In a professional core that could then be much reduced from its present level of 160,000 (not including air force and navy), there would no longer be any need to supplement highly skilled technicians with young men of low educational level who are promised good pay and conditions in exchange for obeying orders and not asking awkward questions.[51]

## 4. *The Gay Contribution*

Gay men are oppressed because we deviate from the norms of the gender system. We are perceived as 'effeminate', i.e. insufficiently masculine. What this basically means, as I explained in Chapter Two, is that we have failed to repress the maternal culture within ourselves and to develop the masculine culture of violence. Our homosexuality, which we arrive at by more than one route, is a particular symptom of our deviance at the level of gender. We do indeed share this deeper deviance with a proportion of heterosexual men. But whereas their practice of heterosexuality induces them to continue the road of masculinization, our practice of homosexuality has the opposite effect, consolidating our deviance. And in the context of the gay movement, our pride in our gayness leads us to throw off still more of the masculinity we have internalized and to 'be what gay is'.

The gay movement has two great common denominators, which are shared by all tendencies however much they may differ on everything else. It always insists on the *right to be gay* and on *gay pride*: the first aimed at the outside world, the second at changing our own consciousness. Every individual act of coming out, every small victory against repressive legislation, educational content, medical practices etc. advances our struggle on this double front. But the right to be gay, in our society, means the right to be effeminate. This is what we are, relative to the masculine norm, and this is what everyone, gay or straight, knows in their heart, even when they pretend to the contrary. Gay pride, accordingly, means pride in being effeminate. Every step forward by the gay movement is a blow against the norm of masculinity.

In this struggle, the gay movement links up with other forces at work among men today, in a synergetic relationship of mutual support, even if this takes time to recognize. In particular, this means the movement of (heterosexual) men against sexism. For all men, the norm of masculinity means a degree of self-oppression, even if this is far greater for some than for others, and there are different and even conflicting responses to it (e.g. the queer-basher and the soft heterosexual). If the characteristic self-oppression of the queer-basher is a pretty hard nut to crack, we can at least make a start on breaking down those forms of self-oppression, not so distant from queer-bashing, within our own ranks. The more firmly we come to understand our effeminacy as a source of pride, the less need we feel to try and pass as a 'proper' — even though homosexual — man, both in the sense of actual concealment, and in the sense of suppressing the maternal culture within ourselves. The advance of the gay cause aids us to drop this futile striving to keep a foothold in the camp of masculine respectability, which in turn feeds back to make the gay movement more explicitly a movement of effeminate men. On the other hand, a parallel process at work in the movement of men against sexism aids them to drop their inhibitions towards their own gay feelings, and experience the 'de-masculinizing' effects of a gay relationship. And finally, the advance of the gay movement must also have an effect on winning the most effeminate gay men away from the futile course of transsexualism, to which the medical profession encourages them in the interest of shoring up the gender system.[52]

In this perspective, we can see the divisions between gay and straight eventually breaking down, precisely to the extent that the movements of gay men and men against sexism succeed in undermining the norm of masculinity. However far in the future this lies, we should always bear it in mind as a goal. But because straight, by definition, means consonant with the gender system, the ground on which we shall gradually converge with our heterosexual brothers is on our side of the fence. If they are serious about undermining masculinity, then they must accept the fact of their own deviance as defined by the existing order, and as long as they resist the idea (and the reality) of homosexuality, we can only see this as a deep-seated allegiance to the masculine gender that belies their professions of anti-sexism.[53]

We, for our part, refuse to accept that we are permanently set apart as a minority. This is a static view of the situation; viewed dynamically, we are the thin end of a wedge. It is interesting to recall how at the turn of the century the estimate of one homosexual man in 200 was seen as amazingly high.[54] Fifty years later, Kinsey concluded that one man in twenty was what we would term gay. After only ten years of the modern gay liberation movement, this figure again seems far too low. Coming out is a continuous process, and the more we attack the taboo on effeminacy and homosexuality, the more our numbers will grow. But just as the concept of gay or homosexual, as a deviant minority, only came into being at a certain point in historical development, so we can already anticipate the time when the dichotomy between gay and straight will give way to something else.

Gayness is the wedge that splits open the gender system, in which feminine women and masculine men fit together in the sexual division of labour: a double wedge in fact, as the rejection of heterosexuality and all it implies proceeds in parallel among both women and men. In this sense, it is by no means ridiculous to speak of a 'gay revolution', like the short-lived Gay Revolution Party of New York in 1971.[55]

Nor is it simply 'gay chauvinism' to say, as GLF said in Britain too, that gay is better than straight.[56] All that is wrong here is that gay is simply the immediate next step, not the final goal. 'Gay shows the way', as the London GLF *Manifesto* put it, and gayness is a tremendous force against the gender system. But as more and more people follow our lead and the gender system crumbles, we shall have to redefine ourselves, no longer as a deviant minority but as the new majority, able to relate among ourselves both within and across the biological division of sex, and having only pity for the stubborn minority who still cling for a while to the traditional faith.

The gender division of masculine and feminine, as manifested in individual psychology, expresses the sexual division of labour in society, in which women have always specialized in childcare, and men, after first specializing in hunting animals, went on to practise violence against other human beings in warfare. If gay liberation, in the full sense of the abolition of gender, is now conceivable for the first time in history, it is because this sexual division of labour has ceased to be necessary and become an obstacle to human progress, even to human survival. War must be abolished, and this means also the permanent state of war that a ruling class exercises against an oppressed class, a ruling nation against an oppressed nation, and that men collectively exercise against women. In place of violence as the organizing principle of social relations, we must put love. The relative democratization we have seen this century in the Western world, in relations between nations, between classes, and between women and men, is the first step in this direction, and it is indeed necessary to defend the real gains made. But there is still a very long way to go within our own societies, not to mention the reordering of relations between West and East, and between North and South.

As the gender system is the underlying support or substructure for the whole system of class relations, providing the violent masculine personality that is required for all forms of domination, it is not just women and gay men who have an interest in abolishing it. So do the oppressed class in our society, and oppressed peoples at the international level.

And since a new world war would jeopardize the whole future of our species, this interest is ultimately a universal one. Yet it is women and gay men who are directly oppressed by the gender system, and whose perception of this aspect of social relations is accordingly most acute. The struggle against gender is therefore our appropriate contribution to the overall struggle for communism. And gay men have a special role to play within this, as a fifth column within the masculine camp.

How can we best contribute to the abolition of war? Women are generally not called upon to play a military role, and neither are those men who are out as gay. The most immediate tactic that comes to mind is that women should staunchly maintain their opposition to this 'male game', and gay men should undermine the recruitment of soldiers both by spreading homosexuality and by coming out. In the early days of gay liberation in the United States, one slogan ran: 'Suck cock, beat the draft!'

In struggling against an imperialist war machine such as the United States unleashed on Indochina, this tactic was unquestionably correct. But what if you were a feminist or gay liberationist in Vietnam? The photos of diminutive Vietnamese peasant women leading massive GIs at rifle point captured the whole essence of a struggle for national liberation. Some American feminists argued that Vietnamese women, by taking up arms against the United States and its puppet regime, were simply exchanging one set of oppressors for another. Vietnamese feminists, however, thought otherwise, and so no doubt would their American sisters if a similar fate ever befell them.

The violent masculine personality is the psychological aspect of a division of labour that ascribes men the task of fighting. But the relation between the two levels is a dialectical one. Just as there are some men in whom this personality is not properly established, so conversely it is possible for even the least violent of people, men or women, to learn the military art and to practise it, at least in a situation of genuine defence. The traditional argument for democratization of the armed forces can be extended in the feminist perspective. For the only army that can mobilize large numbers of women for a combatant role is an army whose task is a genuine defence of 'hearth and home'. An army in which women can play a full part is already an army that is deeply committed to peace, to the abolition of war; an army with a built-in contradiction between the military function and the mentality that has traditionally been the support of this; an army whose anger at the aggressor is not a channel for pent-up masculine violence, but is tempered by sorrow and compassion. Something of this is always to be seen in the armies of smaller or weaker countries defending themselves against an invader.[57] It goes without saying, moreover, that the participation of women in the armed forces makes a significant contribution towards freeing them from domination by men, and this is testified to by all those countries today in which women receive military training, even if only in a secondary militia role, from China to Israel.

Just as much as women, gay men typically find warfare repulsive. It is a terrible thing to contemplate using a machine-gun against the beautiful young men in the aggressor army. Christopher Isherwood, for example, has specifically argued the case for pacifism on this basis.[58] But if you say, as he did, I refuse to kill another human being in any circumstance, then you abandon the ground of political debate, the ultimate criterion of which must be what is best for human society as a whole.

I was in my teens when national service was abolished in 1958, and along with other gay men of my generation heaved a sigh of relief. But the experience of the last two decades has scarcely been that this has weakened the culture of violent masculinity. On the contrary, these years have seen an escalation in the practice of violence, particularly arising out of the frustrations of underprivileged adolescents, yet expressed not just in gang warfare among themselves (let alone attacks on their oppressors), but equally against old people (mugging), women (rape) and gay men (queer-bashing). One aspect of the present situation, in fact, is a contradiction between the unmitigated culture of masculine violence in which boys grow up (especially the glorification of butchery on tv) and the relative de-institutionalization of violence in our society. Maybe there is a certain vague recognition of this problem by those who say 'they should bring back national service' (and these include working-class women as well as *Daily Telegraph* readers) as an answer to the rise in crimes of violence. A democratically organized militia system open to both sexes might well provide a certain framework of *self*-discipline.

Together with the participation of women in the military, it would be quite feasible to demand not merely that homosexuality in the forces should cease to be both grounds for discharge and a criminal offence, but that gay men should be integrated into the forces in an up-front way, being positively encouraged to come out and defended against persecution just as is our right in any other situation. In the ranks, the queer-bashing mentality can still be particularly oppressive, as shown by the suicide of a gay soldier after bullying by his comrades reported in the press in August 1980: by no means the first of its kind. Just as in all other fields, in the forces too gay men should be able to *be ourselves*. And by showing that an effeminate gay man, or a woman, can also be a good soldier (in the double sense of good at the military art, and a defender rather than an aggressor), progress would be made towards breaking down the connection between the military function and the mentality of violent masculinity, as a step on the way towards the abolition of both war and the warrior altogether. Precisely in that field of 'manly activity' where we feel least at home, gay men have an important role to play.

Our relationship to the feminine specialization in the sexual division of labour, i.e. childcare, is of a completely different order to our relationship to the masculine specialization of warfare. War is an unqualified evil, and today humanity can at last prepare for its abolition. Our intervention in the military task is at most a temporary necessity designed to help hasten the end of this dreadful business altogether. Childcare, on the other hand, is a permanent requirement of human society, and it will play an even more important part under communism. In this field, the specialization that has up till now been allotted to one sex has rather to be redistributed to involve both sexes equally.

I referred in Chapter Two (p. 103) to the exclusion of gay men from childcare as an aspect of our oppression. Indeed, while the gender division is at least softening sufficiently to allow an increasing number of heterosexual men to play a part in the maternal function, if still almost always a secondary one, gay men, though better equipped for this than most heterosexual men, are precisely excluded. The reproduction of the gender system requires each heterosexual couple to bring up 'their' children as if they were its private property. Gay men even have great difficulty in being permitted to adopt the large number of children who desperately need parents. If a certain ideology in recent years has perceived it as something positive that the 'gay lifestyle' is unfettered by 'breeding', I see this as simply a false consciousness of adaptation to our present oppressed and marginalized position. Lack of any common work, such as caring for children provides, has a lot to do with the difficulties experienced in maintaining meaningful relationships, monogamous or otherwise, which is one of the main causes of gay unhappiness.

In the last few years, the rights of lesbian mothers have been a major front of the anti-gender struggle, but the next generation of children need gay men as parents too. Not just as 'role models' for a gay minority seen as permanently set apart from the mainstream. But precisely as a major intervention towards the erosion of the gender system, helping to end the enforced masculinization of young boys, and allow them to retain their share of the maternal culture that is so essential to humanity.

It was one of the greatest contributions of GLF to the gay movement, and to the communist movement in general, to say:

> We intend to work for the replacement of the family unit with its rigid gender-role pattern by new organic units such as the commune, where the development of children becomes the shared responsibility of a larger group of people who live together...We intend to start working out our contribution to these new [gender-free] models now, by creating an alternative gay culture free from sexism, and by setting up gay communes. When our communes are firmly established, we plan to let children grow up in them.[59]

This alternative to the existing gay male subculture is

essential to our own salvation here and now, and I am convinced that the lack of fulfilment to be gleaned in the gay ghettos of our cities today, after ten years of 'gay liberation', will lead sooner or later to a new wave of gay radicalism.

Those of us who refuse to fit the categories of gender, who dissolve the barriers by making ourselves out of a bit of feminine here, a bit of masculine there, cannot but be incomprehensible from the standpoint of the gender sytem, which is so deeply rooted in normal personal identity. Our deviance, of course, works both ways. The straight world seems just as ridiculous to us as we seem to it.

The problem was that we were very much a minority, and could see no way things could be otherwise. We were subject not just to incomprehension, but to the day-to-day repressive action of the ideological apparatus, to queer-bashing in its hundred and one guises, let alone the sporadic pogroms that devastated our ranks. As one of our defences, we invented camp.

Camp is not just a device anyone can use to deflect hostility. The particular way it does this is based on the volatile relationship between the gender system and its deviants. We are not what we seem from the normal standpoint to be. Being male, we are taken as men like any others, but we turn out to be as much feminine as masculine. By using drag, we externalize the 'woman' within and cause a new level of illusion; the person who appears as a woman is really a male, even though a male who is not a proper man. In the GLF practice of radical drag or 'gender-fuck', both our femininity and masculinity could be externalized simultaneously. At the same time as we produced the illusion, we proclaimed it to be just an illusion, still leaving the real mystery of our being intangible.

Camp originated as a way of taking this gap between appearance and reality and playing it so as to deflect the hostility we arouse. It said to the outside world that, precisely because we were not what we seemed, we need not be taken seriously. We were really just children still, playing our little games. It proposed a new division of labour: we'd leave to the straight majority the serious things of life — earning a living, bringing up children, defending the country, not to mention science and philosophy — if they would leave us the tiny space on the margins that we needed for our harmless frivolity.

How could we have done anything else? Our gayness automatically sets us outside the family, and a society built around the family unit. We could offer no alternative principle of social organization, and could only seek tolerance for a marginal existence on the sidelines of history. Yet the traditional seriousness of the straight world, however necessary, was as one-sided as the frivolity it expelled and left us to represent. Isn't this itself an aspect of the gender system, the drive of the masculine ego to impose itself and its principles on the world in an ultimately undialectical way? However serious the problems facing Earth today, doesn't the particular gay sensibility that could not be tolerated in the past also have something special to offer, in a new synthesis of seriousness with gay frivolity?

Lost souls, deprived of a place or even a definition in society, we have time and again plumbed the very depths of despair, the secret inwardness of our outward revels. Unfettered by the meanings that the straight world gave to its strivings, we came face to face with the ultimate hollowness of all things. The frivolity of camp hid the meaninglessness we could feel inside. Suicide was so often the most honest way out.

Today all this is radically changed. The gender system is in crisis, and our species can only survive if we manage to reorganize our society along non-gendered lines. Suddenly the gay minority find ourselves with a part to play in serious affairs, and no unimportant part at that. Instead of the self-mocking defences of camp we develop an entirely new gay pride. We demand our way back into society, to make our particular contribution to the mainstream.

On our horizon today is the vision of liberation. Freeing our heads from the ideology of oppression, we have moved from stubborn resistance to exploring new needs. No longer accepting society's definition of us as perverted, we have come to understand that it is society that is perverted and needs our help. The abolition of gender is not just a requirement of gay liberation, but of human liberation in general.

And the abolition of gender will involve, among other things, returning to society the peculiar sense of the absurdity of it all that it led us to cultivate, in our own one-sided way, while the straight world was cultivating its seriousness.

The suicidal conflict between the two superpowers, each imagining it can impose its particular pattern of civilization on the planet by brute force, shows very clearly the crucial need for a higher camp. Humanity can only survive if those who claim to have something to offer can offer it in the humility of knowing that no new principle of civilization is anything more than a new mask for consciousness, a disguise that has no more tangible substance to it than the sequins and eyelashes of the drag queen, or the masks of Astoreth, Apollo or Jahweh in which our ancestors believed they saw an ultimate reality. The ultimate reality of the consciousness that guides us is precisely a non-reality, not in the sense that the stuff of consciousness, the vibration, the field of force, does not exist (or there would be nothing to be non-conscious of), but in the sense that any pattern it is given captures merely a fleeting moment of the infinite flux, before melting away in an ironic parody of itself.

It is this higher camp that our species desperately needs. Our planet is too small now for us to erect new gods to rule us in place of the old crumbling ones, even the latest of false gods — Humanity. Instead of an ultimate meaning, consciousness offers us simply the ultimate game — a never-ending game — advancing in an infinite paradox of contradictions. And once we look at things in this way, we might be equipped to face the task of organizing the material side of life rather more successfully: cherishing the biological base that offers us access to the infinite, as something both to protect and to develop.

The stakes involved in the future course of the gay movement are high ones, because our particular movement is indeed a strand in the general movement for communism. If we become conscious of this connection with the totality and allow it to guide our own struggles, then the predictions of Edward Carpenter, more than seventy years ago, may yet come true:

It is possible that the Uranian spirit may lead to something like a general enthusiasm of Humanity, and that the Uranian people may be destined to form the advance guard of that great movement which will one day transform the common life by substituting the bond of personal affection and compassion for the monetary, legal and other external ties which now control and confine society.[60]

# Afterword:
## Beyond Communism

> I will only, in conclusion, say that in this
> view Creation is a stupendous and perpet-
> ually renewed work of Art, an everlasting
> evolution and expression of inner mean-
> ings into outer form, not only in the great
> whole, but in every tiniest part; Nature is
> a great vehicle, an innumerable network
> and channel of intelligence and emotion;
> and this whole domain of the universe the
> theatre of an immense interchange of
> conscious life.
>
> EDWARD CARPENTER[1]

Communism is the name we give to a society organized
according to the principles of reason. Not a reason represented by a minority of philosophers, whose ideal societies
cannot avoid reflecting the division of labour between those
who 'know' and those who do not. But that reason which is
the common possession of all human beings. If anything, in
fact, it is those who are not privileged, having no special
access to education, who understand best that the good
society can only be based on equality. Equality not in the
sense of everyone being 'the same', as anti-communists
charge, but rather that of an equal claim to happiness, and to
the material and cultural wherewithal that is a precondition
for happiness. This equality is the expression of love, it is
the only way love can prevail. And all of us whose minds are
not too distorted by a jealous concern for our privilege, or an

abject adaptation to oppression, know that love is better than hate, and the only way we can be happy.

Twenty thousand years ago, the terrible ignorance of our ancestors led them to create a universe full of evil spirits, and live in fear of their own creations. Yet even so, the claims of human happiness were better recognized than in most of the intervening period. The rise of warfare, of the gender system, the state, class and private property, was the price we paid for accelerating our development, heading towards the point at which humanity as a whole, united into a single planetary society, enlightened by science and with unprecedented power to rearrange and improve our material environment, can establish a society free from both the ignorance of the primitive world, and the oppression of the intervening period.

The very forces of scientific technology that make communism possible, however, give us the potential for self-destruction, at a point when we still have to resolve the divisions between nations, between classes, and between the sexes. We are so near to the good society, but at the same time so terribly far. We may stretch out our hand from the present quicksand and pull ourselves onto firm ground; or the gap may prove too great and we sink down forever. It is impossible to say, at this time of writing, which way things will turn out. Even if we avoid the disaster that has in the last thirty years become possible at any time, it is unlikely we shall be over the hump, at least reaching a 'lower stage of communism', in the lifetime of anyone who reads this book. We have the choice, therefore, between despair, or a struggle inspired by hope.[2]

In so many of my contemporaries I have seen despair enter and consume the soul, whether it leads to heroin or hare krishna. For those of us outside the mainstream of society, the choice is posed with particular starkness. We cannot merely plod along, pretending nothing exists outside our own four walls, our nine-to-five job, our little hobbies or our parochial island home. We are more inclined to raise our eyes to the horizon, but in terror at what is to be seen there we are also more likely to fall.

My own particular inspiration has always been the search for knowledge. Yet after trying hard for three decades to find the causes of things, it's rather what I don't know that seems to expand every year. Hope can certainly not be based simply on conquering the universe with theory, a goal that now strikes me as more than a little megalomaniac. No matter how far the frontiers of human knowledge are extended, at that point there is always an abyss, a great nothing, which knowledge can never cross.

On a clear night we can see with the naked eye galaxies that are not a few feet above our heads, as our ancestors used to think, but a trillion miles away and a billion years back in time. Every few years, moreover, the hypotheses of cosmology undergo yet a further radical change, from steady state to big bang, then to the big bang itself as 'white gusher' to a black hole, then to the possibility of plural universes, and so on. We do not know, we shall never know, whether the six veils we have lifted are six out of six, six out of seven, six out of a million, or six out of an infinity. All we know, at the edge of all our knowledge, is that there is still this abyss ahead.

Yet to turn away from knowledge is to turn directly into despair. For there are things that we do know, and that our science has established relatively firmly in the last few decades. We can locate ourselves in a three-tier system of evolution: the evolution of the physical universe, from big bang through to the formation of galaxies, stars, ultimately planets; the evolution of life, from the first macromolecules, up through the viruses and single-celled organisms, to the mammalian world and homo sapiens; and that other, peculiarly human evolution, for which the right word is often hard to find: society? production? consciousness?[3]

Marxism has been so important in my own intellectual development that I must once again take it as a point of reference. There is no doubt in my mind that our developing metabolism with our natural environment, as mediated by production, is the guiding thread that has brought us from the first proto-humans, through the gatherers and hunters, agriculture and class society, up to the rise of scientific technology. Yet isn't this just a means to an end? The point of communism, after all, is not more efficient production but human happiness. And happiness isn't just a question of enough to eat, a comfortable home, good sex, etc. as the utilitarians maintain. Once the needs of the body are satisfied, it's the claims of the spirit that start to dominate.

Spirit? — or shouldn't I say 'brain'? For there's no doubt that the brain is the biological organ involved. Yet there is this thing called 'consciousness', meaning that after the processes of the human brain have been described, as you might describe those of a computer, there's something irreducible left over, i.e. what all this *feels* like, whether it's the input through our senses, our emotional state, or the processes of reasoning and imagination that seem to need no precipitating factor outside the brain itself. However epiphenomenal this appears from the conventional standpoint of physical (including biological) science, from the human standpoint it is all that matters. For nothing in the universe matters except in so far as it affects, either actually or potentially, the consciousness of conscious beings.

'Sentience' is in some ways a better word than 'consciousness'. There is no doubt that the higher animals, for example, feel. A worm or a fly may feel as well, even if it beggars our imagination to even try and conceive what their feelings might be like. This is the reason why we should do everything we can to avoid cruelty to animals. 'Sentience' is the category of Buddhism, in this respect far more scientific (if that term can be used here) than Christianity, which seeks to divide living beings rigidly into those that have souls and those that do not. Yet the evolving side of human sentience is not the side that we share with the animals. Bodily happiness, for an animal, is all-important. The very idea of spiritual happiness for an animal is, I believe, quite inappropriate.[4] This is where our cerebral cortex distinguishes us, and as it is this side of sentience I am particularly concerned with here, I shall stick to the term 'consciousness'.

Standing at the present make-or-break point in human history, we can see ourselves as almost absolute beginners in the evolution of consciousness. In our Western civilization, this is still terribly restricted by our childish inability to manage our bodies in a reasonable way. In the civilizations of Asia, where the spiritual disciplines have been far more developed, they are held back by the underdevelopment of science. In both East and West, consciousness is distorted by the division of labour, which reduces the majority to servants of the more conscious few, by the gender system, and by the division of our planet into separate and conflicting societies. And given an untold number of planets on which life might exist, it would be a similar arrogance to that of Ptolemaic astronomy to see our own as more than one of millions where intelligent life has developed. By that very token, it is most unlikely to be among the pioneers.

Yet these so necessary lessons in modesty are themselves a sign of increased awareness. They enable us to ask the question 'what is our consciousness part of?' in a new and unprecedented way, to see the evolution of human consciousness as part of an overall evolutionary process, an essential dimension of the evolving universe. Physicists may see the existence of life and consciousness, on one planet or a million, as merely contingent. Seeking to grasp the process as a totality, however, it seems scarcely conceivable that such a principle as consciousness, totally *other* than the physical world that is its necessary base, should exist, and most probably scattered here and there throughout the physical universe, unless it played some fundamental part in the pattern of the universe as a whole. If this seems idealist from the conventional point of view, this point of view simply stems from a certain empire-building tendency in physics, which because of its rapid and early success foolishly claims to possess the ultimate truth about the universe. We need only to look within ourselves for a moment to know this is a lie, and today it is increasingly being recognized as such, even among physicists themselves. We feel! We are sentient beings! We share a developing consciousness! And this side of the universe, this 'inside' to the physical world's 'outside', demands to be taken into account.

Nikita Khrushchev showed his one endearing feature, a certain closeness to his native soil, by remarking that Soviet cosmonauts had gone up into space and found there was no God. But it is undeniable that the Christian God, and more than the Christian for that matter, has been made untenable by the scientific advances of the last few hundred years, so that he has either to be jettisonned altogether, or transformed until he bears no recognizable similarities to God the father of Jesus. He is forbidden to interfere in physical processes (no more miracles!), he must no longer have his portrait painted, and most recently his grey beard has been torn away and his sex changed from male to female.

Yet Buddhism, and even the Christian Gnostics,[5] understood long before modern anthropology that we humans make gods in our own image. And unlike the humanists of today, they did not set out to erect Man (or even Woman) in place of the God-father. At a certain level of consciousness, which we are belatedly beginning to catch up with in the West, it becomes clear that the divine principle is already within us, indeed that it is nowhere else.

Even the great spiritual teachers of Asia, however, who understood the divine as a wider kind of consciousness of which each individual consciousness is part, remained stuck in a static conception of the universe. The spiritual quest necessarily takes a different tack once we have learned that beings much like ourselves exist scattered throughout the universe, having evolved, like we have, as part of the evolution of matter, life and consciousness as a whole, yet with most probably a few million years' experience also of the kind of deliberately planned evolution that our own planet is just about able to conceive of, but not yet able to undertake.

The 'web of consciousness', then, that all these myriad points compose, has a structure very different from that seen for example by Buddhism, and an evolving structure at that. Anything more, we shall only begin to comprehend if we are able to link up into this universal consciousness for ourselves. And I sense that the precondition for this is not to send rockets to the stars, or to cross the universe through a black hole,[6] but rather for the human species, organized as a communist society, to pursue — among its other activities — a kind of collective meditation. Even keeping our radio ears open for signals from other life forms, I suspect, will fail to produce the desired results. Who in their right mind would want to link up with us? Wouldn't they rather wait to see whether our planet can make it, whether our evolutionary path is a through-way and not a dead end, before extending the helping hand that might eventually be forthcoming?

Humanity is the arrow, not the target, in a metaphor from Teilhard de Chardin.[7] For all the criticisms that may be made of Teilhard's writings, I believe his concept of convergence is immensely fruitful, expressing the insight that our species, once conscious of its evolution, will steer ourselves towards that 'omega point' of transcendence which we can see as our necessary goal. If this is a convergence with the divine, the only divinity I can comprehend in it is the great web of consciousness itself, as it wraps the material world in its sentient folds. Yet how do we know that once we manage to link into this level of the evolutionary process, to shift our standpoint from that of our own planet to that of the universe as a whole, the very relationship between consciousness and its material base may not prove very different from how it seems today, with this matter being, after all, merely the raw material out of which consciousness makes itself?

# Notes

## Notes to Preface

1. Mao Zedong, 'On Practice' (1937), *Selected Readings from the Works of Mao Tse-tung* (Peking, 1971), p. 81. (Translation modified.)
2. Bertold Brecht, 'Praise of Communism', translation from a poster.
3. See Aubrey Walter's Introduction to *Come Together: the years of gay liberation (1970-73)* (London: Gay Men's Press, 1980).
4. After Mao Zedong's death and the fall of the 'gang of four', this was listed among the towering crimes of Jiang Qing, Mao's comrade and partner for almost forty years.
5. As in my Introduction to Karl Marx, *The First International and After* (London: Penguin, 1974), pp. 56 and 69.
6. See my article 'Ten Years of Gay Liberation', *Politics and Power 2* (London: Routledge, 1980), pp. 187-88, where I quoted an example of this difficulty from *Gay Left*.
7. Quoted from Rudolf Bahro, *The Alternative in Eastern Europe* (London: New Left Books, 1978), p. 364.

## Notes to Chapter One

1. See for example Lynda Birke and Sandy Best, 'The Tyrannical Womb: Menstruation and Menopause', and Janet Sayers, 'Psychological Sex Differences', in Brighton Women and Science Group, *Alice Throught the Microscope* (London: Virago, 1980).
2. See below, Chapter Two, pp. 68-69.
3. In particular, all reference to the abolition of the family is deleted in the current (1979) reprint. See Chapter Four, p. 204.
4. It might seem particularly surprising that the biological reductionist variant of feminism ever gained a certain currency,

given that it classes both gay men and straight as indifferently part of the enemy. The New York 'effeminists' of the early 1970s, led by Kenneth Pitchford, actually maintained that the revolutionary movement of women would in due course violently eliminate the male sex. Gay men, however, or at least the effeminist ideologists who supported this process, would be spared until last. Is there anywhere else in the world where such a paranoid philosophy could have been taken seriously?

5. See in particular Mary Daly, *Gyn/Ecology* (London: Women's Press, 1980). The middle chapters dealing with foot-binding, suttee, clitoridectomy, etc. are more impressive than the 'meta-ethics of radical feminism' with which the book starts and finishes.

6. See for example Peter Farb, *Man's Rise to Civilization* (London: Paladin, 1971).

7. The 'myth of matriarchy' was criticized very succinctly by a group of American feminist anthropologists in the early years of the present women's movement: *Women's Liberation: An Anthropological View* (Pittsburgh, 1971). But like all myths, it dies hard.

8. See Fanina Halle, *Woman in Soviet Russia* (London, 1933), pp. 394-96.

9. This preference to avoid conflict, on the assumption that land is unlimited, greatly facilitated the settlement of European colonists in the New World. Time and again, the indigenous peoples only realized the need to make a stand when it was already too late.

10. See for example Ashley Montagu (ed.), *Learning Non-Aggression* (London: OUP, 1978). Rather than 'aggression', I have preferred to reserve the term 'violence' for the deliberate dehumanization of other human beings as originally involved in warfare, later and somewhat more subtly in the practices of priesthoods, bureaucracies and exploiting classes in general. For those in the front line of oppression, i.e. soldiers, violence requires a hypertrophy of aggression, but aggression in itself is a necessary component of all animal existence, giving emotional encouragement to self-assertion. Violence, on the other hand, can also be separated from aggression. But even with those who practise oppression coolly and calmly, from a palace, a business office or a general headquarters, this still requires a mentality which rejects any human empathy and in this sense is equally violent.

11. See for example Laurel Holliday, *The Violent Sex* (Bluestocking: Guerneville, Ca., 1978).

12. I have stressed how the masculine specialization in warfare has very different effects from the much earlier specialization in hunting. In an age when we need no longer kill animals for food, and are learning to appreciate our common heritage with them, it may be tempting to flatten this difference between killing human beings and killing other animals. But the argument that violence is coterminous with males as a sex cannot be re-established in this

way. For in gathering/hunting societies, the gathering that women perform equally includes the killing of animals, albeit the smaller and more defenceless ones that you can 'gather' and kill even with a baby on your back.

13. See Peter Farb, op. cit., pp. 133 ff.

14. The 'broad spectrum' adaptation is transitional in this respect too. The Northwest Coast Indians, for example, have an elaborate hierarchy based on success in warfare, yet at the same time, all warriors of appropriate age still take part in hunting and other productive activities.

15. In exceptional cases, even agriculturalists do have somewhere to run to, e.g. in the European colonies. Marx relates in Chapter 33 of *Capital* Volume 1 ('The Modern Theory of Colonization') how a certain Mr Peel, an English capitalist, paid £50,000 (in the early 19th century!) to transport 3,000 workers and their equipment to Western Australia, but arriving at his destination, found himself left without even a servant to fetch his water. 'Unhappy Mr Peel, who provided for everything except the export of English relations of production to Swan River!' (London: Penguin, 1976, p. 933). What Marx omits to point out, writing as he did from the standpoint of the European working class, is that in one crucial respect 'English relations of production' were very much exported to Australia, the English colonists substituting agriculture for gathering/hunting, and expropriating the land from the indigenous peoples. In the long run, moreover, agricultural land was not unlimited even in Australia, and capitalist relations developed there too, even if in an attenuated form compared with 19th century England.

16. Karl Marx, 'The German Ideology', *Collected Works*, Vol. 5 (London: Lawrence & Wishart, 1976), p. 31. Marx's emphasis.

17. Quoted in F. Engels, *The Origin of the Family, Private Property and the State* (London: Lawrence & Wishart, 1972), p. 237.

18. Karl Marx, *The Revolutions of 1848* (London: Penguin, 1973), p. 67. In the 1888 edition, Engels added a correction here, referring to the discovery of primitive communism.

19. The title given this book by its English publishers, *The Alternative in Eastern Europe* (London: New Left Books, 1978), unfortunately suggests that Bahro's arguments are not directly relevant to the West. But as the book's original title indicates, Bahro has very much to say that bears on the problems of the advance towards communism on the planetary scale, and by no means excluding the particular problems of Western Europe. As soon as he was expelled from East to West Germany, Bahro knew immediately where in the political spectrum he wanted to work, i.e. for the development of a socialist tendency within the *Grünen* — the ecology party.

20. *The Origin of the Family*, loc. cit., p. 230.

21. Marx speaks here of the '*distribution*, and indeed the *unequal* distribution, both quantitative and qualitative, of labour and its products' (his emphases). 'Division of labour and private property are, after all, identical expressions: in the one the same thing is affirmed with reference to activity as is affirmed in the other with reference to the product of the activity.' Moreover, Marx maintains that the first form of this division 'lies in the family, where wife and children are the slaves of the husband' (*Collected Works*, Vol. 5, loc. cit., p. 46). Thus there are the beginnings here of a more radical critique, but one that Marx was unable to develop.

22. op. cit., p. 145.

23. ibid., p. 139.

24. ibid., p. 137.

25. Translated in R. Schlesinger, *The Family in the USSR* (London, 1949), pp. 54-55. This was a consistent theme in Kollontai's writings, even if it is played down by her socialist feminist admirers today, for example Alix Holt, whose *Selected Writings of Alexandra Kollontai* (London: Allison & Busby, 1977) is indeed somewhat selective in this respect. In *Women's Labour in Economic Development* (1923), for example, Kollontai developed her critique of 'bourgeois feminism' in this way: the bourgeois feminists 'absolutely refused to take into account that woman bears a twofold responsibility towards society and that the "natural right" which they were so fond of quoting not only demands that women should effectively contribute to society but also that they should provide society with healthy offspring'. 'In their zeal to establish equal rights and prove woman in every respect equal to man, the feminists were bound to disregard the natural characteristics of women which mark them out for a special place in the collective' (Schlesinger, op. cit., p. 45).

26. For a representative socialist feminist view, see for example Heidi Hartmann, 'The Unhappy Marriage of Marxism and Feminism', *Capital and Class* 8 (London, 1979):

> Marx's theory of the development of capitalism is a theory of the development of 'empty places'...Just as capital creates these places indifferent to the individuals who fill them, the categories of Marxist analysis, 'class', 'reserve army of labour', 'wage-labourer', do not explain why particular people fill particular places. They give no clues about why *women* are subordinate to *men* inside and outside the family and why it is not the other way around. *Marxist categories, like capital itself, are sex-blind* [pp. 7-8, her italics].

This is the space that the concept of patriarchy is designed to fill. Veronica Beechey, however, has indicated very clearly the whole raft of 'problems that arise if patriarchy and capitalism, or the social relations of reproduction and the social relations of production, are treated as independent structures': 'On Patriarchy', *Feminist*

*Review* 3 (London, 1979), p. 78. Yet in her view, 'a satisfactory theory of patriarchy should be historically specific and should explore the forms of patriarchy which exist within particular modes of production' (p. 80).

27. See Stuart Schram (ed.), *The Political Thought of Mao Tse-tung* (London: Penguin, 1969), pp. 334-37.

28. Translated into English as *Women and Russia* (London: Sheba, 1980).

29. Quoted from *The Times*, 23 July 1980.

30. See above, p. 30.

31. See above, p. 43.

32. See above, p. 34.

33. loc. cit., p. 71.

34. The confusion induced by this passage from Engels is compounded on the other side of the fence by those who seek to defend the dogmas of orthodox Marxism against any new ideas. Such a person is Etienne Balibar, a collaborator of Louis Althusser's, who picks Engels up on this point in *Reading Capital* (London: New Left Books, 1971). Here Balibar speaks of 'a surprising text, which not only plays impudently [I think he means 'imprudently'; the French edition has *impudemment*, but this could be a misprint for *imprudemment*] on the term *production*, but demands the application of the technological model of the advance of the productive forces to the forms of kinship, presented as social relations of procreation' (p. 224). Of course Engels was mistaken in his view of kinship, but Balibar's purpose here is to combat the idea that the concept of 'social relations of procreation' could have any validity, i.e. that procreation could be anything but 'natural'. Balibar is in fact a past master at such ideological operations, and wages a similar defence of orthodox dogma, this time against ecological ideas, in 'Irrationalism and Marxism', *New Left Review* 107 (London, 1978).

35. See Laurel Holliday, op. cit., pp. 215 ff. ('How to Have a Girl').

## Notes to Chapter 2

1. *The Origin of the Family*, loc. cit., pp. 128 and 133. In the first of these passages, *'Widerwärtigkeit der Knabenliebe'* is translated as 'abominable practice of sodomy', which is considerably less accurate.

2. Translated in *Bernstein on Homosexuality* (Belfast: Athol Books, 1977).

3. See Jim Steakley, *The Homosexual Emancipation Movement in Germany* (New York: Arno, 1975), pp. 30 ff. Also W. Herzen,

'Antithetical Sexual Sentiment and Section 175 of the Imperial Penal Law', in *Bernstein on Homosexuality*, loc. cit. It is characteristic of the time, however, that Herzen, who accepts Ulrich's estimate that 1 in 200 men are homosexual, regards this as an 'amazingly high incidence' (p. 30)!

4. See note 1 above.

5. The WLSR was formally founded only in 1928, but the international movement dated from the first International Congress for Sex Reform which Hirschfeld convened in Berlin in 1921. The League was in no way a specifically homosexual organization, but it provided the best framework available at the time for the gay movement. Its platform called for 'a rational attitude towards sexually abnormal persons, and especially towards homosexuals, both male and female', and demanded 'only those sexual acts to be considered criminal which infringe the sex rights of another person'. See Jeffrey Weeks, *Coming Out* (London: Quartet, 1977), pp. 137 ff.

6. The exception to this, in Germany, was the Community of the Special (Gemeinschaft der Eigenen) led by Benedict Friedländer, who rejected the theory of an innate 'anomaly' only at the price of elitism. The *Eigenen* championed a male supremacist sexual practice that combined heterosexuality and paedophilia, and regarded both conventional heterosexuals and gays as *Kümmerlinge* (stunted). See Jim Steakley, op. cit., pp. 43 ff.

7. *The Early Homosexual Rights Movement* (New York: Times Change, 1974), p. 65, from where the Batkis quotation is taken.

8. Francesco Saba Sardi, in a 1972 article 'La società omosessuale', states:

> Under Nazi rule...it was a specific type of homosexual, weak and 'decadent', who was the object of persecution, certainly not the rough barrack-room bugger. The mincing queen of the boulevards and gay ghettos was taken away; he was not sufficiently war-like. The rough SA or blond SS man, however, so loved by their sergeant or *Sturmbannführer*, were deemed more virile and militaristic, more worthy of trust and membership in their 'service', if they did not abandon themselves to frivolous affairs with women. [Quoted by Mario Mieli, *Homosexuality and Liberation* (London: Gay Men's Press, 1980), pp. 159-60.]

But as I have argued elsewhere, it is essentially a slander put about by the Left that the Nazis in any way condoned or promoted homosexuality; they consistently viewed it as part of the 'degeneracy' they were set on stamping out. If there is any grain of truth mixed in with the slander, it is simply that when male homosexuality disguises itself as a cult of 'manliness' and virility, it is somewhat less obnoxious from the fascist standpoint. See my Introduction to Heinz Heger, *The Men With the Pink Triangle* (London: Gay Men's Press, 1980), pp. 10-11.

9. See Chapter Three, p. 149.

10. See David Thorstad, *Gay Liberation and Socialism* (New York, 1976), and the interview with him in Rosa von Praunheim, *Army of Lovers* (London: Gay Men's Press, 1980), pp. 190-91.

11. For a relatively sophisticated statement of this position, see Don Milligan, *The Politics of Homosexuality* (Edinburgh, 1980). The more vulgar end of this particular spectrum is represented by Tony Cliff, leading theorist of the (British) Socialist Workers Party, in his Introduction to *The Word is Gay* (London: SWP, 1979): 'we should look forward now to the first leader of the London workers' council being a 19 year old black gay woman!' (p. 3). What a classic of opportunism...

12. Andy, 'Gay Liberation This Way?', *Come Together* 3, London, 1971; reprinted in Aubrey Walter (ed.), *Come Together: the years of gay liberation* 1970-73, loc. cit., p. 58. As always, a conspiracy theory of this kind suggests the need for a counter-conspiracy, and this explains the support that terrorism enjoyed for a while in London GLF, as depicted in Aubrey's Introduction (pp. 28-30).

13. This concept pervades all approaches to sexual politics by the softer Left, for example the International Marxist Group and the milieu of 'Beyond the Fragments'. 'Feminist and Gay politics are an essential part of people gaining control over their lives, the part of the process whose aim is control over decisions concerning our bodies and identities'; editorial in *Gay Left* 10 (London, 1980).

14. In my 1973 article 'Towards a Marxist Theory of Gay Liberation' I myself made a last desperate effort to attach gay liberation to orthodox Marxism, arguing that women's special-ization in childcare was, at least in capitalist society, simply a convenient arrangement, and completely ignoring the converse male specialization in violence. In this way, I sought to locate gay oppression at the level of gender, thus explaining the mass emotional hostility to gay people, while reducing the gender system in its present form to women's economic dependence on men. I've made a self-criticism of this article in a 1980 Postscript to its current reprinting in Pam Mitchell (ed.), *Pink Triangles: Radical Perspectives on Gay Liberation* (Boston: Alyson, 1980), and certainly have never seen any more convincing attempt to argue this connection.

15. Particularly by Sheila Rowbotham in S. Rowbotham and J. Weeks, *Socialism and the New Life* (London: Pluto, 1977); also Chushichi Tsuzuki, *Edward Carpenter 1844-1929* (London: CUP, 1980).

16. Edward Carpenter, *My Days and Dreams* (London: 1916), pp. 97-98.

17. Edward Carpenter, *The Intermediate Sex* (London: 1930), pp. 116-17.

18. Edward Carpenter, *Towards Democracy* (London: Allen &

Unwin, 1949), pp. 220-21. This edition, the most recent, unfortunately misprints 'affectation' as 'affection'.

19. C. S. Ford and F. A. Beach, *Patterns of Sexual Behaviour* (London: Methuen, 1970).

20. (New York, 1974).

21. Ford and Beach, op. cit., p. 139.

22. ibid., p. 140.

23. It is useful to compare the data on female homosexuality. There is only information for this among 17 of the societies in the Ford and Beach survey, and in many of these a penis substitute is employed, no matter how redundant this is in terms of clitoral stimulation. Even among the Australian Aranda, when women stimulate one another's clitoris, 'one of them will say to the other, "a man will come with a big penis and cohabit with you"' (p. 141). The space for female homosexuality, in other words, seems to be as strictly confined to that compatible with the heterosexual role as is the case with male homosexuality.

24. See below, pp. 110-111.

25. 'Three Essays on the Theory of Sexuality', *Standard Edition*, Vol. 7 (London: Hogarth, 1975), p. 222.

26. See in particular Paul Hoch, *White Hero Black Beast* (London: Pluto, 1979).

27. The causation here is a circular one, for it is the economic dependence of child-rearing women on men in the family that makes the price of male labour-power higher than that of female.

28. This situation is exposed very well in Heinz Heger, *The Men With the Pink Triangle*, loc. cit.

29. Recognition of this marks the very starting-point of the struggle for gay liberation. As it was expressed in the *Principles* of London GLF (December 1970): 'Legal reform and education against prejudice, though possible and necessary, cannot be a permanent solution. While existing social structures remain, social prejudice and overt repression can always re-emerge'. Quoted from Aubrey Walter (ed.), *Come Together...*, loc. cit., p. 48.

30. Not that 'psychonazism' is in any way confined to the Latin countries. When I was at school, our teenage years were regularly punctuated by lectures from a certain Dr Mathews, whose warnings against homosexuality were couched in a peculiarly intimate mixture of vulgar Freudianism and Christianity.

31. Quoted from Mario Mieli, *Homosexuality and Liberation*, loc. cit., p. 72.

32. In the language of the traditional French gay ghetto, the 'femme' and 'butch' gay men are known as *tantes-filles* and *tantes-gars*, i.e. girl-queens and boy-queens. Here the language itself exposes all 'butch' pretensions, setting the tone for the marvellous insights of Jean Genet in *Our Lady of the Flowers*.

33. Mario Mieli is particularly perceptive on the 'repressed roots of

anti-gay violence'; loc. cit., pp. 153-58.

34. Mario Mieli builds a whole political tactic on this, 'women and queens together' (loc. cit., pp. 185-92). But even though I agree with him about the need for a common struggle against the gender system, I don't accept that this is as free from contradiction as Mario assumes, or that the contradictions can be overcome by the force of Eros, which too easily resolves all problems in Mario's book. In my view, the struggles of women, gay men, and men against sexism are convergent rather than simply parallel in their assault on the gender system, and what we should work towards is a 'strategic alliance', as was already spoken of in the London GLF *Manifesto* of 1971.

35. London GLF *Manifesto*, 1971 (1979 edition, pp. 8-9).

36. Even in the heterosexual context, when a couple have lived and worked together for many years, they can often grow together into a strong bond of companionship characterized by increasing similarity.

37. This concept was an important one in the early GLF. See 'Being What Gay Is' and 'Brotherhood' in *Come Together* 13 (London, 1972); Aubrey Walter (ed.), *Come Together...*, loc. cit., pp. 181-84.

38. 'One penis plus one penis equals nothing' only in the contorted arithmetic of David Reuben; *Everything You Always Wanted to Know About Sex* (London: W. H. Allen, 1969), p. 143.

39. The situation for a gay child growing up in a normal family has been compared with giving a Jewish child to be brought up by anti-Semites. The comparison is very apt, apart from the difference that gayness is actually acquired in the family situation.

40. 'Group Psychology and the Analysis of the Ego', *Standard Edition*, Vol. 18 (London: Hogarth, 1971), p. 108.

41. To be published by Gay Men's Press early in 1982.

42. The gay liberation movement has firmly rejected the idea of 'bisexuality', as this is represented today. Either it serves as a cover for gay men still unwilling to come out, or it refers to those men who extend their masculine sexual practice by taking gay men as objects as well as women. Even in GLF, 'there was at least a substantial minority of gay men whose attachment to male privilege was complete and grotesque, summed up on one memorable occasion when one of the most active members of GLF from its earliest days stood up and proclaimed: "I'll fuck anything, man, woman or dog!"' (Aubrey Walter, Introduction to *Come Together...*, loc. cit., p. 34). Mario Mieli also has a nice metaphor for the 'bisexuals' (op. cit., pp. 203 ff.). But besides those gay men, such as Mario himself, concerned to 'explore our secret passion for women' (ibid., p. 191), as the gender system becomes more eroded we can expect a shift in categories and definitions that will gradually create a space for a genuine bisexuality unstructured by

gender. The hang-ups about homosexuality in the 'men against sexism' movement, however, show that we are still a long way from this.

43. S & M is another way in which the 'father' intervenes in the gay relationship, in this case essentially as object rather than subject, i.e. as a function of the effeminate gay man's rejection by his father, and the emotions arising from this. According to Fred Halstead, whose credentials on this subject are incontestable, 'I would say 90 per cent of leather people are masochistic, if not more . . . it is just more attractive to be dominated' (Rosa von Praunheim, *Army of Lovers*, loc. cit., pp. 93-94).

44. See Chapter Four, p. 204.

45. John Rechy, *The Sexual Outlaw* (London: Futura, 1979); Guy Hocquenghem, *Homosexual Desire* (London: Allison & Busby, 1978).

46. See Paul Hoch, op. cit.

47. Adam Mars-Jones, in an unpublished essay on Mario Mieli's book written before its appearance in English, very sensitively rendered the central concept of 'trans-sexuality' as 'pansexuality', since, as Mario himself makes clear, 'I shall use the term "trans-sexuality" [*transessualità*] throughout this book to refer to the infantile polymorphous and "undifferentiated" erotic disposition . . .' (*Homosexuality and Liberation*, loc. cit., p. 25). But this terminological option was impossible to adopt in translating the book, as Mario's concept is in fact designed to 'express . . . at one and the same time, both the plurality of the erotic tendencies and the original and deep hermaphrodism of every individual' (p. 26). This use of 'trans-sexuality' is precisely a question-begging one, assuming that the 'woman' and the 'man' already exist, in latent state, within the infant.

## Notes to Chapter 3

1. Introduction to the First Edition of *Capital* Volume 1, loc. cit., p. 92.

2. I attacked this attitude several years ago in an article written jointly with Aubrey Walter, for the short-lived 'broad left' magazine *7 Days* (London, 8-14 March 1972). It was significant of orthodox Marxist misunderstanding of the ecological critique that our article, which we called 'Coming to Terms With Nature', was retitled 'Long Live Nature' and illustrated by a picture of a fox! See also John Mathews, 'Marxism and the Environment', *Politics and Power* 1 (London: Routledge, 1980).

3. See John Gofman, *An Irreverent Illustrated View of Nuclear Power* (San Francisco, 1980), and Mike Prior, 'Nuclear Power', *Politics and Power* 1, loc. cit.

4. 'Labour is, first of all, a process between man and nature, a process by which man, through his actions, mediates, regulates and controls the metabolism between himself and nature' (*Capital* Volume 1, loc. cit., p. 283). 'In London, for example, they can do nothing better with the shit of 4½ million people than pollute the Thames with it, at monstrous expense' (*Capital* Volume 3, chapter 5, 4).

5. See John P. Holdren, 'Global Thermal Pollution', in John P. Holdren and Paul R. Ehrlich (eds), *Global Ecology* (New York: Harcourt, 1971), pp. 85-88.

6. Tidal power involves tapping energy from the moon's rotation (and on a much smaller scale, the rotation of the earth round the sun), yet it would only slow this down by an absolutely imperceptible amount, even if continued for thousands of years.

7. See John Mathews, op. cit. New technological advances are being made all the time. The artificial splitting of water by sunlight, or photolysis, is reportedly only two years away (*New Scientist*, 20 August 1980), thus making possible the storage of solar energy in hydrogen fuel.

8. Approximately 10 per cent more males are conceived than females, but at every step through life male mortality is higher. In Britain at the turn of the century, the number of surviving males fell to that of surviving females by the age of 3 or 4. Today, with a reduced mortality all round, there are still more males than females until about age 35, and this break-even point is steadily rising. The lead in male births over female in the advanced countries today is in the region of 6 per cent. See also Jalna Hanmer and Pat Allen, 'Reproductive Engineering: The Final Solution', in Brighton Women and Science Group, *Alice Through the Microscope*, loc. cit.

9. *Gyn/Ecology: The Metaethics of Radical Feminism*, loc. cit., pp. 276 ff.

10. See Chapter One, pp. 54-55.

11. In China this was particularly criticized during the Cultural Revolution as the 'productive forces theory', but after the death of Mao Zedong it is once again ascendant, with the overriding priority given to 'modernization' over the transformation of social relations.

12. The Soviet system is not even without its own 'socialist' variant of the anarchy of production. Despite the system of central planning, the continued existence of the class division leads to decisions being made at every level that are governed by individual and sectoral interests, not by the interest of society as a whole. If anything, this problem is rapidly becoming still more acute in the

Soviet system than in the West, even during the present recession. See for example Emmanuel Todd, *The Final Fall* (New York: Karz, 1980).

13. The life expectancy of a male professional worker is several years longer than that of a male manual worker in Britain today. In the United States, the proportion of cancer deaths directly attibutable to industrial processes, which in the past was estimated at as low as 5 per cent, is now recognized by the Department of Health, Education and Welfare as 38 per cent, in a 'conservative estimate'. See Samuel S. Epstein, *The Politics of Cancer* (New York, 1979).

14. Letter to Marx of 7 October 1858, Engels' emphasis. See my Introduction to Karl Marx, *Surveys from Exile* (London: Penguin, 1973), p. 26.

15. See for example J. B. Priestley, *English Journey* (London: Penguin, 1975), originally published in 1934.

16. 'Constant revolutionizing of production, uninterrupted disturbance of all social conditions, everlasting uncertainty and agitation distinguish the bourgeois epoch from all ealier ones. All fixed, fast-frozen relations, with their train of ancient and venerable prejudices and opinions, are swept away, all new-formed ones become antiquated before they can ossify. All that is solid melts into air, all that is holy is profaned, and man is at last compelled to face with sober senses, his real conditions of life, and his relations with his kind' (Karl Marx and Frederick Engels, 'Manifesto of the Communist Party,' *The Revolutions of 1848*, loc. cit., pp. 70-71).

17. Rudolf Bahro, a very spiritual atheist, describes capitalism as the epoch of society that is par excellence 'distant from God'; and in his book the Soviet system, too, is still 'following the capitalist road' (loc. cit., pp. 411 and 7).

18. There was of course a certain lack of synchrony here. The Latin American countries had already thrown off Spanish and Portuguese rule, based on an earlier form of merchant capitalism, before the annexation of Asia and Africa on the basis of industrial capitalism came to a head.

19. 'This stratum of workers-turned-bourgeois, or the labour aristocracy, who are quite philistine in their mode of life, in the size of their earnings and in their entire outlook, is the principal prop of the Second International, and in our days, the principal *social* (not military) *prop of the bourgeoisie*...In the civil war between the proletariat and the bourgeoisie they inevitably, and in no small numbers, take the side of the bourgeoisie, the "Versaillais" against the "Communards".' [1920 Preface to the French and German editions of *Imperialism*, Lenin's emphasis; *Collected Works*, Vol. 22 (London: Lawrence & Wishart, 1964), p. 194.]

20. *Collected Works*, Vol. 33 (London: Lawrence & Wishart, 1966), pp. 499 and 500. In my Introduction to Karl Marx, *The First*

*International and After*, (loc. cit.), I made a particular point of stressing how 'imperialism has radically differentiated the historical trajectories of metropolis and colony, and virtually reversed the direction of the revolutionary process' (p. 69). Orthodox Marxist reviewers, however, were upset by my insistence that this was not just a temporary phenomenon tied up with the export of capital, but existed already in Marx's day and before.

21. I have surveyed Mao's contribution to Marxism in my pamphlet *Mao Tse-tung, Marxist* (London: Anglo-Chinese Educational Institute, 1977).

22. See Rudolf Bahro, op. cit., especially chapter 11.

23. Although the burden of the arms race is proportionately much greater on the Soviet economy than in the West, the atrocious performance of Soviet agriculture and light industry shows that far more is wrong with Soviet planning than simply the military burden. Yet the domination of the Soviet economy by the demands of the armed forces is a major factor in maintaining its inflexible economic system. The Soviet people accordingly have a further interest in getting rid of the arms race. See for example David Holloway, 'War, Militarism and the Soviet State', in E. P. Thompson and Dan Smith (eds), *Protest and Survive* (London: Penguin, 1980).

24. Quoted from R. Schlesinger (ed.), *The Family in the USSR*, loc. cit., p. 394. As I argued in Chapter One, this 'full development of masculinity and femininity' is precisely the basis of *inequality*. But even in orthodox Marxist terms, equality is never synonymous with mere 'equal rights'. As Engels wrote in *The Origin of the Family*, 'the peculiar character of the supremacy of the husband over the wife in the modern family... will only be seen in the clear light of day when both possess legally complete equality of rights' (loc. cit., p. 137).

25. The Czech exile Zdenek Mlynar, former secretary of the central committee of the Czechoslovak Communist Party, relates in his book *Nightfrost in Prague* (London: Hurst, 1980) how after the invasion of August 1968, when the Czech leaders were brought to Moscow for 'negotiations', Brezhnev not only told them he had requested and received confirmation from President Johnson, before invading their country, that the United States still held to the Yalta and Potsdam conventions; he went on to say that the Soviets would prevent the West from intervening in support of Czech independence 'even at the cost of risking a new world war' (p. 241).

26. Eritrea, a former Italian colony, was awarded to Haile Selassie (the original Ras Tafari), emperor of Ethiopia, after the Second World War, in recognition of his services for the Allied cause.

27. One element that is generally ignored in analyzing Soviet policy, but is certainly far from negligible, is the tsarist tradition of

a world empire, originally conceived in terms of Orthodox Christianity. After Constantinople fell to the Turks in 1453, Ivan the Terrible declared: 'Two Romes have fallen, the third shall be Moscow'. This strand in Russian expansionism was still very pronounced in the 19th century, and Marx and Engels paid particular attention to it, though their writings on this subject have suffered considerable suppression by the Soviet regime and its supporters. Engels' 1889 pamphlet *The Foreign Policy of Russian Tsarism*, for example, has never been made available, and it was only in 1969 that *Marx's Secret Diplomatic History of the Eighteenth Century* (1856) was reprinted.

28. op. cit., pp. 238-39.
29. 'Notes on Exterminism', *New Left Review* 121 (London, 1980).
30. Cf. Alva Myrdal, 'The Superpowers' Game Over Europe', *Protest and Survive*, loc. cit., p. 87.
31. The Trotskyists are particularly guilty here, and they also share the Soviet analysis of Western economic problems: see for example Ernest Mandel, *The Second Slump* (London: New Left Books, 1979).

## Notes to Chapter Four

1. 'Manifesto of the Communist Party', *The Revolutions of 1848*, loc. cit., pp. 79-80.
2. ibid., pp. 72-73.
3. ibid., pp. 79.
4. The perspective of the 'world countryside' surrounding the 'world town' was first put forward by Nikolai Bukharin in 1926, building on the passage from Lenin quoted in Chapter Three, p. 145 above. See Stephen F. Cohen, *Bukharin and the Bolshevik Revolution* (London: OUP, 1980), p. 258. More recently this theme was taken up by the Chinese Communists; see for example Lin Piao (Lin Biao), *Long Live the Victory of People's War* (Peking, 1968).
5. As Marx developed this theme in his 1844 'Introduction to the Critique of Hegel's Philosophy of Right': 'a class with *radical chains*, a class of civil society which is not a class of civil society, a class which is the dissolution of all classes, a sphere which has a universal character because of its universal suffering and which lays claim to no *particular right* because the wrong done to it is not a *particular wrong* but *wrong in general* . . . a sphere . . . which is, in a word, the *total loss* of humanity and which can therefore redeem itself only through the *total redemption of humanity*. This dissolution of society as a particular class is the *proletariat*'. [*Early Writings* (London: Penguin, 1975), p. 256. Marx's emphases].

6. See Mario Mieli, *Homosexuality and Liberation*, loc. cit., p. 228.

7. 'That union, to attain which the burghers of the Middle Ages, with their miserable highways, required centuries, the modern proletarians, thanks to railways, achieve in a few years' ('Manifesto of the Communist Party', loc. cit., p. 76).

8. ibid., p. 67. An assertion which Engels had to qualify in the 1888 edition; see above, Chapter One, note 18.

9. ibid., p. 7.

10. A good case could be made that the privilege of men over women is no less substantial, and at the very least this overlaps with the class division to make working-class men, for example, that much less oppressed, and middle-class women that much less privileged, thus muddying any attempt to draw clean-cut lines between the 'people' on the one hand and the 'enemy' on the other. Some people try to get round this problem by confining the 'enemy' to the tiny minority at the summit of privilege, whether you prefer to call them 'finance capitalists', or, in a more modern terminology, 'white heterosexual ruling-class men'. But then the main bulk of privilege is located within the 'people' themselves. The categories of 'people' and 'enemy' are simply not appropriate to the situation we face in the advanced capitalist countries today.

11. 'The Class Struggles in France', *Surveys from Exile*, loc. cit., p. 71.

12. 'Speech on the Hague Congress', *The First International and After*, loc. cit., p. 324; and letter to H. M. Hyndman of 8 December 1880.

13. *The State and Revolution*; chapter 3, 1.

14. See in particular *The Proletarian Revolution and the Renegade Kautsky*.

15. There are major differences among states conventionally lumped together as fascist, in particular the respective degree to which they rest on a mass middle-class movement or on the military. Italian fascism was the most civilian, while the Latin American dictatorships often have so slender a popular base that their dynamic is quite different to European fascism.

16. I have refuted this argument in greater detail in 'Marxist Strategy in Britain', *Problems of Communism* 11 (London, 1978).

17. Barry Hindess, *The Decline of Working-Class Politics* (London: MacGibbon, 1971).

18. Quoted from Paul Addison, *The Road to 1945* (London: Quartet, 1977), p. 232.

19. See *Observer* colour supplement, 18 March 1979.

20. At the start of GLF, many of us believed that the state could not tolerate gay people openly struggling for our rights, and that we would meet with heavy repression. We were proved wrong, and though there are still those who claim that, with the deepening economic crisis (and when hasn't it?) the moment of repression will

rapidly arrive, the gay movement can scarcely choose any other course but to exploit to the full the space it has won.

21. 'The Civil War in France', *The First International and After*, loc. cit., p. 237.

22. See my Introductions to *The Revolutions of 1848*, loc. cit., p. 47, and *The First International and After*, loc. cit., pp. 20-22.

23. In my view, the best example of this at the present time would be the circle around *Politics and Power* magazine.

24. 'Critique of Hegel's Philosophy of Right. Introduction', *Early Writings*, loc. cit., p. 251.

25. This led Engels, arriving in Manchester in 1844, to get involved with the utopian communists around Robert Owen and write for their newspaper the *New Moral World*. When he and Marx developed their ideas of historical materialism, however, Engels had to change tack. He switched his allegiance to the Chartists and started to write for the *Northern Star* — in no way a communist journal, but definitely an organ of class struggle.

26. Despite the definite gains that these revolutions brought, including gains specifically for women, at the same time the gender system which inducts male children into a culture of violence was inevitably reinforced. The speed and tenacity with which the 'new class' crystallized in all these countries should also be seen as significantly conditioned by this reinforcement of the gender system. It is worth reflecting on the fact that since its establishment in 1917 there has only ever been one woman member of the Soviet Politbureau (E. A. Furtseva, 1957-61, i.e. during the Khrushchev liberalization). See also Chapter Three, p. 149.

27. See Edward Thompson, *William Morris* (London: Lawrence & Wishart, 1977), especially his 'Postscript', p. 791.

28. 'Critique of the Gotha Programme', *The First International and After*, loc. cit., p. 346. Marx's emphasis.

29. See Stanley Moore, *Three Tactics: The Background in Marx* (New York: Monthly Review, 1963).

30. The sense of loss felt by the English utopians of the late 19th century is expressed very poignantly by Edward Carpenter, writing in 1927 at the age of 83: 'What is to be done? Though I have written on the Cure of Civilization generally I grieve to say I have no panacea for the present mass of human ills, & sometimes certainly they seem intolerable'. [Quoted from Keith Nield's entry on Carpenter in the *Dictionary of Labour Biography*, Vol. 2 (London: MacMillan, 1974), p. 90.]

31. (London: Women's Press, 1979).

32. 'At the risk of seeming ridiculous, let me say that the true revolutionary is guided by a great feeling of love'; Che Guevara, 'Notes on Man and Socialism in Cuba', *Che Guevara Speaks* (New York: Merit, 1967), p. 136.

33. In the 19th century, certain otherwise very radical socialists

were quite militantly anti-feminist. See for example my Introduction to *The First International and After*, loc. cit., pp. 16-17, note; also Edward Thompson, op. cit., pp. 374-75.

34. In Spanish, *'amaos los unos los otros'* expresses this inclusion in a considerably more forceful way. I don't know whether the embarrassment this causes is in any way a reason why the proportion of men to women in Hispanic churches is unusually low.

35. This can be illustrated from the current ideology of the nuclear disarmament movement. In *Protest and Survive*, for example, Edward Thompson writes that 'the deformed human mind is the ultimate doomsday weapon' (loc. cit., p. 52), and Ken Coates that the movement must rely on 'the light of our reason, the generosity of our hopes and the warmth of our love for one another' (p. 245). They recognize the need for a profound cultural change, yet they are still chary of linking up with the anti-gender movement which is the only possible vehicle of this.

36. Peter Stansill and David Mairowitz, *Bamn* (London: Penguin, 1972). Our article was 'Wham, Bamn, Thank You Ma'am', *7 Days*, 2-8 February 1972.

37. See Chapter Two, p. 93.

38. Aubrey Walter and David Fernbach, 'Wham, Bamn, Thank You Ma'am', loc. cit.

39. *North-South: A Programme for Survival* (London: Pan, 1980).

40. Rudolf Bahro, op. cit., p. 364.

41. In *The Alternative* Bahro recognizes male domination as one of the basic social relations, together with the dominance of town over country, and of mental work over manual work, that 'already provide the fundamental elements of the social *division of labour* and of the *state*, and moreover an entire epoch before private property in the means and conditions of production makes its historical appearance' (loc. cit., pp. 46-47, Bahro's emphases; cf. above, Chapter One, pp. 37ff.). In private conversation with me (London, March 1980) he has acknowledged that the sexual division of labour is the most ancient of social contradictions, and correspondingly the most difficult to erode. Yet though his Kuan Yin is indeed the loving mother, I have been unable to convince Bahro (a heterosexual man) that the gender division must be challenged here and now, as a vital part of resolving the contradictions of class and imperialism on which Bahro shows such a deep understanding.

42. I think my own experience here was fairly typical, in that I severed my connections with the socialist Left, after getting involved in gay liberation, not in anger and rejection, but simply out of a need to explore new ground without restraint by traditional dogma. The bitterness only came later, when our former comrades refused to even try and understand what we were on about.

43. The most fascinating work on the subject has been done by Angus Calder, who just 'missed' the War; *The People's War* (London: Panther, 1971). See also Paul Addison, *The Road to 1945*, loc. cit.

44. George Orwell, *Collected Essays*, Vol. 2 (Penguin: London, 1971), pp. 67-68.

45. See my article 'Tom Wintringham: Britain's Forgotten Marxist', *History Workshop* 11 (Oxford, 1981).

46. During the War, the most fertile soil for socialism was in fact the armed forces. It is often said that the forces vote decided the 1945 election. An index of the politicization of the British army at this time is given by the 'Cairo parliament', a political debating society elected by the two hundred thousand soldiers stationed in Egypt in summer 1944. This gave a two-thirds majority to the Left (Labour, Common Wealth and Communist), to the horror of the Tories at Westminster.

47. Common Wealth was by no means a negligible quantity. Though its strength was essentially a temporary function of its non-acceptance of the electoral truce, winning three by-elections in 1943 and 1944, a handful of Common Wealth candidates could still attract 110,634 votes in the 1945 General Election, a higher figure than the Communist party, which was then at its peak.

48. A programme of survival developed from this starting-point would also require a far greater degree of self-sufficiency in the production of food (above all), energy and raw materials.

49. See also my article 'The Impasse Facing CND', *Politics and Power* 3 (London: Routledge, 1981).

50. In Britain this demand has generally been very muted, presumably because the workers' movement has never perceived the army as a serious threat. Even the Leninist minority, who profess to do so, have claimed that nothing can be done about it (as about so many other things) until 'after the revolution'.

51. The intake of conscripts with a relatively high level of education has already forced a considerable measure of democratization in several West European armies, by comparison with our own all-professional forces. These range from relaxed dress codes in the Netherlands through to trade unionization in Norway and 'co-determination' between officers and men in Sweden.

52. See Janice Raymond, *The Transsexual Empire* (London: Women's Press, 1980).

53. Cf. Mario Mieli, op. cit., especially pp. 191-92 and 210 ff.

54. See Chapter Two, note 3.

55. See 'Gay Revolution Party Manifesto', in Karla Jay and Allen Young (eds), *Out of the Closets* (New York: Douglas, 1972), pp. 342-45.

56. Cf. Jeffrey Weeks, *Coming Out*, loc. cit., p. 265 (chapter 16, note 5).

57. In Britain in 1940, there were many women who wanted to bear arms. When the Home Guard was still a spontaneous popular movement and had not yet been taken in hand by the War Office, some women did unofficially join, and a private 'Amazon Defence Force' was also formed. Dr Edith Summerskill requested in Parliament that women should be allowed to join the Home Guard on equal terms with men, but this was flatly refused in favour of an unarmed Home Guard Auxiliary along the lines of the WAACs. The distortion of national defence by the gender system was made quite explicit; for example, the men's desire to defend 'hearth and home' would be undermined if 'hearth and home' joined them in the firing line. [J. Langdon-Davis, *Home Guard Warfare* (London, 1941), pp. 55 ff.] Tom Wintringham, on the other hand, supported the demand of women for weapons, explaining that 'whenever a people has been fighting for its life, the women have joined in' (*Picture Post*, 15 June 1940).

58. *My Guru and His Pupil* (London: Eyre, 1980), pp. 4-5.

59. London GLF *Manifesto*, 1971, p. 15. As Aubrey Walter points out in his Introduction to *Come Together...*, loc. cit., p. 21, this passage was bowdlerized when the *Manifesto* was reprinted in 1979.

60. See Chapter Two, p. 68.

## Notes to Afterword

1. *The Art of Creation* (London, 1919), p. 33.

2. This despair is the 'seventh enemy' in the catalogue of perils compiled by Ronald Higgins, *The Seventh Enemy* (London: Pan, 1978), a discussion of the world crisis which I value precisely because its author proceeds from a different starting-point than my own, in his case an Establishment one, yet our paths are convergent and we are very definitely on the same side — the side of hope.

3. Taking the universe as a four-dimensional whole, what from our standpoint is past, present and future are all essentially copresent. There is no reason, moreover, why the totality of being should be restricted to the universe as we know it. This may be simply one bubble in a wider sea, its apparent finitude being merely the finitude of our knowledge. Yet for us, and for all other intelligent life we might get in touch with, evolution has to be a reality. Time is an arrow pointing in one direction, this being a basic precondition for that ripple between matter and consciousness which we call life.

4. Here I differ with Peter Singer, author of *Animal Liberation* (London: Paladin, 1979), who seeks to apply a common ethical

framework to animals and humans on the Kantian basis of each individual being an 'end in itself'.

5. See Elaine Pagels, *The Gnostic Gospels* (London: Weidenfeld, 1980).

6. See Adrian Berry, *The Iron Sun* (London: Cape, 1977). Not science fiction, but a do-it-ourselves manual.

7. *The Phenomenon of Man* (London: Fontana, 1980), pp. 283ff.

# Other new titles from
## GAY MEN'S PRESS

**Noel Greig and Drew Griffiths**   UK £2.50/US $5.50
**Two Gay Sweatshop Plays**
   These are two of the most acclaimed productions by the men's company of Gay Sweatshop. **As Time Goes By** surveys 100 years of gay oppression and struggle, from Victorian England through Nazi Germany to contemporary New York. 'A triumph' (*Irish Times*). **The Dear Love of Comrades** depicts the life of Edward Carpenter, champion of socialism, feminism and gay liberation at the turn of the century. 'This play will be a part of theatre history' (*San Francisco Update*).

**Cracks in the Image: stories by gay men**   UK £2.50/US $5.50
   Sixteen short stories by some of today's most exciting new gay writers, British and American. A rich and varied collection which presents gay men and the world as revealed by our own lived experience, often quite contrary to popular image. Candid, witty, sober, perceptive and engaging.

**ALSO AVAILABLE:**

**The Men With the Pink Triangle**   UK £2.50/US $4.95
by Heinz Heger
   For decades, historians have ignored the persecution of homosexuals by the Nazi regime. Now a man who survived six years in the Nazi concentration camps has finally told about that terrible era. **The Men With the Pink Triangle** is the intensely personal story of a young Austrian student who was abruptly arrested by the Gestapo in 1939 for being homosexual. He spent the next six years in German concentration camps; like other homosexual prisoners, he was forced to wear a pink triangle on his shirt so he could be readily identified for special mistreatment. 'One of the Ten Best Books of 1980' (Richard Hall, *The Advocate*).

# Other books from
# ALYSON PUBLICATIONS

**The Men With the Pink Triangle***　　　　　　　　　　$4.95
by Heinz Heger

The true life-and-death story of homosexual prisoners in the Nazi concentration camps. (See full description under Gay Men's Press.)

**Beyond the Fragments:**　　　　　　　　　　　　　　$6.95
**Feminism and the making of socialism**
by Sheila Rowbotham, Lynne Segal and Hilary Wainwright

A ground-breaking look at the implications of the women's movement on leftist politics. The authors argue not just for a rhetorical acceptance of feminism, but for a redefinition of priorities, a new approach to theory, consciousness, and political organization. (Publication date: October 1981. Orders received earlier will be shipped immediately upon publication.)

**Pink Triangles:**　　　　　　　　　　　　　　　　$4.95
**Radical perspectives on gay liberation**
ed. by Pam Mitchell

The American left and the gay movement have a great deal to offer each other. The essays in this book give new insight, from a progressive viewpoint, on such subjects as pornography, pedophilia, community building, and theories of gay liberation.

**Young, Gay and Proud**　　　　　　　　　　　　　$2.95

One high school student in ten is gay. Here is the first book ever to address the problems and needs of that often-invisible minority, helping young people deal with questions like: Am I really gay? What would my friends think if I told them? Should I tell my parents? Does anybody else feel the way I do?

**Reflections of a Rock Lobster:**　　　　　　　　　$4.95
**A story about growing up gay**
Aaron Fricke

Guess who's coming to the prom! No one in Cumberland, Rhode Island, was surprised when Aaron Fricke appeared at his high school prom with a male date. He had sued his school for the right to do so, and the media had been full of the news.

Yet for the first sixteen years of his life, Fricke had closely guarded the secret of his homosexuality. *Reflections of a Rock Lobster* is his story about growing up with this secret. With insight and humor, Fricke tells how he first became aware of his homosexual feelings in childhood, then learned to hide them from adults, and then to repress his feelings completely, before he finally developed a positive gay identity.